WANT TO MAKE MORE MONEY WRITING?
A SCRIPTWRITING PRO SHOWS YOU HOW!

Every year over 200,000 scripts are written for information and retail videos. This is the only book that teaches you step-by-step how to write for this lucrative market. Barry Hampe, a successful writer-director, shares with you his writing techniques and ma[illegible]u get started in this growing [illegible]t.

This information-pack[illegible]n exercises, actual sample [illegible]d insider's knowledge of how [illegible]'s fastest-growing market for writers.

VIDEO SCRIPTWRITING

"A lively, affirmative, upbeat and informative book that is also enormously practical.... Hampe's advice can help you write excellent video scripts."

—Richard Walter, screenwriting chairman, University of California, Los Angeles; author of *Screenwriting: The Art, Craft and Business of Film and Television Writing*

"Wonderful!...There is something for everyone—from rank beginner to old pro."

—James B. Young, Ph.D., executive director, Hawaii Public Television

BARRY HAMPE is an independent scriptwriter and filmmaker who has written—and often produced and directed—many information videos and documentary films for broadcast television; for sales, training, and corporate communication; and for retail sale.

How to Write for the $4 Billion Commercial Video Market

BARRY HAMPE

PLUME
Published by the Penguin Group
Penguin Books USA Inc., 375 Hudson Street,
New York, New York 10014, U.S.A.
Penguin Books Ltd, 27 Wrights Lane, London W8 5TZ, England
Penguin Books Australia Ltd, Ringwood, Victoria, Australia
Penguin Books Canada Ltd, 10 Alcorn Avenue,
Toronto, Ontario, Canada M4V 3B2
Penguin Books (N.Z.) Ltd, 182-190 Wairau Road,
Auckland 10, New Zealand

Penguin Books Ltd, Registered Offices:
Harmondsworth, Middlesex, England

First published by Plume, an imprint of New American
Library, a division of Penguin Books USA Inc.

First Printing, April, 1993
10 9 8 7 6 5 4 3 2

LIBRARY OF CONGRESS CATALOGING-IN-PUBLICATION DATA
Hampe, Barry.
Video scriptwriting : how to write for the $4 billion commercial video market/ by Barry Hampe.
p. cm.
ISBN 0-452-26868-0
1. Video tape advertising. 2. Television advertising.
3. Advertising copy. 4. Television authorship. I. Title.
HF6146.V53H35 1993
659.14'3—dc20 92-29107

Printed in the United States of America

To Sylvie, who always believed . . .

Contents

List of Figures

Acknowledgments

Getting a book made involves a lot of people whose names don't appear on the book jacket. I must thank my agents for their support: Michael Larsen, who not only appreciated my work but found a publisher for it in record time, and his partner in life and work, Elizabeth Pomada, who likes my ideas and writes a world class money letter. I want to thank my editor at NAL/Dutton, Hugh Rawson, who sent me incredibly encouraging letters while I wrote the book. Also, thanks go to my friend John Campbell, who made available his office and his Macintosh system, night after night, for us to print out the manuscript and compile the index. Finally, not just the manuscript for this book, but every treatment and script mentioned here, and every magazine article before that, has had to pass under the critical eye and flashing red pen of *my* partner, Sylvie Hampe, a tough but appreciative reader, one of the great copy editors, and my best friend.

Introduction

This book is a writer's guide to the high-paying world of scriptwriting commercial videos. And while it has been written to help print writers make the transition to scriptwriting, it can also be a valuable tool for producers and directors, for students of video and film production, and for corporate communicators who often find themselves running a one or two person video department, expected to perform miracles against impossible deadlines.

If you've been writing articles for magazines, you already have the basic research and organizational skills required of a commercial scriptwriter. But the actual writing of a script *is* significantly different from writing a magazine article. I've written plenty of both—and edited two magazines—so this book will show you what the differences are and how to make the transition.

If you've been producing or directing videos—either without a script or from a script written by someone else—and want to (or need to) become proficient at writing your own scripts, you already know about such things as relying on the images and understand how visual sequences go together to tell a story. But you may need some help with researching the topic, organizing the overall structure of the video, and putting believable words in the mouths of the actors or narrator.

What This Book Can Do for You

When I began scriptwriting, my approach was that of a documentary director and editor, not a writer. The distinction is important. A writer trades in words on paper, evoking images in the mind. But a video director finds or creates actual images before the camera. And a video editor organizes the material that has been produced to give it form and meaning.

I've made documentary films for which no script ever existed and in which no word of dialogue or narration was ever spoken, and I've written and directed scores of commercial videos. So this book can help you learn how to plan a program on paper—which is video scriptwriting.

If you are presently a freelance writer, this book can show you how to write for the lucrative and growing market for commercial video scripts. I can't teach you to be talented and I can't teach you to be creative. But I can show you the fundamentals of commercial scriptwriting from the perspective of a producer-director-editor who is also a writer. And I can take you through the business of scriptwriting from creating a demonstration script and getting your first assignment to negotiating an agreement and getting paid for your work.

If you are a corporate communicator, expected to do all things brilliantly, from troubleshooting equipment to writing and producing videos, this book can help.

If you are a producer or director, you'll not only find help in writing the script when you need to, but you'll have a better understanding of how to work with the scriptwriters you hire. You'll know what they are doing—or should be doing—in researching, organizing, and writing the script, and you'll have a better notion of how to talk with them about work in progress. (When all else fails, you can refer them to the appropriate chapter in this book.)

And if you are a student, or a beginning writer, or a wannabe, the process which you'll learn here of research, planning, simplification, organization, and clear, concise writing that goes into commercial scriptwriting should be of value to you in almost any form of writing.

In each chapter you'll find a true story about a client to give you some idea of the way the world of video scriptwriting actually works. Sometimes the names have been changed or omitted to shield the guilty.

You'll find examples of treatments, scripts, proposals, editing logs, and shooting scripts to give you a concrete idea of form and format in video scriptwriting.

And at the end of each chapter there's an exercise to help you develop the skills you need to succeed.

If you want to write scripts, and you have the desire to develop your writing talent and the persistence to make yourself known to potential clients, you should have plenty of video scripts to write.

And when those assignments start coming in, you'll know how to write them, and you'll also know how to deal with your clients and be paid what you are worth.

A Note on Usage

"Filming" Video

In this book, I use the term *video* to include both film and videotape productions. Today, most programs—even if originally produced on motion picture film—are shown on a television screen. It is getting as hard to find a motion picture projector in a corporate or industrial setting as it is to find a noncomputerized typewriter.

Our language has extended the verb *to film* to mean recording sound-image material regardless of whether the actual recording medium is motion picture film or videotape. Today, people talk of *filming* a video.

Where the production was shot on film, I have used the noun *film*.

Clients

Videos and films are most often made with other people's money. The companies, organizations, or groups of people funding the production may be called *sponsors*, *investors*, or *clients*. Throughout the book I've referred to whoever is paying for the production as *the client*. A scriptwriter may, however, be involved with two clients. One is the company or organization funding the video. The other is whoever hired you to write the script—the ad agency or production company which has been commissioned by the funding entity to produce the video.

To differentiate the two, I have called the organization funding the video *the client*. And I've called whoever hired you, *your client*. Sometimes, of course, *your client* and *the client* will be the same.

Gender

When I first began writing about video and film, I found I always used the term *cameraman*, even though I knew the person behind the camera was not always a man. Finally, I asked a production company to schedule a woman on camera on my next shoot, so that the portion of my unconscious where the words are stored would get the idea. From then on I had no problem writing *camera operator* instead of cameraman.

In this book I have tried to avoid any indication of gender, except where it is obviously appropriate. For example, I've tried to refer to clients as *he or she* or *him or her*. If I haven't done it everywhere, it is because, as a writer, I sometimes just can't face inserting an awkward *himself or herself* to break up the rhythm of a sentence or piling up multiple uses of *he or she* and *him or her* in long passages. And I can't force myself to use *s/he,* which I hear in my reading ear as "ess slant aitch ee." Therefore, if you find a *he* without an *or she* or a *him* without an *or her,* I hope you'll accept that this is still the convention in English grammar and can be read, if you so desire, as *she or he* and *her or him.*

1

Commercial Scriptwriting: A Growing Market

No man but a blockhead ever wrote, except for money. —SAMUEL JOHNSON

Commercial scriptwriting—writing the scripts for nonfiction, information films and videos for corporate use, for sales and training aids, and for the retail home video market—is a growing field for writers. It generally pays more than magazine writing, and it pays faster. I did a survey of 173 consumer magazines listed in the *Writer's Market*—excluding literary and "little" magazines, which pay very poorly—taking the highest figure mentioned under nonfiction for each magazine. The average payment per article for all the magazines in the survey was $419.96. The median payment for the 173 magazines was $250 per article. In the same survey, 57 percent of the magazines paid *on or after publication;* only 43 percent on acceptance.

Then I sent a questionnaire to production companies in twenty-five of the one hundred largest cities in the United States, asking what they paid for a freelance writer to research, organize, and write the treatment and script for a fifteen minute video. While the size of the response hardly makes this a scientific survey, the results are interesting. The average fee paid by all the respondents for such a job was $1,800. One producer wrote that the average he pays a freelance scriptwriter is $3,500, and several said their average was $2,750.

Commercial scriptwriting takes about the same amount of work as researching, outlining, writing, and rewriting a nonfiction magazine article. But where an article might bring in $300 to $500—after it has been accepted, and whenever the publishing company decides to cut the check—the script for a ten to fifteen minute commercial video can pay five to ten times as much.

And you get one-third to one-half the money in advance!

Plus expenses.

Over 200,000 Scripts a Year

Commercial video production is a growth industry. Businesses now routinely include sales and training videos in their corporate planning. The fact is that, today, a significant percentage of the population *can't* read. And of those who can, many *won't*. Every executive has more things arriving daily to read than he or she has time for. So does every family. Look at the pounds of paper that come through your mail slot or get stuffed in your mailbox every week. Do you read it all? Most organizations have learned that if they want to communicate with an audience, they'll have a much better chance of getting their message across if they present it on video.

In the late 1980s, one trade publication estimated that commercial video and film production was a $4 billion a year industry. And the market has grown considerably since then. Since the rule of thumb in the industry is to allow 10 percent of the production budget for the script, we're looking at a $400 million market for scriptwriters. At an average of $1,800 a script, that represents more than 220,000 scripts a year that somebody is going to have the chance to write.

It could be you.

What Is a Commercial Video?

Most often, a commercial video is a message from a sponsor: a business, a government agency, or even a nonprofit organization.

It could be an orientation program for newly hired employees. Or an update on changes in employee benefits for everyone in the organization.

It could be a sales video for a new resort development or for a new product coming to market.

It could be a public information program, such as one I wrote for the Hawaii Department of Transportation to inform motorists and area residents about a major highway construction project.

Or it could be an appeal for funds from a nonprofit community-service organization.

Commercial videos include all the customary areas of industrial filmmaking—training and education, sales, and public relations. In addition, commercial videos include new forms of corporate and organizational communication. In today's high tech workplace, the Xeroxed—or even desktopped—newsletter is giving way to the video newsletter. One department store I know of does a weekly video news program for its employees.

Similarly, many organizations are beginning to put out what might be called video annual reports.

A developer I work with wanted to reach all the residents of a housing development with a message about a specific problem, and decided to create a ten-minute video which could be mailed to every family in the development.

Who Are Your Clients?

They're all around you. Every city has several video and film production companies. They produce television commercials, and they produce most of the commercial videos that get made. A certain amount of the production they do is already scripted when they get the job. Very few production companies can afford the luxury of a full-time staff writer. What they may have is a hyphenate—a producer-writer or director-writer or even an account executive–writer. Production companies are always glad to know about talented freelancers who can be brought in on a project.

More and more, clients are asking their advertising agencies or public relations firms to create commercial videos. In many cases, such agencies may have one or more writers who are terrific at getting a message across in thirty or sixty seconds (or in a newsletter or brochure) but who really are not prepared to sustain a video script for ten minutes, fifteen minutes, or a half hour or more.

Both the agencies and production companies have busy times when they are swamped with work. They're delighted to know of someone who can handle an assignment which comes in unexpectedly at such a time.

Many businesses have set up a video section within their corporate communications division, only to discover that while they may have an excellent—and very creative—technical staff, they don't have anybody who knows how to research, organize, and write a good video script. The print writers are too dependent on words, and the video tekkies don't necessarily know how to research and organize a topic. So they're looking for scriptwriters—and they'll hire freelancers.

The federal government has always been a major user of films for training and for communication with the public. Today, when there is not necessarily a huge difference in cost between a brochure or pamphlet and a ten to fifteen minute video (and virtually no difference in cost between a slide show and a video), we are beginning to see state and municipal governments get on the video bandwagon. Quite often they have an idea of what they want, but no idea of how to accomplish it.

The first thing they need is a scriptwriter.

Nonprofit organizations have also learned that one of the best ways to get a message to the public about the good works they are doing is to produce a video. Usually their budgets are tight. They'll call a production company and ask, "How much will it cost to make a ten minute video?" There is no honest answer to that question, at least not without asking a series of qualifying questions first. How long a video runs on the screen has little or no relationship to how much it will cost to produce. These are the things that affect the budget: How many people and how much equipment? For how many days? At how many locations? With how many actors? And how many of what kind of graphics and special effects? Quite often, the production company will suggest that the organization start with a scriptwriter, then come back and the producer will work out a budget based on the script. I've gotten a number of referrals this way.

As you become an experienced scriptwriter with a good knowledge of the production process, you'll often find yourself functioning almost as a consultant to your client. At that point you may jump into hyphenateship yourself and become a writer-producer or a writer-director or even a writer-producer-director.

What Does It Take?

Commercial scriptwriting requires a different approach to writing from prose or fiction or even playwriting. A commercial script is more technical than literary. And a successful commercial script will be far more visual than verbal.

It is based on solid research of the topic to be portrayed on video. And it requires a sound sense of fundamental structure and visual organization. Essentially, a commercial video script is a carefully planned blueprint for communication in a visual medium.

What's in It for You?

The money's good. An average video scriptwriter can command several times the hourly rate of an average magazine writer—for about the same amount of work.

The perks can be great in terms of travel and meeting interesting people. The first part of any script project is research, and that usually means a trip to the location. The location could be the billion dollar Gold Coast on the Big Island of Hawaii, or a casino in Las Vegas, or the *Queen Mary* in Long Beach, or a store down the street from your house. Wherever it is, you'll probably need to take a look at it. And that often means travel at the client's expense.

If you like to mix with the stars—or like to be able to say you have—scriptwriting is a way to do it. Several years ago I wrote an hour show about a celebrity golf tournament. Two planeloads of TV and film people flew to Maui from Hollywood for the event. As part of the deal, my wife and I spent a week in a luxury hotel, mingling with Burt Lancaster, Donald O'Connor, Leslie Nielsen, Richard Crenna, Barbara Eden, Jerry Lewis, Robert Stack, and others.

If you stay at it long enough, sooner or later you may find yourself writing for or about the folks whose names and faces are familiar on *Entertainment Tonight*. TV stars will often hire out as spokespersons for commercial videos. And as the writer, you put the words in their mouths. Over the years I've written scripts for commercial videos featuring Jim Nabors, Dick Van Patten, Dolly Parton, Wally (Famous) Amos, Bob Denver, and Alan Hale. And I've written for many of the entertainers—comedians, musicians, and radio and TV personalities—in my former hometown of Honolulu and my current hometown, Las Vegas, who are called on to be spokespersons or MCs, or even to play little scenes in someone's video.

If you become accomplished at scriptwriting, you'll have the satisfaction of being able to do—for pay—what most other people cannot do at all. On my way back from a scouting trip to the Big Island's Kohala Coast, I called my office from the airport and got a message to call one of the local production companies. The producer told me they had shot eleven twenty-minute videotapes of a special event for one of their clients, and now they needed a script. I took on the job and then discovered that the tapes had been shot with little or no pre-planning, and that much of the footage was unusable. What I had to do was salvage the few decent shots from among what often looked like home movies, create a structure, and write some pickup scenes that could be shot inexpensively to cover essential material which was missing from the footage. I'm proud of that script and proud of the video that was made from it. The video isn't anything spectacular. It may never win any awards. But the client loves it. The P.R. firm that contracted the job loves it. And the production company knows that I saved their reputation with the client after a shoot got out of control.

Sometimes you get a chance to do something that you're just pleased to be a part of. Such a job was a script I did for the Hawaii Family Stress Center. A private, nonprofit institution, they had a 99.9 percent success rate in preventing child and spouse abuse. But they didn't have much money. One of the production companies I regularly work with agreed to produce the video for just their out-of-pocket costs, and I wrote the script for about a fifth of my usual rate. The resulting video has helped them to raise money both from private sources and from the state legislature so that they can continue and expand their work. It made a difference. And I'm glad I was able to help.

A Client Story: The Last Magazine Job

Several years ago, I fell into what seemed like a terrific opportunity for a freelance writer. An in-flight magazine serving Hawaii but published on the mainland needed a Hawaii-based writer-editor to assign stories, deal with writers and photographers, do some writing, and make sure that the Hawaiian words and references in the magazine were correct.

For instance, there was the writer trying to do an article on Hawaii's Big Island from guidebooks and a Hawaiian dictionary who wrote, "Hawaii's cowboys are called *pipi kane* which means 'male cow,' which sounds funny but seems to make sense to the Hawaiians." I faxed off a correction saying *pipi kane* (literally "male beef") means bull not cowboy. The word for cowboy in Hawaiian comes from the Spanish drovers who brought the first cattle to the Islands. When they were asked what they were called, they said "Espaniolos." The Hawaiians called them *paniolos,* and that became the word for cowboys.

I did that kind of editing and wrote feature stories for the magazine for six months, bringing in a few thousand dollars a month for less than half-time writing and editing. And then, with no notice, the magazine suspended publication, owing me over $5,000, which I have never been able to collect. And that was my last magazine writing.

I'll stick to scripts. When I write a script, I write a letter of agreement with the client, usually for payments of one-third in advance, one-third on delivery of the treatment, and one-third on delivery of the script. I start with a positive cash flow from the advance, and if any payment isn't made on time, all work stops. If the client fails to pay for the treatment, I stop work and don't write the script. So the most I can lose, if the client shouldn't pay, is a third of the fee on that script with that client. I like that a lot better.

Exercise: Calculate Your Pay

Calculate the time you would spend querying, researching, planning, organizing, writing, and rewriting a 2,000 word magazine article.

Divide that time into the amount of your latest magazine sale or $420, whichever is more. The number is your hourly rate for magazine writing.

Now divide that same number of hours into

$1,000
$1,800
$2,500

The numbers you get here are your low, average, and preferred hourly rate for writing a ten to fifteen minute commercial video.

2 The Scripting Process

> The *art* of scriptwriting has to do with the creative and conceptual considerations underlying the genesis of a television script. The *craft* of scriptwriting deals with the most effective and systematic means of implementing those creative decisions—and doing so with the greatest possible professionalism.
>
> —J. MICHAEL STRACZYNSKI,
> *The Complete Book of Scriptwriting*

How is a script created? I've found that most clients, and even some writers, have the idea that the job of the scriptwriter is to write the narration for the video, which they consider the important part. These are the same people who confuse writing with typing.

Functions of a Video Script

Commercial writing—especially scriptwriting—is mostly thinking. A script is a set of decisions about how to tell a story in images which limits, organizes, and visualizes the material that will go into the finished program. Very little of what a video scriptwriter does is "writing" in any literary sense. A commercial video script is not art or literature any more than a blueprint is a building. A video script is a plan for a work still to come.

Limits and Defines the Scope of the Production

A video scriptwriter starts with a blank page and writes onto it *everything* to be included in the video. Whatever you don't write into the script won't be seen in the finished program. As a video scriptwriter, you'll learn to write with a stopwatch in one hand. Almost always, your agreement with the client, or with the production company or ad agency which hired you, is to write the script for a video of so many minutes in length. And you'll usually be given far more material than can be covered in the minutes available. As a scriptwriter, you have to narrow the focus, eliminate whatever is not needed, and concentrate on the essentials.

Organizes the Material for Presentation to an Audience

The best way to save time in a video is to bring up a topic just once, deal with it thoroughly, and move on. To do this, you have to know how you are going to start, how you are going to end, and how you are going to get from the opening scene to the final fade-out economically and effectively. If you know how to organize a magazine article, you'll have no trouble planning a video script. In any event, we'll go into the process in detail in Chapter 5.

Visualizes the Topic So It Can Be Recorded on Video

When I was editing *Hawaii High Tech Journal*, a writer who had done several magazine articles for me told me he had started writing scripts on science topics for local educational television. He showed me one. It was nothing but narration. That, he said, was what the producer wanted. And that may explain why educational programming can often be so boring. If the writer puts all the information in the narration, and then the ETV producer-director repeats most of it visually, the result has to be so much redundancy that the program will seem slow and dull.

Word processors and video cameras are not necessarily natural enemies, but it often seems that way. Writers use words to paint pictures in the mind. But videos show the actual pictures. As a video scriptwriter, you have to stop depending on words to make your point and begin to think in pictures.

My teacher, Sol Worth, taught graduate students in the Documentary Film Laboratory at the Annenberg School of Communications at the University of Pennsylvania how to make a film by having them come up with an idea and then form into teams, each of which filmed, edited, and finished a documentary during the year. Early in the first semester, Sol asked each student to write a one hundred word statement which began, "I want to make a film about . . ." These were graduate students and the statements were often abstract: "I want to make a film about hate." "I want to make an antiwar film." "I want to make a film about how the world always beats you up."

Then Sol would jump in and ask, "How would you show that? Give me an image. What would we see first? What next? How can you make an audience *see* what you mean?"

This is your job as a video scriptwriter: To make the audience see what you mean.

To show, not tell.

Scriptwriting Assignments

Writing a commercial video script usually takes the form of one of four different kinds of assignments:

Writing from Scratch

Someone wants a video made and you are asked to write the script for it. All that may exist at this point is a want or a need. For example:

> Our customers are first time home buyers and we want to tell them that owning a condominium is not like renting an apartment. They are responsible for preventive maintenance.
>
> We need a video to show our employees their options under the new profit-sharing plan.

Your job is to research the background information, to find out who will be the audience for the video and precisely what the client wants to communicate to them, to seek out interesting ways to visualize the program, and then to plan, organize, and write the script for the video that will be produced.

Documenting a Unique Event with the Outcome in Doubt

This is a common public relations assignment. The client plans a special event—anything from the opening of a new store to the testing of a new product to the sponsorship of a worthwhile activity such as the Special Olympics—and wants a video made about it. Documenting a unique event is all planning—knowing what should be included so it will be recorded while the event is going on.

If you are lucky, you'll be brought in at this stage to plan a script for the eventual video. Even though you can't be sure what will happen, your job is to give the project an organizing structure—to predict the kinds of things that will probably happen, organize them for presentation to an audience, and come up with a plan so that everything that should be in the video will be recorded. What you will most likely write is a treatment for the potential video along with an outline of probable content and a shot list of scenes that must be recorded.

After the event is over, you'll write the script, organizing the actual footage into a coherent whole, adding a spokesperson, if necessary, and other scenes as background or follow-up, and writing a final narration.

Scripting Existing Footage

What often happens is that someone decides that it would be a good idea to have a video of some event (usually at the last minute) and hires a camera operator to shoot some footage. This could be anything from shots documenting a unique event to footage of a process such as the construction of a building. Sometimes the client will have a need for a video and will already have footage that was shot for some other purpose. In any event, you'll be asked to take the existing footage and turn it into a finished video. In effect, you'll do a paper edit of the footage, organizing the scenes into a coherent structure and adding narration and pickup shots as required.

The problem is that the client thinks this should be a simple job for you since everything is already shot; all you have to do is put it together and write the narration. Actually, it's more work than writing a script from scratch. The reason is that you have to find or create meaning and structure out of footage that very likely was shot without a plan, whereas if you were writing from scratch, you'd start with the plan and then determine the content. To use the existing footage, you first have to look at all of it, log it, and transcribe the sound bites you'll probably want to use. And that's time-consuming. Only then can you begin to organize it and write the script.

Scripting When a Rough Cut Exists

Finally, you may be brought in as a writer during post production after a video has been shot and edited to rough cut, to write the narration. You pretty much have to accept the director's or editor's structure. You may be able to fine tune the editing a little bit—shortening or lengthening a scene or suggesting that some scene occur earlier in the video to set up a later scene. But that's about it. You haven't been hired (and aren't being paid) to do a complete re-edit of the video.

For this reason I suggest taking a look at the rough cut before making a final commitment to do the job. You may not want to do it. Or you may know how to do what the client wants, but you wouldn't want your name on the finished product. (It's also possible that the client or the production company doesn't like what they've got, and they're hoping you'll do a re-edit on paper for the price of a narration script.)

The Process of Creating a Script

Writing a commercial video script is very much like writing a magazine article. Your work starts when you receive the assignment. For a magazine article, this comes from an editor; for a video script, it comes from your client—from a production company or ad agency, or directly from the end user.

Research

As with writing an article, you begin with research. You have to find out the who, what, when, where, why, and how that will make up the content of the video. And you'll also be researching the locations to shoot in and the things and people to show.

Organizing the Material

The next step is to organize the material to make up the structure for the video. You have to decide what you start with, what you end with, and how you build up the scenes in between.

The Treatment

Next, you'll usually write a script treatment. A treatment is often called an outline of the proposed video, but I prefer to think of it as a description of the script that will be written. It states the purpose for making the video, lists important points to be included, tells the visual or cinematic style of the video, and then outlines the content that will be included. I try to make a treatment as complete as possible, because it is the first approval point for the client. I don't move on to writing the script until I have an approved treatment.

The Script

The script is the blueprint for the video, written from the approved treatment. It tells everything that is shown and everything that is said.

Storyboard

For some clients, the script may then be translated into storyboards. A storyboard is a series of drawings, like a comic strip, showing each scene, with the dialogue or narration written in below. Preparing the storyboards is not the writer's responsibility, but you may want to meet with the artist who will do the drawings to discuss what you had in mind for each scene. You should also review the storyboards, if possible, before they go to the client, to be sure they are accurate.

Equipment

These are the tools you need to work as a video scriptwriter:

- A computer with a good word processing program. I recommend a reasonably powerful laptop that you can take with you when you are doing research, and that you can take to the ad agency or production company when rewrites have to be done quickly. For more on scriptwriting with a computer, see Appendix 1.

- A VHS videocassette recorder to let you play back existing footage and rough cuts. Preferably the VCR should display minutes and seconds of running time rather than a continuous number.
- A good, well-adjusted color monitor for video playback.
- A still camera to take with you when scouting locations.
- A microcassette audio recorder for recording interviews.
- A stopwatch to time the scenes as you write them.

A Client Story: The Writer Without a Stopwatch

I have a friend and client whose company specializes in graphic design and print advertising. He's my client when he needs writing and I'm his client when I need graphic art. One day I was in his shop picking up some artwork, and his designer was all excited because they were getting ready to do their first thirty second TV commercial. I wished them well and left, wondering who had written the spot. I found out when my friend called a few days later, wondering if I'd look over the rough storyboard the designer had done, with an eye to "polishing" it for him. I said, "Sure, fax it over."

When the pages kept coming until there were six 8½ × 14 pages with fifteen storyboard panels, I knew there was a problem. The first thing I did was read the narration against my stopwatch. Incredibly, it timed out to four and a half minutes! I called my friend back and said that when a script runs nine times longer than the time it has to fit in, "polishing" won't help. In fact, carving, grinding, and sanding won't either. You have to start all over with a concept that will fit a thirty second time spot.

Exercise: Compare Scriptwriting with Magazine Writing

Compare the process of commercial scriptwriting with the process of writing a magazine article. Make a list of the similarities and the differences. If you have already been writing magazine articles, the similarities list shows you the things you already know how to do.

Pay special attention to the differences. These represent the new skills you have to learn.

3 Think in Pictures

> In most good films, the set-up begins with an image. We see a visualization that gives us a strong sense of the place, mood, texture, and sometimes the theme. . . . Films that begin with dialogue, rather than with a particular visual image, tend to be more difficult to understand. This is because the eye is quicker at grasping details than the ear.
>
> —LINDA SEGER, *Making a Good Script Great*

As a scriptwriter, you have to give up your reliance on words to tell the story. Oh, you'll still write a lot of words, but most of them will be used to describe the pictures the audience will see on the video screen. In a script, you tell the story with pictures.

Audio information—narration, dialogue, interviews, and music—may help the audience interpret the video. But it won't take the place of solid evidence in the form of concrete visual images.

From the very start of the scripting process, your research, planning, organization, and writing must be pointed toward answering the question, What will the audience see? As writer of the script, you have to show to the client, the director, the camera operator, and the video editor—and through them the audience for the video—the images that make up the story you want to tell. You do this with a well-visualized, coherent script which clearly communicates your intentions to the people who will read it.

For a long time I made documentary films which were, for the most part, unscripted. We'd shoot all the film in the budget, and I'd go back to the editing room and spend the next six weeks—or six months—looking at what I'd shot and trying to organize it into a coherent whole which would carry a message to an audience. From learning about editing structure, I learned the structure of scriptwriting. From culling through thousands of feet of film and many hours of videotape, I learned about visual evidence.

Visual Evidence

Communicating with an audience through an existential, visual medium is far different from communicating in a face-to-face or voice-to-voice situation. Audiences have the perverse habit of assuming that whatever they think you are communicating is what you intended to communicate. As far as they are concerned, the message that they get from your video is the only message there is. And since you can't go along with every print to talk with the audience, you have no opportunity to defend yourself—to revise, clarify, or explain what you actually meant.

Consider these two sequences from a public relations program made to recruit students for a famous university. The video brought out many of the strong points of the school, including its academic reputation and the high percentage of Nobel scholars on the faculty. But two sets of visual evidence stick in my memory:

The university is located in a cold and windy northern city with a long, bitter winter. But there were absolutely no shots of cold, snow, or wind in the video. There was, however, a rather idyllic sequence of students sunbathing and swimming at a lake, which almost certainly was shot during summer school, not during the regular academic year. The narration explained that the students enjoyed their outings at the lake and added, almost as an afterthought, "Of course it's not always like this. It can get pretty cold in winter."

Then in a sequence on the life of a student, the videomakers chose to show an attractive female graduate student living with two other young women in an expensive town house close to the campus. Again the disclaimer in narration, "Of course not all students live like this," followed by a reference to the availability of student dormitories for most undergraduates. Which were never shown.

The visual evidence in this video is that if you go to that university, you'll live in an expensive town house and enjoy sunny afternoons on the beach, narrative disclaimers to the contrary notwithstanding.

What your finished video shows, far more than what it says, will be taken as evidence for the truth of its message. That's why it is important to think of the images that you write into the script as visual evidence. The question is not whether *you* can argue the case for what your images mean; you'll never get the chance. The only real test is whether the images can stand on their own and argue the case themselves.

Distorting the Evidence

What about when people's behavior seems to contradict the words they themselves are saying? As a consultant to Marriage Counsel of Philadelphia, I worked with therapists to develop training materials for student counselors. I remember an unedited tape of an intake interview which showed a marriage counselor working with a husband and wife. To understand this couple, you had to watch their behavior as well as listen to the words they said.

If you simply had an audio recording or a transcript of the words being spoken, you could easily come away with the feeling that, while all was not right with the marriage, at least the couple was trying. But if you looked at the body posture and behavior of the husband and wife, you couldn't escape a quite different conclusion.

The wife was eager to please the marriage counselor, trying to put a good face on things, quick to cooperate. The husband said little and did nothing. At one point the counselor asked them to turn their chairs so that they were facing each other and talk directly to each other about their problems. The wife immediately moved her chair. The husband didn't budge. He sat slumped down, hands in pockets, present—but not there. It was clear from the visual evidence that she was living on hope, desperately hanging on to the marriage, but he had already left home.

Suppose you had the job of cutting down this fifty minute sequence into an editing script for a short training video, with the marriage counselor introducing the case and then giving a summary of it at the end. The temptation always is to organize the material to keep *what is being said* flowing smoothly. In fact, many writers like to get a verbatim transcript to work from.

Working this way, the long pauses where the husband said nothing might be cut out of the script because they are "uninteresting." Indeed, working from a transcript, they would not even be noticed. And the scene in which the husband didn't move his chair might be eliminated because "nothing's happening." The visual evidence would then have been altered so that it seemed to support the verbal statements that everything was going to be okay. And it would unquestionably come as a shock to the audience for the marriage counselor to say (as the actual marriage counselor said to me) that there was very little chance of this marriage lasting, and that a divorce might be the best solution for both parties.

"Visuals" vs. Visual Evidence

To the best of my knowledge, the term *visuals* came in with television and was the direct result of transferring word people—writers and radio broadcasters—into a newly created visual medium that had no history and no traditions. These television people used the word *visuals* the way pre-vérité filmmakers sometimes used the word *sound*. They'd say, "I've got some good 'visuals' to go with the doctor scene." It was a reminder to themselves that without pictures, it wasn't TV, just as filmmakers used to have to remind themselves that they needed some kind of sound to go with their silent footage.

All that is ancient history. But the notion of visuals continues to pop up from time to time. And it means, quite specifically, pictures used to illustrate a verbal point. For a beginning scriptwriter, the problem with the notion of visuals—or illustrating a statement with pictures—is that it can lead to thinking that the statement is the only important thing. Which leads to believing that as far as the pictures are concerned, close enough is good enough.

It isn't.

I once had to screen all the films and videos I could find on early learning in children. Most had been made in cooperation with some academic expert on child learning. It was obvious, in many of these films, that the narration had been written to follow the theory of the expert, and then the images had been shot as visuals. Unfortunately, all too often the behavior shown was not the behavior described. The narration might say, for example, that at a certain age young boys join together in inseparable gangs. Which is generally true. But what we might see on the screen would be several boys at a playground—each playing by himself. There was no evidence, visually, to support the small boy gang thesis.

Did the script say:

> Group of boys playing

Or did it say:

> Nine-year-old boys playing together as a gang

The first is what was shot. It was as if the director or the expert or both had decided that everyone knows that at a certain age young boys gang together, so it will be enough to show a bunch of boys—regardless of what they are doing—for everyone to get the point.

The second is what you have to write into the script to protect yourself from a lazy director or an expert who has never learned to think in pictures.

Finding Concrete Images

The more specifically you can describe your script in terms of concrete images, the better your chance of communicating through video. Similarly, the more abstract or interpretive your idea is, the more important it becomes to build up evidence for the idea through concrete images.

To be recorded on video, an image has to be solid, tangible, and existential. Images are described with concrete nouns and action verbs. A concrete image can be understood in a single shot. For instance, there's no problem for a director in recording the image-idea:

> The boy runs toward the camera.

Just turn the camera on, tell the boy to run, and shoot what happens.

The problem gets trickier with the addition of adjectives. In one shot, how do you think a director would record this image-idea?

> The *frightened* boy runs toward the camera.

Probably the director would try to have the boy act frightened—his face contorted, breathing heavily, looking over his shoulder, bumping into things, and so on. The director might also try to shoot in a situation that helps the audience infer fright from the setting: At night on a dimly lit street. In a dark forest. On a battlefield.

Let's try another. How do you think a director might shoot this image-idea in one shot?

> The *intelligent* boy runs toward the camera.

It can't be done.

That idea takes two scenes in sequence. First a scene that establishes the boy's intelligence, and then the shot of the boy running.

You can't record abstractions, such as:

> Economics is the dismal science.

Nor can you record the absence of something:

> On Tuesday, the mail didn't come.

Yes, of course, you can record two actors talking. One says, "Happy Tuesday, did the mail come?" The other says, "No." Or you could put the statement in narration. The point is, you can't take a picture of something that doesn't exist or never happens.

The best you can do, in either case, is to shoot and organize a sequence of concrete events from which you *hope* the audience will infer your meaning. For instance, you could build up a montage cutting from a desk calendar showing a day of the week to a mail slot or in-box showing the mail arriving. When you get to Tuesday, you cut to an empty in-box and hold the shot long enough for everyone to get the idea that the mail isn't coming. Just be aware that this isn't a picture of the mail not coming. It's circumstantial evidence—an inference from a string of images.

See for Yourself

That's why field research is so important to a scriptwriter. You can't describe what you haven't seen. And you can't use as visual evidence what you don't even know exists.

The alternative to field research is what I call "cubicle copy," which is what you get when the scriptwriter sits in his or her cubicle and substitutes verbal flash for visual evidence. Cubicle copy is the commercial video equivalent of the car chase in a screenplay—all action and no substance. It may have exploding graphics and a lot of classy visual effects, but there will be a lack of authenticity and verisimilitude in the script and in the resulting video.

Seeing What Is There

As a scriptwriter, you not only have to think in pictures, you have to learn to see like a camera. When you are out scouting a scene, a setting, or a location, you have to learn to see what is *actually there*. Otherwise your brain may instruct your eye to filter out whatever the brain considers unimportant.

Most people see what they are looking for, not what they are looking at. I'm always fascinated by the way people look at snapshots. As far as they are concerned, all that is important in the picture is what they *want* to see. They'll show you a crowd scene, underlit and partially out of focus, and say, "Here's Jennifer and the baby." Or a close-up of a bush, which they say is a snapshot of Uncle Jasper. And if you look closely, sure enough, you'll see a tiny Uncle Jasper way in the background.

When I was serving time at a small ad agency, the art director brought in an assignment to do a TV commercial for a shoe store. He had scouted the location and done storyboards detailing how the commercial would be shot. His experience, however, was all in print, so he asked me to direct the videotaping. It was a low budget spot that had to be done on location in half a day. As I was busy with other things, I didn't take the time to scout each location myself, but relied on the art director's storyboards.

One scene called for an overhead shot of a woman walking up the street and passing underneath the store's marquee to go inside. The art director told me we could shoot the overhead scene from the fourth level of a parking garage across the street.

From ground level, the marquee was a dramatic copper-clad structure with the store's name in illuminated letters. Very strong, visually. But when we got to the fourth floor of the garage and set up the camera, we were looking down at a copper-clad box containing several years of accumulated trash.

He had blocked the mess inside the marquee out of his mind when he sketched the storyboard. He saw it the way he would draw it, not the way a camera would have to shoot it.

Writing from Existing Footage

As a scriptwriter, you may sometimes come into a project after the completion of principal photography. Someone hands you a dozen rolls of videotape and says, "Here's what we shot. Write the script." Then you have to review the footage, take notes on it, and decide which scenes to use. Which means you have to see what is actually there.

Learning to see what is there can be especially hard for the person who is new to working with video. The snapshot mentality comes into play, and you tend to see what you *need*, rather than what is there. For example, in a documentary about a protest march there was a shot of an empty street, with a cold looking police officer in the foreground, standing by a police barrier. The narration at this point said, "Twenty thousand people took to the street in protest. . . ." But what the visual evidence said was *nobody was there*.

The script needed to say:

> Crowd shot: many people parading down
> the street.

Even better would be to know, based on your field research, that you could write the scene this way:

> Montage: Many people arriving at
> assembly area. Marshals organize the
> crowd. Large group sets off, chanting a
> protest song. Many people parading down
> the street.

Overcoming Your "Education"

Most of our experience in looking at films and videos, from grade school on, has been in interpreting them. And I take the word *interpreting* quite literally to mean translating from visual imagery to some form of verbal response—either written or spoken.

For example, I was working with a graduate class in the use of visual communication in education. I showed a short, artistic film about Aphrodite rising from the sea. Then I asked, "What did you see?" At first, the responses were either generalities about beauty, art, mythology, and the human condition, or they had to do with creative writing, the classics, and how to use film in the classroom. "Yes," I said, "but what did you see? What is in the film? What happened within the frame? What was the first shot? What was the next shot?"

With a great deal of difficulty, and with everyone contributing, the class was slowly able to start recreating and describing from memory the sequence of shots that made up the film. And as they got into it, they got better. When they came to the last few shots, where the naked Aphrodite is shown dancing in the moonlight at the edge of the sea, several people remembered that the "just born" Aphrodite had the white outline of a swimsuit on her otherwise beautifully tanned body.

We can only speculate as to whether the filmmakers noticed that flaw when they were putting the film together. Perhaps they did and thought they could get away with it. Or perhaps they never saw it at all.

Finding Accurate Analogs

A scriptwriter, working with existing footage, is pre-editing that footage—doing what is often called a paper edit. If you were there when the footage was shot, you have another problem: you know everything that happened. It takes only a little bit of the footage to spark your memory, so that you can recall the entire event. But your audience wasn't there. So the footage you choose for the scene has to stand as an accurate analog for everything you remember.

Here's a problem that came up in one of my videos. I had separate sequences of two different mothers and their two-year-old children working and playing together. Let's call one the Bad Mother. Her own behavior was pretty neurotic, and she tended to see only her little boy's "faults," never his good points.

The other was clearly a Good Mother. She talked freely with her daughter, paid attention to her, and encouraged her to do things on her own. The Good Mother was a Scandinavian, and she liked everything clean and neat. I recorded her daughter helping her mix the batter for a cake.

In editing the video, I put the two mother-and-child sequences back to back, the Bad Mother first. Each sequence ran about four and a half minutes, cut down from nearly two hours of original footage.

In the sequence with the Bad Mother I had focused on the little boy, because it was his behavior I was interested in. I had sidestepped and cut around the mother's neurotic outbursts as much as possible, because I wanted the audience to watch the behavior of the boy, and not waste their time trying to psychoanalyze his mother.

In the Good Mother sequence I was especially interested in the way the mother and daughter talked with each other, and I had concentrated on one point where the daughter is handing eggs to her mother to break into the mixing bowl. At the second egg, the daughter gestures as if to break the egg herself. The mother exclaims, "No! Please, dear! Let me do that," and the little girl hands over that egg. But when she picks up the third egg, she persists, and finally does crack the egg on the edge of the bowl.

I had been focused on their talk, leaving in as much of it as possible. When I ran the two sequences, I realized I had made a big mistake. I had included almost all of the footage in which the Good Mother worries about neatness, clucks about the mess, and says "Don't . . ." to her daughter. In the forty-five minutes or so of original video, this negative talk totaled no more than a minute. But when all of it was cut into a four minute sequence, it made up a disproportionate fourth of the edited version.

As a result, while I had neutralized the Bad Mother, I had inadvertently ended up making the Good Mother look pretty bad. By the time the daughter tries to break an egg on her own, an audience would be quite likely to miss the point that while the mother protests and asks her daughter not to break the egg, she could easily have stopped her, but didn't. I was afraid they might see it, instead, as just one more case of a fussy mother worrying about the mess. So I re-edited.

In the final version, the concern of the Good Mother for neatness is shown, but it doesn't overpower the important behavior of the child. And it doesn't turn a really good mother into a villain. The visual evidence of the sequence was brought back in balance with what had actually happened.

Selecting Footage

When you're reviewing existing footage for use in a script, you have to see it for what it is. In selecting footage to use, you might ask yourself these questions:

What is the main image in the shot?
Is the shot in focus?
Is the camerawork acceptable?
Is the sound (if any) usable?
Is the shot long enough to use? (Time it with a stopwatch if necessary.)
Does it present visual evidence to support the thesis of the video?
Could the scene be misconstrued or misunderstood by an audience?
How will this scene work in sequence with what precedes it in the script and what follows it?
Is there a better shot somewhere else?

What about Talking Heads?

Interviews—whether a two-shot with the interviewer asking the questions and interviewee answering, or a close-up of the person giving answers without including the questions—are a staple of video production. They're cheap and easy to do and can often be highly informative.

They can also be boring.

An interview is only as good as the performance of the person being interviewed and the relevance of the answers to the theme of the video. Interviews are often visually uninteresting, and as visual evidence they leave much to be desired. The fact is that while an interview is prima facie evidence that the person shown said the words that were spoken, it carries no evidence whatsoever about the truth value of the statement itself.

As a scriptwriter, you'll occasionally have to include interviews or statements from people as part of the video. But never get in the habit of relying on them. One good reason is that statements on camera are a terribly inefficient way to tell your story. A normal speaker will only say 125 to 150 words a minute. That's not much. Just one double-spaced page from the manuscript for a newspaper or magazine article contains more than 250 words. Which means it would take the average speaker about two minutes to cover the information on that one page if he or she didn't pause, say "uh," repeat phrases, and do all the stuff that's normal in conversation.

If you can show a picture of the topic, you can cut down substantially on the words which must be spoken. As a writer, I've always looked askance at the statement "A picture is worth a thousand words." As a scriptwriter, however, I take it literally.

When Is a Video Not a Video?

A video is not a video when it isn't visual. If a video isn't composed primarily of visual evidence, then (even though it may be shot on videotape and played on a TV screen) it really isn't a video. For example, videotaping someone giving a lecture does not produce a video as we mean the term here. It produces a lecture which has been recorded on videotape, just as videotaping the pages of a book results in a book which has been recorded on videotape.

Some ideas just aren't video ideas. They belong in an article, or a pamphlet, or a speech, or an audio recording, or a wall poster. And there's nothing wrong with that. Unless you—or the client—try to force them to become a video. Try this some time: put a short video on the VCR, but turn off or block out the picture, leaving just the sound. If you can easily follow what's going on, then too much of the information is coming in the audio channel, and not enough through visual evidence.

The Word Trap

The trap for any beginning scriptwriter is to get caught up in words—narration or dialogue—with no pictures on the screen. I've actually seen what were called "scripts" which contained nothing but narration. The idea, I presume, was that the video director would fill in with "visuals." The underlying assumption was that the verbal explication of the theme for the video was the most important thing.

And that's *not* thinking in pictures.

Start with the images. Know what you are going to show. Don't worry about verbal explanations. An audience today knows how to look at pictures. You don't have to tell them what they are looking at, unless there is no way they could know without some narrative explanation. Build up the visual evidence and when you have it organized, go back and see how little you need to put into narration.

Script people doing what they do, even if you're mainly interested in what they have to say. Select the location so that it becomes a part of the evidence of the scene. If you need to include an expert on juvenile delinquency who is proposing alternatives to putting adolescents in adult prisons, plan to videotape him at the prison, rather than in his office. You'll have the visual evidence that says this man is talking about concrete reality, not just some theory he's concocted.

Organize your video so that it presents a visual argument for the statement you are trying to make to the audience. Point out the visual evidence, if you must, in the narration. Lead up to a strong visual conclusion, and when you have made it, stop.

Use Your Eyes

For heaven's sake, look at videos and films—especially documentaries and other nonfiction programs. Learn to look with a critical eye. Commercial videos and documentary films, like any other creative form, range from excellent to lousy. Try to find the ones that appeal to you and analyze what it is you like about them. Do the same with the ones you dislike.

Form your own opinion. Hundreds of books about film theory and film analysis have been rushed into print in the last two decades to cash in on the popularity of film and video studies. Unfortunately, most have been written by people who are teachers, not by writers, producers, or directors, and many of them are not very good.

Ask people in the business to recommend examples of good commercial videos for you to watch. And find out why they consider those particular videos good. If there's a chapter of the International Television Association (ITVA) near you, see if you can get a look at the winning videos in their annual competition.

A Client Story: Sometimes You've Got to Teach the Client

I wrote, produced, and directed a documentary film for a client who was a print writer and the editor of the newsletter for a non-profit mental health organization in a large eastern state. He had gotten a grant for his organization to do a community education project on the release of mental patients from institutions. An important part of the grant was a series of public forums on the problem to be held in major cities across the state. He thought they would be interesting and controversial and should be a central part of the film. My experience was that public forums are dull, talky, and generally a waste of good film. Since we had access to shooting situations which could deliver powerful imagery, I didn't want to waste time and filmstock having people *talk* about the problem when we could *show* people *living* the problem. But the client had been adamant about what he wanted. And I had, reluctantly, gone along.

But not completely. As I told my crew, "Constraints tend to melt away in the face of good footage." We had shot some pretty good footage in halfway houses and mental institutions which yielded a few strong, visually compelling scenes in the edited film. And virtually every one of them was the result of ignoring the client's original instructions. But because of the client's insistence that we concentrate on the forums, we had missed several other opportunities for dramatic visual evidence.

Finally the day came when I showed him the edited version of the documentary. The strong scenes that we had were there, as were many long statements from the forums. When the film ended, the client leaned back in his chair, eyes closed, one hand on his forehead as if pressing out a difficult thought. "What I would really like to have," he said, "is more of those scenes that show the actual people in the community as they really are. And that's less talky."

"Rick!" I finally managed to say, "that's the film I proposed in my original treatment. The one you turned down flat."

My print of that film sits in the rack gathering dust, a reminder that I hadn't managed to teach the client, early enough, to think in pictures.

Exercise: Make a Stick Figure Script

Take a magazine article, either one you wrote or an interesting article you've found in a magazine. Using a scratch pad (or storyboard forms if you have them) turn the article into a script, by using stick figure drawings—no description of the image and no narration to explain the scenes. See how far you can get just thinking in pictures. Each stick figure drawing should suggest to you the content of the scene it represents. Looking at the drawings, you should be able to talk your way through the whole script, in the form: "The first thing we see is. . . . Then we see. . . . Then the narrator will have to explain this part while we look at. . . ."

When you have it completed, show someone else your stick figure script and talk him or her through the video. See if you feel that you are making sense. Ask the other person if he or she understands and can "see" the video.

Script Research

The reason why so few good books are written is that so few people who can write know anything.

—Walter Bagehot

In my view, video scriptwriting is mostly preparation. Long before you have to type FADE IN at the top of page 1 of your script, you'll have:

- researched the subject thoroughly,
- organized the material for effective presentation to an audience,
- outlined your approach to the video in a treatment, and
- gotten approval of the treatment from your client and the client.

Start with the Nature of the Project

The first step in preparation is brief research into the nature of the project. This may take nothing more than a phone call. It may be covered in your initial meeting with your client. However it is accomplished, there are certain things you need to know before you can agree to write the script or can even provide an estimated price for your work.

How Long Is the Video?

In general, the longer the video, the more work you'll have to do in creating the script. This is not a straight-line relationship. A six minute video may take the same amount of preparation, research, approvals, and meetings as a fifteen minute program. And it may take just as long to write, because you have to work in a tighter space. Similarly, a half hour show probably *won't* take twice as much time for research and preparation as a fifteen minute video although writing the treatment and the script *will* take twice as long.

What Is the Topic?

Early on you need a sense of what your client and the client think they are producing. Get them to describe their fantasies about the program, so you have an idea of what they think they are eventually going to see on the screen. You'll research the content of the video in much more detail later, but you need an overview to evaluate the job you're going to have to do.

Is the Proposed Length Realistic?

Can a video of the proposed length cover everything the client expects to be in the program? If not, is the proposed length too short or too long? Most of the time, you're not going to mess around with the proposed length of the video to any great extent. If the client wants a fifteen minute video, your job is to figure out how to cover the material in that length of time.

But sometimes clients have completely unrealistic expectations of what can be presented in a video minute. Then you have to be prepared to say, "I don't see how we can cover all of this material in the time allotted." To make your point, you may have to outline the content, assigning running times to each element, and then add up all the running times to show how long you estimate the program will actually run.

What Is the Style of the Proposed Video?

What kind of program will you be writing? Will it be classic documentary style with a voice-over narrator? Is it going to be a drama with actors and dialogue? Will it depend heavily on still pictures and graphics, or will it have a lot of action or live video? Will there be lots of interviews and talking heads? Will there be an on-camera spokesperson? Is anyone thinking about special effects, animation, or other video magic?

How Much Research Will Be Necessary?

What are you going to have to do to learn enough about the topic to write the script? With whom will you need to talk, and how easy are they to get to? What books, articles, reports, studies, pamphlets, and other written materials will you need to read? What location sites must you visit? Is there existing footage to review? Are there photographs or other visual elements you'll need to see?

What Is the Production Budget for the Video?

There are two important reasons for the scriptwriter to know the size of the budget. The first is that you need to know what you have to work with. You don't want to be writing in helicopter shots and a location trip to the Source of the Nile if you have only enough budget for two days of shooting in the studio. In an ideal world, the budget wouldn't be set until after the script is completed, and you would be able to write the show exactly the way you think it should be done. In the real world, however, the budget is usually set before the writer gets involved. Either the client comes in with a figure in mind, or the client goes to your client and asks, "How much will it cost to do a ten minute video about our new fall line?" And your client issues a "ball-park figure" which is supposed to be an estimate but quickly becomes graven in stone.

The second reason you need to know about the budget is that your fee is inextricably related to its size. One rule of thumb is that the cost for the script should be 10 percent of the production budget, but this is not a simple, straight-line matter. The production budget may be quite low, and your fee may have to be 20 or 25 percent of the budget—or more—or it won't be worth taking the job. If you are being asked to write a script to existing footage, the "production budget" may only include scripting, editing, and post production, or about one-half to two-thirds of what a full production would cost. So your fee quite reasonably could be 20 percent or more of the production budget. In my experience, writing a script from existing footage takes more of the writer's time and is often a more difficult task than writing from scratch. Therefore it should command a higher fee.

What Are the Deadlines for the Script and the Video?

Are the deadlines realistic? Or are you going to find yourself working around the clock to meet your obligations? I don't mind walking on water to meet a client's needs, but I won't do it as a matter of routine, and I don't do it at my basic rate of pay. When I perform miracles, I expect to be paid as a sorcerer.

Content Research

Once you've agreed to take on the job, you'll start researching the content of the video. And quite often the nature of the content will clue you to the form and style of the video. Your goal is to become, in a very short time, an expert on the narrow topic which is the subject of your video.

Purpose and Audience

A commercial video is made for some purpose. What is it? Why is the client willing to spend thousands of dollars to have this video produced? Is it a sales tool? A public relations vehicle to enhance or improve a corporate image? A training video for employees?

You should be able to write in one sentence what the proposed video will be used for. (And that sentence should appear in the opening of your treatment.)

Identify the target audience. Whom does the client want to reach? Potential customers? Current customers? Women under forty? Men who play golf? Executives of Fortune 500 companies? Tourists visiting your area? Travel agents? Stockbrokers? Entering freshmen?

As with the purpose, you want a clear statement of intended audience. Often the nature of the target audience will be determined by the purpose of the video. The target audience for an employee training video will be employees. But which employees? New hires, old hands, or everybody? Don't assume you know. Ask.

Is the client hoping for a multipurpose, multiaudience video? The client may hope to use the video for more than one purpose with more than one audience. Sometimes this is possible. Sometimes it isn't. I wrote a script for the Hawaii Department of Labor and Industrial Relations about how an occupational safety and health inspection is conducted. They wanted to show it to employers to inform them of what to expect when such an inspection occurs and to motivate them to bring their facilities up to OSHA standards. As a secondary audience, however, the state wanted to use the video as an aid in training new occupational safety and health inspectors. We agreed that this would be no problem as long as we aimed the information toward the employers' point of view and did not try to go into detail on how inspectors should inspect.

The rule of thumb is that a video which tries to be all things to all people will end up meaning nothing to anyone.

Important Content Points

A major focus of script research is to learn from the client the important content points to be included in the video. I take the position that while I am an expert on writing video scripts, the client is an expert (or should be) on his or her business.

Benefit. If you are writing a sales video, the most important content element is the *benefit*. What do the buyers get for their money? What sets this product or service apart from other products or services? What can you promise the viewer that the client can deliver? Common benefits are that the product or service:

Enhances the buyer's image
Offers higher quality (than the competition)
Offers lower price (than the competition)
Is a new and better way to do something
Increases safety and security
Saves the buyer money
Saves the buyer time
Has excellent service and support

In the Department of Labor video, the benefit to employers was to learn how to prepare for an occupational safety and health inspection.

Copy points. Copy points are other important content elements which should be included in the video. For the documentary *Light in Art*, one important point was to discuss the three primary colors and show how they combine to make other colors and white light.

In an employee orientation video for a supermarket chain,

a copy point was constant innovation to keep the stores successful.

In a student recruiting video for Cannon's International Business College of Honolulu a major copy point was that all students learn to type, but that doesn't mean they are going to work as typists. If they can't type, they're locked out of the modern business world with its reliance on computers.

In a video for Kentucky Fried Chicken, an important point was to show that the stores and menus were changing to meet changing customer needs. And this would result in job security and room for advancement for current employees.

In a video for a resort hotel, a copy point was to encourage hotel guests to visit the shops and boutiques on the resort grounds.

As you research the video, you'll come up with a list of major points which must be included. One way is to ask for them. Ask the client, "What information *must* be included in the video?"

Get the details. As you pick up the benefits and copy points, get the details behind them. If you don't know how primary colors combine, you need to find out. Have someone explain it. Ask for a good reference book.

If someone tells you willingness to innovate has kept the stores successful, get examples. Ask for success stories. And explore the negative cases. Have there been innovations that didn't work? This could lead to something you can use. In researching the supermarket video, I learned that the chain—let's call it "Yourstore" (not its real name)—had tried on-site bakeries and pharmacies in the stores more than forty years before. They weren't successful at that time and were removed. Today, several supermarket chains have bakeries and pharmacies. But knowing about the attempt that failed let me write about Yourstore as a company running way ahead of the pack:

```
                SPOKESPERSON
        And Yourstore was
        experimenting, then, with
        new ideas to meet the
```

customers' needs . . . ideas
like pharmacies in the stores,
and bakeries right on the
premises, with that good
baking smell in the air . . .
ummmm.

NEW CLERK
Some supermarkets have
those today.

SPOKESPERSON
That's right. But don't forget,
this was nearly forty years
ago . . . So Yourstore was
way out in front!

Scout the Location

Get out and see the places where the video will be shot. Remember, you can't write about what you don't know about. Reality is often far more interesting than the stuff you can make up sitting at your desk and looking out the window. When I was researching the script for the Department of Labor, I went on several actual occupational safety and health inspections. The inspector simply introduced me as a consultant to the department. As a result, I had a good feel for what happens during an inspection and for what the situation would look like. Even though we didn't shoot the video at any of the locations where I had gone on inspections, my script included the sorts of situations likely to be encountered at any similar site. For instance, at a construction site the inspector asked to see if all the electrical equipment had ground fault circuit interrupters installed. These shut down the equipment if there are electrical problems. That became a scene in the script.

Take along a camera and shoot pictures of the location to use as a memory aid when you're writing. If you've been shooting your own pictures for magazine articles, you're probably accustomed to using slide film. For location scouting, however, I use print film, because prints are easier than slides to work from.

You don't need reproduction quality, just a picture good enough to jog your memory.

Meet the People

If possible, you should interview the key people who have information about the topic of your script. It doesn't have to be a long interview; a half-hour may do it. What is important is to get the story from each person's unique point of view and have the chance to ask specific questions. Each person you interview will put his or her own spin on the information. By talking with several people you'll often turn up contradictions which have to be resolved. And each person you talk with becomes a resource you can go back to for more information.

I was working on a project for a hospital which had a successful drug and alcohol treatment program. It ran an inpatient program at the hospital and an outpatient program at several locations. Most of my information, however, was coming from either the marketing director at the hospital (the client) or the account executive at the ad agency (my client). I finally insisted that I needed to talk to the directors of the two programs. When I did, I learned that much of the information I had been given was not quite right, and in one critical area it was dead wrong. My information indicated that the hospital had dropped its intervention program—in which a counselor, members of the family, and the person's employer confront the person abusing drugs or alcohol and pressure him to get help. When I got to the director of the inpatient program, he said, "Not true! It's one of our most successful programs."

If you can't conduct the interviews face-to-face, do them on the phone. But face-to-face is better, because you get a lot more visual information. You see the facility, you see the person, and you meet others who are involved—any of which may lead to a scene in your script.

Auditioning the interviewee. Another reason for conducting interviews face-to-face is that you may want to use some of the people in the video. The interview is an opportunity to see how they present themselves, how they react to questions, and how they speak. Then you can select the ones who are credible and eliminate the long-winded, the insecure, and those with annoying mannerisms. Often I'll use a small tape recorder for the interview, although I always take notes as well, because I never want to put myself at the mercy of a bad battery or a jammed tape. I do this in part just to see how people react to the recorder. If they freeze up in an informal interview, they'll never make it in front of a camera, lights, and several crew members.

Suppose you know that for political reasons you are going to have to have the president of the company in the video. In the interview you discover that the president has a grating voice and speaks poorly. With this information, you may be able to craft a scene in which the company president is seen doing something with workers or other executives—being active and showing leadership—while a voice-over narrator does the talking.

Immerse Yourself in Detail

Your script has to be accurate. The producer and director are relying on you to give them correct information in the narration and in the visual scenes. They won't be checking up on you, unless it becomes obvious that something you wrote is wrong. And they don't employ fact checkers to be sure you've got it right.

Be sure you get the correctly spelled full name and title of everyone you talk with. The easiest way is to get a business card. But if they don't have a card, get it written down. And double-checked. Before the video is finished, you'll find yourself responsible for subtitles identifying speakers and for much of the information which goes in the opening and closing titles.

One of my most embarrassing moments came with a magazine article I did on a woodworker and furniture craftsman. My editor told me the man's name was Roger Worldlie, which he thought fitting because Roger had traveled a lot. That seated the name in my mind. Then I interviewed him in his store, which had a sign with his name on it out in front. And I got his business card and picked up other written information about him. When the article was published, I was pleased with it and sent several copies to Roger. A few days later I called to ask how he liked the piece. He said, "It's really very nice, and the pictures are beautiful, but, Barry, my last name is Worldie, not *Worldlie*."

Double-check the details: names, dates, spellings, locations, titles.

And then triple-check.

Collect Paper

Everywhere you go in researching the script, you have the opportunity to gather details in writing. If someone is telling you about a process, ask if there is a description in writing that you can take with you. Ask for brochures and annual reports. If someone has written a memo that relates to the content of the video, ask for a copy.

Don't be put off by size. Make it your goal to collect several pounds of paper on each script assignment. You may have to carry home a two hundred page report to find the one paragraph that will help your script.

Printed documents tend to have names of people, projects, and locations spelled correctly and are probably a better source than your notes. They often include maps and photos which can be helpful. And somewhere in all that paper you may find a clear explanation of something you didn't understand when you were interviewing the project manager.

Printed matter is also a source of questions in preparation for an interview and of follow-up questions as you get to know more about the project.

Writing from Existing Footage

When footage exists, it just adds one more piece of research to everything else you have to do. If the video will be made completely from the existing footage, you don't have to scout locations or audition possible on-camera speakers. But you still have to become an expert on the topic. Which means you still have to do all the basic content research. And you have to view the footage. Yourself. Just as you can't send someone out to do your interviews for you, or to scout locations, you can't rely on someone else to view the footage.

Window Print Dubs

For viewing the footage, you ask your client to copy all the original footage to VHS tapes in what is called a window print dub. When the footage was originally recorded, in addition to picture and sound, the videotape equipment recorded a time code on the tape. This permits a readout shown in HOURS: MINUTES: SECONDS: FRAMES which looks like this:

01:23:27:05

which is one hour, twenty-three minutes, twenty-seven seconds, and five frames. There are thirty frames to a second. Time code is used to locate a specific frame of the tape for editing.

When the tape is played on a machine which can read time code, the numbers change rapidly as the tape progresses. The frame numbers go by in a blur, the seconds change every second, and so forth.

In a window print dub, the videotape copy is recorded with a small "window" in the picture, usually along the bottom, in which is printed the time code from the original tape. As you view the tape on your VHS machine, the time code in the window tells you the address on the original tape of the footage you are watching.

When the original footage is dubbed to VHS, be sure you request a separate VHS reel for each original reel. This adds a few dollars to the cost of the dubs, but it will save you hours later on. If you don't do this, you'll end up with reels 1, 2, 3, and 4 of the original all dubbed onto one VHS tape. When you are writing the script, you'll want to check each scene on the tape as you write it. And you'll find yourself trying to go from a scene on reel 1 to a scene on reel 4, and you'll have to wait anywhere from two to five minutes while the tape fast forwards through reels 2 and 3. Then back to reel 2 and another wait of several minutes, and so on. It all adds up, and there's nothing you can do during those long waits. If you have each reel of original dubbed to a separate VHS reel, however, you just pop out reel 1, put in reel 4, and save a lot of time.

Logging the Footage

You log each scene with the tape reel number, the starting time code, a description of the scene, a summary or a transcript of what is said, and your comments. Figure 4-1 shows a sample page from the tape log for reel number 6 of the original footage for a video for First Night Honolulu. I began logging this footage when I knew very little about the project or who was involved. So people are identified generically: "woman," "man," "girls," "singer w/guitar," "rope trick guy." This is so I, or anyone else who needs to use the log, will know who I mean. It turned out that the "rope trick guy" was comedy magician Ken Noyle. If I were to identify him in the log as Ken Noyle, the director and editor might or might not know who I meant. But *everyone* who looks at the footage will know who the "rope trick guy" is.

First Night is a New Years' Eve celebration which emphasizes art and performance. As I got some experience with the footage I decided it would be helpful to have a category for each scene. For instance, C stands for crafts; V for voice or sound bites; M for music; X for technical entries such as black (no picture), end of reel, and so on; and J for jugglers, magicians, and acrobats.

FIGURE 4-1

Excerpt from the Footage Log, *First Night* Video

First Night Tape Log Reel 06 (2)

RL	TIMECODE	CAT	DESCRIPTION	COMMENT
06	06:06:49	C	Man getting face prepared for plaster, pull to 3 shot	
06	06:07:29	C	CU wetting plaster swatch for mask	
06	06:07:37	V	Girls in silhouette at plaster masks	NG
06	06:08:04	M	Black, then see singer w/ guiter, pull wide to 2S	
06	06:08:35	M	Hawaiian slack key guitarists in palaka shirts in tent, playing guitars	NICE
06	06:09:39	M	Slack key guitarist tells story to start song	
06	06:10:24	M	Slack key guitarist - CU hands on guitar, start of song	
06	06:10:35	M	Slack key guitarist continues story about someone "sitting under a pineapple tree" laughter "sitting under a pineapple tree, thinking about what he's gonna do, and a pineapple fell in his head . . . and his hand slip all the way down to the bottom, says, hey you got two different sounds here. I'm going to put them together"	
06	06:11:01	M	Slack key guitarist starts a song, then says, "Now you know what slack key is all about." Plays La Paloma	
06	06:12:08	M	Good CU of slack key guitarist as he continues La Paloma	
06	06:13:25	X	Black	
06	06:13:28	J	Comedian w/ rope - Indian rope trick	
06	06:14:36	J	Rope trick guy says "When the applause finally dies away." It stops. He says "All right." Looks in audience, says "Could you put your purse down so you can applaud with the other people ma'am?"	
06	06:14:46	J	Continues with the rope trick	

The log uses time code even within the description to tell when things happen. I use certain notations such as CU and ECU (close-up and extreme close-up) and 2S (two-shot—two people in the frame) because they are comfortable to me. You can use any shorthand you want, as long as it means something to you and will also have meaning for those who have to use your log or the script you write from it.

I don't feel compelled to put a comment after every shot. If I especially like a scene, I'll note it as GOOD or NICE. If it is unusable for some reason, I'll note it NG for no good. The description should tell why: out of focus, too dark, sound bad, or whatever.

The important thing is that the log should help you find scenes you want to include in the script. This is why I categorized the First Night scenes. Then I had the computer sort them into a separate log with all the music scenes together, all the craft scenes together, and so on. This gave me two logs: one chronological by reel and one sorted by category. When I wanted a music scene in the script, I could find it in the category log. Then I could look it up in the reel log and see what else was happening near it.

When a Footage Log Exists

Even if a footage log exists, you have to look at all the footage. *You can't write about what you haven't seen.* I would *never* write from someone else's log without at least having reviewed the footage and made my own notes. The way you log footage is intensely personal. You have no way of knowing what the other person knows about what constitutes a usable scene or how scenes go together to make a finished video. You don't know if they are any good at this, or what their visual sense is like. And it doesn't matter who they are. Even if the log was made by the producer or the director or the camera operator, you don't know what they had in mind when they logged it, or what kind of video they would make. Also, it's my experience that people who know the footage—who were there when it was shot—log in a kind of personal shorthand which often is meaningless to me.

If I were going to use someone else's log, I would probably photocopy it with space to make additional notes of my own. This would save writing down time code and basic description. But I'd still have to look at all the footage.

Why You Can't Write or Edit from a Transcript

I've known many directors who shot a lot of interviews, dubbed the audio from the videotape to an audio cassette, and sent it out to a stenographer to be transcribed. There's nothing wrong with this. But then they would sit down with the transcript and try to edit the video by cutting and pasting what was said into a "script."

It's never really successful.

The first and most obvious reason is that editing by audio track gives up the strength of the visual medium. You build a video with pictures, not with words.

The second reason is that while it is easy to join the words in a written transcript, it's not so easy to join the actual spoken words on videotape. For one thing, the voice inflection may be wrong, going up when it should be going down, seeming to ask a question when it should be making a statement. For another, the person speaking may not look the way you want or may not be where you want him or her to be.

If there's a lot of talk, a transcript can be great. But you're still going to have to go back to the footage and annotate the transcript with time code, so you'll know where to find a statement when you need it and can cross-reference it to the visual description in your reel log. Of course, if you can get the audio transcribed before you start logging footage, you can enter it into your computer and make it part of the footage log.

Judging the Footage

Because I've directed and edited a lot of videos, I can never look at someone else's footage without thinking that I'd have done this or that differently. It's a trap to beware of. Especially when you first start working with video, be careful about substituting your judgment for that of the working pros. You have a lot to learn, and it's not your job to grade the people who produced the footage on how well they've done. Your job is to find the good stuff so you can use it in your script.

On the other hand, I've found that if I keep getting angry about the footage I'm looking at, there's probably something wrong with it. The other side to that coin is that quite often I've been called in *because* there's something wrong with the footage, and the people who have it don't know how to get a script out of it. In that case, if I'm being well paid to solve the problem, I can handle the anger.

Planning the Program

As you research the video script, you should be thinking about the kind of program you are going to write. During the research phase, you may encounter various factors that push you in one direction or the other. If the purpose is to evoke emotion, you may want to go with a dramatization using actors. If the client has a treasury of graphics, paintings, or photos on the subject, you may decide that they are the most dramatic way to present the topic. If the audience will be children, you may want to consider computer animation or even puppets.

Will you use an on-camera spokesperson? If so, you'll be looking for locations in which to shoot the spokesperson.

By the time you complete your research you should have a pretty good idea of what will go into the video and how it will be presented.

The next step is to take this mass of information and organize it.

A Client Story: Doing the Research on Camera

In Chapter 1, I mentioned a video that I "saved" through scripting. Here's what happened. A chain of restaurants had opened several new locations and had added some new items to their menu. They decided to make a "day" out of officially opening (or re-opening) the restaurants, having them blessed by a minister—which is a tradition in Hawaii—and having live music, balloons, prizes, and freebies at each of the five locations. Members of the executive staff traveled from location to location accompanied by a Dixieland band and my client's video crew. Customers were encouraged to visit all five stores that day and get a special "passport" stamped to win a prize.

In spite of the fact that there were two cameras in operation all the time, and the same procedure was gone through at each of five restaurants, the footage was woefully incomplete. It didn't contain a complete sequence of a blessing, a complete statement of the purpose of the event by management, or a complete song by the Dixieland band. What it seemed to do was make the same set of mistakes five times. In essence, I had to do the script research after the video was shot. These are excerpts from a letter I sent to my client about the footage:

> There are no shots whatsoever of the special passports (500 to be given out at each restaurant). No shots of anyone receiving a passport. No shots of anyone explaining the passport. No shots of a passport getting stamped at a store.
>
> Although six different radio stations participated, there is only limited footage of two radio DJs, and no radio broadcast audio.
>
> There is only one shot of a drawing for

a door prize (which is also one of the two shots of the DJs).

Too much camera time is spent on people from the P.R. firm riding the bus.

No close-up of an employee wearing the Celebration Day button.

I don't see in the footage any evidence that "each restaurant will be decorated professionally" as indicated in the "Game Plan."

There is . . . no systematic coverage of the new menu items. There is one shot of the menu, close-up of the word NEW, and no return to what is NEW.

There is no complete coverage—establishing shot, MS, CU while the sound continues—of the Country and Western band at Westridge Shopping Center or the Hawaiian music group at Windward City Shopping Center.

No footage of the 20 × 30 posters announcing Celebration Day.

We have no interviews or statements from (company executives) such as:

"This is an important marketing test for use on the mainland."

"We're introducing a new image, brighter more complete restaurants, rather than take-out places, and a new menu."

"This is going to be great for business."

With just a little research and planning the footage could have been so much better. And that's what the scriptwriter brings to the equation.

Exercise: Prepare a Research Checklist

Based on the information in this chapter, prepare a research checklist for yourself. This should give you an outline of the things you need to find out before you can write the script.

Now take a magazine article, perhaps the one you used for the exercise in Chapter 3. Using the checklist, make a time estimate of how long it would take you to research that article for a script.

With this information you should have a very concrete idea of what you have to do to research a video script and how long it will take. And that's the first step in pricing your work.

5 Finding the Organizing Structure

The three most important facets of story craft are: (1) structure; (2) structure; (3) structure.
—RICHARD WALTER, *Screenwriting: The Art, Craft and Business of Film and Television Writing*

Two tasks which have never been terribly popular with writers—and which seem to have fallen into even greater disfavor today—are outlining and rewriting. For years I sat down with my notes, scribbled out three or four topic headings on a scratch pad—which I called my "outline"—and began writing. When I had written a first draft, I'd go through it, cross out the redundancies, and then cut it apart and Scotch tape it back together in a way that seemed to flow smoothly. Then I retyped it, which I called "rewriting." I honestly thought I was outlining and rewriting, when I was actually doing something else entirely.

Then a friend asked me to look over the script for an hour long video he was getting ready to direct and tell him why he was having so much trouble in pre-production planning. The program was called *An Insider's Guide to Oahu* and was being produced to play on cable television in hotel rooms in Waikiki. As I read through the script, I realized from the way topics were raised and dropped that the script had been written as if it were a circle-the-island tour starting and ending in Waikiki. This is certainly one way to organize the material, but nowhere in the script did it say this was what was being done. An Oahu resident would realize it. But a tourist probably wouldn't.

The effect was that the script seemed to jump around from topic to topic, back up to tell more about some topic mentioned previously, and then jump away to something completely different. For instance it jumped from Hanauma Bay, Oahu's wonderful undersea preserve, to the riding stable and rifle range in Koko Head crater; to Sandy Beach, home of some of the best body surfing in Hawaii; to a sequence on Hawaiian food at the plate lunch trucks at Sandy Beach; to Sea Life Park, where the whales and dolphins play; then back to two more beaches, Waimanalo Beach and Kailua Beach. Which is exactly the order in which you would reach each of these places if you were driving counterclockwise around the island on Kalanianaole Highway. Over the weekend I wrote a seven page, single-spaced memo analyzing the script. Boiled down to essentials, it said the script had many good scenes but no strong underlying structure to help make sense of them.

The producer hired me to do a rewrite—in a hurry, of course, because shooting days with local and national celebrities had already been scheduled. Having said that the script needed to be reorganized, I knew I had to find an organizing structure that would pull the material together into a coherent whole. Consciously or unconsciously, I went back to the way I used to edit documentary films. When all the film was shot, I would go through the footage and break it down into a lot of little rolls of film. Each roll contained one scene and was labeled with a piece of tape proclaiming its content. Then I'd sort all the rolls of film and line them up on the film rack over my editing table in the order in which I thought they should appear in the finished documentary.

This became a sort of existential outline, organizing the material in sequence for presentation to an audience. The first little rolls of film on the left side of the top shelf on the rack would be edited together to make the opening. The pieces of film that made up the ending would be lined up on the right side of the bottom shelf. In between, the rolls of film were sorted so that like things went together and the presentation could flow smoothly from the opening through the presentation of visual evidence to the ending, stopping at each topic once, dealing with it, and moving on.

I went through the original writer's script and wrote a brief description of each scene or piece of business on a 3 × 5 card. Then I sorted these into categories such as beaches, boats, food, history, places to go, sights to see, water sports, and so on. Finally I taped the cards to the wall in my office in the order in which I thought I should write about the topics. I had created a paper editing rack on which to organize a paper movie.

It worked. It organized the material in a way that made sense to me and to the director. And because I had to write some scenes out of sequence, so they could be shot when the celebrity hosts were available, the organization let me know what was supposed to happen in the script before the scene I was writing and what would follow. Which allowed me to mention previous and coming scenes in dialogue, even though they hadn't been written yet.

Get Organized

The single most important task of the commercial scriptwriter is creating a structure which organizes the information you've gathered for presentation to an audience. Several times I have been asked to rewrite the work of someone else. Invariably, the writer had done a pretty good job of gathering the information but simply didn't know how to put it together so it would make sense to an audience.

I think one reason writers are put off by the idea of outlining is the way they were taught. For a writer, outlining is a means to an end, organizing the material so you can write about it. In the hands of a junior high school teacher–bureaucrat, however, the outline became an end in itself. If you were ever graded on how you prepared an outline, or were given a bunch of memory rules about outlining, such as, "You can't have 1 under A unless you have another subtopic to make a 2," you've probably been turned off about organizing in advance.

Become an Expert on Your Subject

The way I wrote *An Insider's Guide to Oahu* gave me a whole new approach to outlining my data before I begin to write. It doesn't matter whether you're writing a magazine article or a video script; if you're going to be any good at it, you have to know what you are writing about. You have to become enough of an expert on the topic that you could take an oral exam on the subject or go on talk radio and talk about it. If you're not ready to do that, you're really not ready to write about it.

When I used to write a first draft with next to no organization, what I actually was doing was taking the important stuff in my notes and other background material and making it mine by writing about it. By the time the first draft was done I really understood the topic, and then I was able to reorganize and rewrite so it would make sense to someone else.

In video scriptwriting, you use the process of outlining the material and writing the treatment to become an expert on the subject. It's sort of like cramming for a test. You're trying to be consciously aware of everything you know about the subject for the relatively short time it takes to write the script. At the same time, to help you organize the material and to jog your memory about details, you create an existential outline.

The Existential Outline

When I was rewriting *An Insider's Guide to Oahu,* I wrote everything out on cards and taped the cards to the wall. Unfortunately, each time I moved a card, I moved a little bit of wallpaper along with it. So I needed a better system. I went to a plastics company and bought several scrap ends of Plexiglas—one to two feet high and two to three feet long—left over from jobs which had been cut to size. Because I didn't care about the exact size, I got them for the scrap rate—pretty cheap. In place of 3 × 5 cards, I began to use Post-it Notes, which would stick easily to the Plexiglas and could be moved around at will.

Then, as I'd go through my notes and all the other material I'd collected about the topic, I'd jot down a few words about each separate bit of information on a Post-it and stick the Post-it on the biggest sheet of Plexiglas I had. This became a kind of preliminary sort of the material, setting up the major points to be covered and organizing the Post-its in clusters around related topics. If three different people talked about, say, environmental health at three different places in my notes, each of the references became a Post-it, and all three Post-its were stuck on the Plexiglas next to each other. If a Post-it referred to detail too extensive to transcribe, I'd code it to show the place in my notes where the full information could be found. When I had reduced *everything* to Post-its, I'd get another sheet of Plexiglas and reorganize the information in sequence in the way I thought I should write about it. (Recently I discovered foam core display boards which can be bought at any art supply house. They work as well as Plexiglas but cost less and are much lighter in weight.)

The next evolution of the existential outline came when I discovered several companies were selling sticky substances that could be used to give any kind of paper the sort of movable stickiness of Post-its. For instance, Dennison's Tack a Note is like a glue stick which lets you rub on the sticky stuff. Moore's Tacky Tape is an applicator for applying sticky stuff in a tape strip. Both are useful. So, now, instead of having to hand write the references onto Post-its, I type the information using the outline utility in my word processor. I don't worry about form or typos, but I do continue to put similar things together. When I have everything typed into the outline, I format it to print out in two inch wide columns (the width of a Post-it). Then I print out the outline, spread sticky stuff on the back, and cut it up into Post-it size chunks. These get organized onto Plexiglas the same way I organized the Post-its. In addition, I still use Post-its for topic headings, random thoughts, creative ideas, and other information which supplements the typed data.

Organize in Sequence

My system is to organize the typed chunks and Post-its—let's just call them notes—in sequence, running down the Plexiglas in columns. This is the point at which you have to narrow the scope of the video, trim away the fat, and concentrate on the essentials. The stated running time of the video you're writing tells you how much you can include. Remember, a ten minute video with wall-to-wall narration can handle no more than fifteen hundred spoken words. If time is critical—for instance if the script *must* be finished in eight minutes—I'll let each column represent a unit of time, such as thirty seconds or a minute. Then the heading for each column becomes the running time: the first column might cover the start to one minute of running time and be labeled "0-1," the second column would be labeled "1-2," and so on.

The production budget tells you whether you can think big or have to keep it small. You'll have discussed the budget with your client, and you'll have a good idea of how many days of shooting you can write for and how lavish you can be in post production.

The notes get stuck on the Plexiglas board in the order of presentation. They become a sort of storyboard made out of press-on notes. And they're easy to change. As you build up the structure of the script by adding notes to the Plexiglas, you'll be constantly revising the order of presentation until it feels right, makes sense to you, and flows visually from beginning to end. Even after you've started writing, you may find that something you thought would come late in the script needs to move toward the beginning, and that something else will have to be moved to take its place.

That's the great part about this system. It's not a junior high outline that you turn in for a grade. It's just bits of paper stuck on a piece of plastic to help you get organized so you can do your job better.

The Structure of a Video Script

In the first course I took in creative writing at the University of Pennsylvania, Professor Bruce Olsen defined the famous "Beginning, Middle, and End" this way:

> The beginning is the point in your work
> before which nothing needs to be said.
> The end is the point beyond which
> nothing needs to be said. And the middle
> runs in between.

That's a simple statement of a profound idea. And it's helpful when you have a lot of material you're trying to cram into a limited framework of time. For the opening, you can ask yourself how deep into the material you can go before you start the video. And for the closing, you're asking, in essence, how soon can I stop?

The Opening

The opening should catch the viewers' attention, excite their interest, and suggest what the film is about.

The first two minutes. What happens in the first couple of minutes after the video starts has an immense bearing on the audience's reaction to the video. You've got everything going for you before the opening fade-in. The audience expects the experience they are about to have to be worthwhile or they wouldn't be there. Even captive audiences assume there must be some value, or they wouldn't have been "captured" to view the production. And then the program starts and the audience is invited to enter the separate reality unfolding on the screen. And in the space of the next couple of minutes either you deliver the goods or you lose them.

It's impossible, today, to find an audience in the Western world that hasn't been strongly conditioned by hour after hour of television viewing. And what do they see? Show after show that begins with conflict and sudden dramatic action, a tease designed to grab their attention and keep them from zapping away to another channel. That's your competition, in the sense that the audience—and even the client—will unconsciously compare your video with what they see on prime time television, not with other documentary, industrial, or training productions.

Does this mean you have to start a video about employee benefits with a murder and a car chase? Only metaphorically. What is true is that you have to hold the attention of even a captive audience, somehow, or they'll mentally wander away.

Every manual on effective communication suggests you start with what the audience already knows and build on it. But if you try to play it safe, you're apt to lose more souls to boredom than you'll save with misplaced relevance. I don't think it's your responsibility to do all the work for your audience. You have no business confusing them, of course, but you don't have to do all their thinking for them. You can ask yourself, "Do I have to tell this to the audience? If I leave it out, will it be missed?" If the answer is no, leave it out. Oh, *you* might miss it, because you know you left it out. But the audience? Never.

As obvious as this seems, there are videos being made with two openings. The first is some sort of preamble with only marginal relevance to the message of the video. It comes on the screen after the opening fade-in. The second occurs a few minutes later when the video actually begins. Don't make the mistake of thinking that because you learned about the elements of the video in a certain order, or because the events to be shown occurred with a certain chronology, you have to present them that way. Starting in medias res was a good technique when Edmund Spenser wrote *The Faerie Queene*, and it's still a good technique today. Your job is to make your audience want to see what will happen next. The best way is to start with a problem and work outward from it in as many directions as it takes. What you are after are the seeds of dramatic conflict. And that applies just as much to a training film on employee benefits as it does to a detective show on TV.

Titles. The opening titles may come before the opening, or after it, but should not stop the progress of the video. Every name and title you see at the start of a Hollywood film has its place established by contract with the various unions, guilds, performers, and craftsmen involved. But most commercial videos are produced without those restraints, and the writers and producers can do whatever they please about the titles. Discuss with your client which titles and credits need to be at the head of the video and which ones can go at the end. On a personal note, I place my credit as scriptwriter in the same cluster with the producer and director. If their credits go at the head, mine does too.

My preference has always been to open the video with a strong scene and then superimpose the title and the major production credits on a weaker scene a couple of minutes into the show. In scouting you want to be on the lookout for an interesting sequence that might be used as background for the opening titles.

If I can't do that, I'd rather get the titles out of the way at the very beginning and then "start" the video with a dissolve or fade-in following the titles. If I'm saddled with a long government disclaimer of the sort that takes a hundred words to say, "We put up the money but we take no responsibility for the content," or with a lengthy list of sponsoring agencies, I try to separate those titles from the body of the video.

Explanation and Exposition

Within or following the opening, you weave in a brief presentation of the theme of the video, the problem it deals with, the main people involved—whatever the viewer needs to know for the video to go forward. Keep this short! Too many scriptwriters, especially beginning scriptwriters, have a tendency to stop the video dead at this point and try to explain everything. Trust your audience and limit this section to the absolutely essential information without which they won't understand the video.

In the theater, exposition was often handled by opening Act

One with the maid on the telephone. In the course of her conversation she would tell us everything we needed to know about the people we were going to see next. It was a lousy opening then, and it still is.

If you don't get caught up in the idea that you have to impose an order on your video based on some sort of exterior logic (first you have to know this, then you have to know that) you'll find that exposition will take care of itself. Let essential information come in when it is needed and relevant. You may play hell with chronology, but your video will flow smoothly from point to point. And that, I'm convinced, is the key to good understanding and retention by the audience.

Presentation of Evidence

You've gotten the audience interested. You've given them a notion of what the video is about. Now you need to present some hard information to keep them interested.

Evidence related to the theme. This may be evidence that supports the theme (or some part of it) or it could be evidence that appears to contradict the theme you've established.

Opposing evidence. If what you presented first was positive, this is negative, and vice versa.

Note that evidence related to the theme and opposing evidence may be repeated several times as you explore a variety of subthemes. They could also be presented simultaneously, as when the narration seems to contradict what is being shown.

Dramatic conflict. The purpose is to introduce something like dramatic conflict into the structure of the video. Dramatic conflict doesn't mean some kind of encounter situation with adversaries yelling at one another. It is a structural tension which keeps the outcome of the video somewhat in doubt—and keeps the audience interested.

You can also provide dramatic conflict without playing opposing scenes against each other if the evidence you are presenting runs counter to the expectations or experience of the audience. In documentaries of human behavior and documentaries of unique events, the outcome is often sufficiently in doubt that there is tension built into the video by the nature of the event itself.

An information video is expected to explore conflicting elements of the situation. This doesn't mean that it has to be passively neutral. But even when it takes a strong position in its theme, it should be able to acknowledge that its position isn't universally accepted. If it were, there would be little reason to make the video.

In an industrial video, the conflict might arise from a technical problem that had to be overcome. Even in a public relations video extolling the virtues of a product or organization, a little conflict can be a good thing. It is now considered the best kind of public relations to raise objections or opposing points of view so that they can be answered. One of the differences between information and propaganda is the willingness of the former to acknowledge that other points of view may legitimately exist, even if they are considered wrong.

Resolution

The resolution is the outcome—which up to now has been somewhat in doubt—in which the conflicting elements are handled and resolved. This is really the point to the video, toward which all the evidence has been leading. If the video is about a scientific experiment, the resolution is the point at which the theory is confirmed or the explanation of why it wasn't. In a video about employee benefits, resolution might be the point at which the employee is told how to sign up for or select the benefits that have been discussed.

The Ending

The ending is the point beyond which nothing needs to be said. It is a final sequence within or after the resolution which ties up the loose ends, drives home the theme, and completes the video for the audience.

The closing titles may come during the ending or after it.

Keep It Visual

The notes making up the structure of the script on your Plexiglas board will probably be primarily verbal content. As you are organizing the structure, keep in mind that you have to keep it visual. Make notes to yourself on how you are going to show the content. If you don't know, you've got a problem. Because the next thing you're going to do is take the structure you've created and use it to write the treatment. And that has to include visual content.

A Client Story: The Little Writer Who Wouldn't

Sometimes I'm asked to function as a consultant to a client when a writer has already been working on the project. In one case a young woman, trying to establish herself as a freelancer, had researched and written about a proposed project to establish a commercial space port on the Big Island of Hawaii. Eventually her first draft came to me. Her research was pretty solid, although in dealing with a state agency she had been far too willing to accept whatever they said at face value, when some probing was needed.

The big problem, however, was the structure of the piece. It had what I call a concentric circle organization. That is, she'd touch on a subject and then swing around and hit two or three other points. Then she'd come back to the first topic and go into it a little deeper before veering off to add more detail to some of the other items. And then she'd come around again. And again.

I put this all down in a memo along with my suggestions of how to restructure the piece and the places where I thought additional research was needed. This writer had come well recommended to me, and I wanted to help her get off to a good start if I could. So I set up a meeting with her and went over her work and my suggestions. When I was finished, I asked if what I had said made sense for the second draft.

"Oh, yes," she said. "But I don't understand why you're telling me all this. Why didn't you just fix it?"

The last I heard she had given up freelance writing and taken a job as a P.R. person with a government bureau.

Exercise: Structure a Video

View some commercial videos on any topic until you find one you like. Outline the structure of the video using Post-its on Plexiglas or cards stuck to anything. Note how the writer has used structural elements to help you follow the theme and stay interested in the message.

If you can find a commercial video that you find hard to watch and difficult to understand, do the same thing with it. Chances are you'll find that its problem is poor structure. Take the existential outline you've made of the bad video and reorganize it so it makes sense and flows smoothly.

Writing the Treatment

It is in the finished treatment that your idea exists in its most comprehensive form short of an actual script.
—J. MICHAEL STRACZYNSKI,
The Complete Book of Scriptwriting

Writing the treatment is, in my opinion, the creative stage of video scriptwriting. It's the place where you integrate all the preliminary work of research and organizing into the first draft of words on paper. In creating an existential outline and organizing the material, you've established an anticipated flow of visual and audio information which you think will be the best way to present the video to an audience. But with the exception of a few notes to yourself, you haven't *written* anything.

In writing the treatment you commit yourself to a structure for the video. And you solve most of the creative problems of the script.

Why Write a Treatment?

So why write a treatment instead of a script? Several reasons:

The treatment represents your first chance to feed back to your client and to the client how you think the video should be made. You expect that they will have suggestions and changes. So you want to use the simplest and easiest form. A script requires full detail and a very formal format. A treatment doesn't.

The production company is going to look at the treatment to see if what you have proposed can be done within the budget. If not, they're going to come back to you for changes. Better to do this while your work is still in outline form and changes are easy to make.

Because the treatment can be explained as a first outline of the proposed script, it is less threatening to the client and to you. If you deliver a finished script and the client doesn't like it, you're in trouble. In the client's mind, you've spent all this time and money and come up with the wrong answer. But if the client doesn't like the treatment, you can say, "That's okay. That's why we do this step. Now, what changes do we need to make before we go to script?"

Approval of the treatment often triggers a progress payment to the writer.

And an approved treatment becomes a legal document if the client rejects the script you've written from it. If you can show that the script you've written is the script described in the approved treatment, then you are owed the final progress payment. And if the client wants substantial changes, you should get a rewrite fee.

Elements of the Treatment

A treatment is often referred to as an outline for the script to come. But I prefer to think of it as an explanation of the video that will be made. The treatment describes the prospective video and demonstrates to the client that the writer understands what must be done. At the same time, it provides a sufficient blueprint for the production that the producer can estimate the cost of making the video. And it represents the client's first decision point on content.

Purpose and Audience

Start the treatment with your understanding of the project—its purpose and the audience for which it is intended. This serves two functions. It reassures the client that you are on track to make the video he or she wants and needs. And it reminds you—and the production company which will make the video—of the same thing.

Within the section on purpose, you may list major sales points, benefits, and people and locations which should be included.

Here's an example from the treatment for a homeowners' video for a housing developer I'll call "Greathouse Properties":

A. PURPOSE

1. The video will be produced to provide useful and essential information to homeowners in properties developed by Greathouse Properties.

2. The video will provide a visual supplement to the homeowners' manual and will refer the viewers to the manual for further information.

3. The video should provide an easy reference for homeowners on:

    a. Their responsibilities,
    b. How to keep their property intact and appreciating,
    c. What to do when things go wrong, and
    d. Whom to call.

4. The video will look at both:

    a. Basic property maintenance, and
    b. Termite prevention.

B. USE

1. The video will be distributed to resident managers, property managers, owners associations, etc.

2. It may be cost effective to give the video to each new owner at closing.

C. **DESCRIPTION**

1. The video will be 10–15 minutes in length depending on how much basic homeowner information is included.

2. The video titles can be customized so that it will appear to be a video specifically created for each new development.

Style of the Video

Next you describe the style in which you think the video should be written, shot, and edited, and the reasons for using this style.

Here are the sections on purpose and style from a recruiting video for Cannon's International Business College of Honolulu:

PURPOSE

The video will show and explain the opportunities at Cannon's International Business College of Honolulu. It will show the attractive features of the school. And it will demonstrate the value of the school.

The video will provide a visual introduction to the opportunities at Cannon's International Business College of Honolulu for potential students and their families. It will be shown:

1. To people who come to the school for information.
2. During recruiting visits to secondary schools.
3. And to people from the neighbor islands or the mainland who may not have a chance to visit the school before matriculating.

The goal is to motivate the viewer to want to come in to Cannon's International Business College of Honolulu and talk about going to school there.

STYLE

The video will be relatively short—not less than ten minutes, nor more than about fifteen minutes.

It will be more visual than talk, and will be backed with a solid contemporary musical theme. The photographic style will emphasize motion. Editing will use quick cuts and dissolves on action. The visual style should approach that of a music video. The people, and the message of the video, should dance across the screen, flowing with the music.

Students and others who appear in the video will be well made up and dressed for success in terms of their peer group.

Testimonial statements from students and graduates will be short and to the point. This is a long commercial, not a short documentary.

Description of Content

The treatment has to describe the prospective video completely enough that the client can decide whether what you have proposed is or is not the video he or she wants produced. It includes all the elements—the people, places, things, and events—which must be a part of the video. And it is organized with the structure that will be used in the script.

The major difference between a treatment and a script is that in a treatment the narration and dialogue are suggested or described; in a script they must be written completely.

To get started, I may do a storyboard with stick figure illustrations on it and no words, like the exercise at the end of Chapter 3. Or I may begin with a shot list: a sequence of visual events that tells the story. I've learned the hard way that if I start with what is said, I end up with a talky script, illustrated with "visuals." And that's a lecture, not a video.

Your problem is to abstract—from all the material you've gathered and observed in the research phase—a sequence of visual events that will give the audience, in a very short time, not only the information, but the feel and flavor of what you have learned over a period of days or weeks.

I tend to write treatments in outline form, describing what is seen and indicating what will be heard. My treatments include every visual scene I intend to write. I try to keep the descriptions brief, while including whatever detail is necessary for the client and the production people to understand what I mean.

Figure 6-1 is an excerpt showing the way I began the treatment for a sales video for the Hilton Hawaiian Village in Waikiki.

The Hilton Hawaiian Village treatment was written for a dramatic video using actors. Figure 6-2 shows the opening of a treatment for a retail video on a helicopter tour of the island of Kauai, to be done in documentary style with a narrator.

Treatment headings. In both treatments, the first heading (A, B) informs the reader (the client) of the copy point being covered under that section. In the Hilton treatment, the second heading (1, 2) tends to be who says what, and the third heading (a, b) adds detail or what we see during the dialogue. In the helicopter treatment, the second heading (1, 2) tells what is seen, while the third (a, b) tells what is heard.

Note that the treatment can also be a place to indicate information you need or decisions that must be made. In the helicopter treatment, I left blank the number of gallons in a ton of water in the hope that someone who knew the answer would tell me. Nobody did, so I ended up calculating it myself when I wrote the script.

Treatment to Script

Sometimes a treatment is a trial balloon. It's a chance to propose a video concept to see how it will be accepted. Especially if the client is less than specific about what is wanted, the treatment becomes a way of forcing the issue and getting a decision before writing a complete script. At other times the information is so clear that the treatment is almost a cookie cutter for the script. For example, Appendix 2 shows an excerpt from the treatment I wrote for an information video about a

FIGURE 6-1

Excerpt from the Treatment for the Script for a Video for Hilton Hawaiian Village

---

A. In the Shell Bar, two couples are seated, being served drinks. It's their last night at the Village.
   1. Roger and Gloria Hofstrau. Fiftyish. He is senior management of a Fortune 500 company. She is active in fund raising and charity work.
   2. Steven and Ginny DeAngelo. In their forties. He is mid-level management with a company such as 3-M. She teaches sixth grade in a public school.

B. Speaking of the Village . . .
   1. Roger is finishing a story about a recent trip.
      a) Ginny says she envies them their opportunity to travel. She and Steve had to budget and save, just for this trip. But it was worth it.
         (1) Planning the trip was a lot of fun.
         (2) Going to tell her travel agent how much she enjoyed it.
   2. Gloria says, well you picked exactly the right place. Hilton Hawaiian Village has just completed a *major* (renovation) rebuilding—like a brand new place. They spent a hundred million dollars or more.
      a) Roger adds that they've watched it grow. It's really an all new resort, in the midst of its Grand Reopening.

C. Destination Resort in Waikiki.
   1. Ginny says that what she likes is that it's not like any hotel she's ever stayed at. It's so much more.
   2. Gloria says in many ways it is like a resort on the neighbor islands.
   3. Steve adds some detail: 22 acres, 4 buildings, 3 swimming pools, etc.
   4. As they talk, we see some exterior shots that give us a sense of size and elegant newness.

D. Joined by another couple.
   1. Mark and Vickie Randall are in their thirties. He's an electronics professional; she manages a bank branch office.

FIGURE 6-2

Excerpt from the Treatment for *Kauai, Your Flight of Memories*

B. Flying out from Lihue.
   1. Interior of helicopter—see Nawiliwili Bay and Harbor.
   2. Alakoko fish pond.
      a) Narration: Legend of the Menehune—built in a single night. 900 feet long. How an ancient fish pond works—grate so small fish can swim in and feed, get too big to swim out.
   3. Waita Reservoir.
      a) Narration says it stores water for sugar cane. Takes one ton of water (______ gallons) to produce one pound of sugar.
   4. Huleia Stream and trees.
      a) Narration: Location used in *Raiders of the Lost Ark.*
   5. Tree tunnel—from the air.
      a) Narrator says it was originally known as the Mahogany Swamp, and tells about the Knudsen family planting the eucalyptus trees to absorb water.
   6. Tree tunnel from the ground. See helicopter flying through the trees.
   7. Aerial of helicopter crossing the woodland.
   8. Aerial of helicopter flying past Kahili and/or Mana Waipuna Falls.
   9. Robinson summer homes.
      a) Narration: Tells about the Robinson family. Largest landowner on the island. Main summer house: 12,000 square feet. Area is a wildlife refuge.
   10. Shot of Niihau.
       a) Narration: Robinson family owns Niihau—the forbidden island. Bought it from King Kamehameha V in 1864. Mixture of past and present. Only Hawaiian spoken there.
   11. Into Okolele River Canyon.
       a) Narration: Owned by the Robinsons and deeded to remain in its natural state. Game preserve.
   12. Flying along a narrow gorge in Okolele River Canyon.

---

highway construction project for the Department of Transportation. And beside it is a portion of the script that resulted from the treatment.

Treatment Length

How long should a treatment be? You'll hear that a treatment should run only a couple of pages. And that may be true if you're submitting a synopsis on spec to a producer (like sending a query letter to an editor). For a commissioned commercial video, however, two pages won't do it. You need a more complete description for several reasons:

1. The production company needs to know what has to be shot and how it will be edited to determine cost.
2. The client is probably not experienced at reading video shorthand and needs enough description to be able to tell what you intend to show.
3. Acceptance of the treatment is often a progress payment milestone for the writer. You want to give your client a document which indicates you've done a substantial amount of work.

My treatment for a fifteen minute video could run anywhere from seven to fifteen pages, depending on the amount of detail that has to be covered and how completely I've written the narration or dialogue. The full treatment for the Hilton Hawaiian Village (Figure 6-1) ran ten pages. The complete treatment for the Kauai helicopter tour (Figure 6-2), which was a thirty minute program, ran sixteen pages. The full treatment for the highway video (Appendix 2) was ten pages long and resulted in a twenty-two page script.

Treatment for a Unique Event

Occasionally, if the video will document a unique event where the outcome is uncertain, a comprehensive treatment can take the place of a script—at least in pre-production. Such a treatment will show that you understand the purpose of the video and will set forth the kinds of things the video director and crew should look for and record. It will include a list of scenes which should be recorded. It might list some conditional shots in the form, If *A* happens then record *B* and interview *C*. It probably will not suggest much in the way of narration other than background information. It may suggest the probable content of interviews. It may propose a tentative structure for the video, or it may defer questions of structure until the footage is shot and the outcome is known. The treatment will meet the requirements of letting the client know the approach to the video and letting the producer estimate the cost of production. A script may be written after the footage is shot.

Figure 6-3 is from the treatment for a documentary film I made called *A Young Child Is . . .* about early learning in young children. I was going to observe very young children with a camera. I knew what I wanted, but I had no idea what I'd get.

The treatment indicates the sorts of things I would be looking for in filming. I think I had it in mind that the paragraph headings in the treatment might become divisions within the film. It didn't work out that way in editing. In the treatment I developed a possible organization of the material, without being unalterably committed to it.

Paragraph 11 in the treatment, headed "Repetition, familiarity, mastery," is a good example of the way you indicate the kind of images you'll be looking for. It doesn't mean you will use these exact images. As it happens, we never even tried to film a parent reading a story. We did shoot in a playground, where we got some film of kids going down slides. But I didn't use it in the finished film.

The story about Johnny in paragraph 14 really summarizes the philosophy of education that will be found in the film.

FIGURE 6-3

Treatment for *A Young Child Is . . .*

Approach to the film:

The approach to filming will be open and documentary in style. We wish to observe the behavior of very young children, recording it on color film with synchronous sound. We wish to explore and document what children actually do (including, if appropriate, what they do in the presence of cameras). Little or no attempt will be made to direct the children's activities, and, in no case, will children be asked or encouraged to "act out" some preconceived activity to illustrate what children are supposed to do.

What we get is what you see.

Filming situations will include, but not be limited to:

1. The behavior of babies less than a year old. We shall be looking for the development of language (patterning sentences, experimentation with words, feedback and reward), the development of motor ability, trial and error efforts toward walking and crawling, and the emotional environment of the very young child.

2. The behavior of toddlers. We shall be looking for concrete examples of exploratory learning, of "play" which gains the child a familiarity with the object or task, and gets him "ready" to use it. We shall also be looking at attention span, and the ways in which these very young children learn from failure, without being defeated by it.

3. The trusting environment. As we film babies and toddlers, we shall be looking for examples of "trust" built into their environment, and the ways in which these children develop a sense of trust.

4. Two-year-olds and the sense of autonomy. In filming children roughly two years old, we shall be looking for the ways in which these children attempt to separate themselves from the background—to define themselves as unique, as individuals—to use as examples of the ways children develop a sense of autonomy. At the same time we shall be looking for examples of sophisticated development of verbal behavior, the self-correcting

mechanism that turns "baby talk" into a reasonable facsimile of adult speech.

5. The "Age of Why?" Here we're dealing with two-, three-, and four-year-olds, looking for some replacement of trial-and-error learning with verbal interaction. Let us be clear about what we expect to find: We do not expect that every "why?" is a reasoned request for information. But, as in patterning sentences before the child has words to fill them with meaning, we do expect to find a new emphasis on verbal behavior—practicing, playing with it, so that he will have the form ready, when he wants to fill it with content.

6. Curiosity. This exists at all age levels, and we want to capitalize on it wherever we find it. We want to look for curiosity as it develops, to see how it develops and how it is turned off.

7. Creativity. Again, one can find examples, perhaps, at all age levels. We shall be looking for them. By "creativity" we do not mean merely artwork, or singing, or anything particularly related to the creative arts. We shall be looking for evidence of children taking what they know and reformulating it into something new, the creative solution to a problem, the development of a "new" word of precise meaning out of two old words, etc.

8. The Age of Initiative. Here we are looking for examples to show that the child has learned to trust his environment, and has gained a sufficient sense of himself that he can now try on other roles, he can begin to accept others and interact with them. He can play with other children instead of alongside others.

9. Verbal behavior of five-year-olds. We want to observe five-year-olds talking with each other and with adults. Our premise is that their verbal behavior can be quite sophisticated, and is a necessary part of the readiness in communication which will lead them naturally into other communication skills such as reading and writing.

10. Decision-making. At all levels we shall be looking for evidence of very young children making decisions on their own, guiding and directing their own behavior.

11. Repetition, familiarity, mastery. We want to show the way in which young children approach novelty. If they don't like it,

they have "a short attention span." But if they do like it, they want it repeated, and repeated, until it becomes familiar and they have a feeling of mastery over it. Examples might be a parent reading a story, and when he has finished the child says, "Read it again," perhaps preferring it to a new story he hasn't heard. Or a young child going down a sliding board. As soon as he has convinced himself he won't be hurt, he wants to slide again, and again, and again.

12. The effects of frustration on young children. In our filming, we expect to find instances where a child finds himself frustrated at what he intends to do. We want to observe this, to see how children deal with frustration.

13. Abstract learning—the learning of colors, numbers, letters, etc. How does a child learn these concepts? What does it mean to say, "He knows the alphabet," or "He knows how to count"? What is evidence that he does, and what is evidence that he doesn't?

14. Learning vs. "Right Answers." Again, we shall be looking for evidence of the difference between learning something, and learning how to give right answers about it. As an example of what we shall be looking for, we have a film clip, five minutes in length, shot in a classroom this past summer. In it, a teacher is working with two seven-year-olds, trying to teach the concept: "2 + 3 = 5." She has a filmstrip projector with a picture of two red chickens and three white chickens on it, and a box of blocks set before the children. At the beginning of the clip, she points to the two red chickens and asks Johnny, "How many chickens do you see?" Johnny answers, "Five." (He has solved the problem, but she doesn't know it. She is looking for the answer, "Two," which is the right answer as far as she is concerned.) She says, "No. How many do you see here?" She then goes through the entire process, counting two red chickens, counting three white chickens, counting blocks for red chickens, "1-2," counting blocks for white chickens, "1-2-3," counting all the chickens, "1-2-3-4-5," counting all the blocks, "1-2-3-4-5." She then says, "So, two plus three equals how much, Johnny?" And Johnny answers, "Four!" He has learned to look for "right answers," and has lost the ability to solve the problem.

Writing a Proposal

Occasionally, you may be asked to write a proposal for a video. You may be involved with a production group trying to get a grant, for example. Or a production company you work with may be replying to a request for a proposal (RFP), which is the customary way government agencies start a video project.

In at least one respect, the proposal for a video is the most important document written for the production. In a few pages, the proposal has to engage the fantasy life of the sponsor, stress the benefits of making a video, and shake loose the money.

The proposal has to convince the people putting up the money that:

1. A video should be made.
2. You know exactly the kind of video that is needed.
3. Your production unit is the only one that can possibly do justice to the video.

The proposal is a selling document. Videos are expensive to produce. The person or organization putting up the money has to be convinced that the benefits of producing a video justify the cost. You may be interested mainly in the content of the video and the production techniques that will be used to achieve that content, but content and technique are not likely to be the sponsor's hot buttons. And, as the old salesman used to say, "You don't sell the steak. Sell the sizzle!"

Demonstrate why this new video is needed.

Push the sponsor's hot button, whatever it is. Stress the direct and indirect benefits of producing the video. Show how the new production will fit into the existing body of work.

For example, when I wrote the proposal that resulted in funding for the production of the documentary films *A Young Child Is . . .* and *Schools for Children* there were already well over two hundred films on early learning in children generally available from various sources. As part of my research, I had spent several months screening most of these films in whole or in part. Clearly, a proposal for two new films in this area had to deal with the question of why additional funds should be spent on new production when so many films already existed.

While this could have been a liability for our project, we were able to turn it into an asset by showing in the proposal that

1. we were familiar with the films in the field, and
2. conditions in education had changed, or were changing, so that new films with a more contemporary philosophical thrust not only were needed but were needed immediately.

This is how the proposal for these two films began:

> General:
>
> There have been many films about young children produced for use with parents, teachers, educators, and the general public. The Vassar College *A Long Time to Grow* series is a notable example. Why, then, should we contemplate producing another such film?
>
> The answer lies in the changes which have occurred in the philosophy of Early Childhood Education since those films were produced, as well as in an examination of the ways in which prior films have been used.
>
> Simply put, it is our contention that half a century of study and research into the ways in which children grow, develop, and learn, regardless of the intent of the original researchers, has been put to the use of finding ways to manipulate children so that they will fit societal preconceptions about how schools should be.
>
> It is our belief that the study of early childhood should be used as a guide to creating a learning situation that will fit the way children are.
>
> We hold tremendous respect and admiration for the massive amount of learning a child has accomplished without schools or teachers from birth to the age of five or six. We are upset by the mismatch between the ways children learn in their very early years, and the ways in which many schools—perhaps most schools—organize the learning situation to "teach" these same children once they have reached some statutory age.

Therefore, we shall produce two films of approximately 25 minutes each about young children and their education, for use primarily in professional education, but with a secondary potential for use with parents and the general public.

The first, *A Young Child Is . . .*, will concentrate on observing and clarifying what young children do, how they learn, and what they need.

The second, *Schools for Children*, will build upon the first, asking, "Since children grow and learn in this way, how should a school be shaped to fit the way children actually are?"

What this proposal says, of course, is that all the other films are obsolete, and isn't it fortunate that we've come along with a proposal to make two new films at just the moment when they are so desperately needed?

Keep It Short

How long is a proposal? The best rule is to be brief. At the beginning of the year in the Documentary Film Laboratory, Sol Worth always asked his students to write a one-page description of the film they'd like to make for their class project, starting with the words "I want to make a film about . . ." By holding it to one page (Sol actually asked for a hundred words, but almost no one ever managed that) he hoped that the students would concentrate on the essence of the film, and not get bogged down in specifics too early in the process. Keep the proposal short, and save the details for the treatment. Be brief, but be complete.

Suggestions for Treatment Writers

Here are some suggestions for organizing and writing the treatment and video script:

Show the Research as Well as the Results

Take the audience through a process of discovery that is similar to your own. Show the good and the bad. If you have the screen time, you can even take the audience down a few false trails. You know what is going to happen in the video, but you didn't when you started your research. Don't deprive your audience of that delicious uncertainty.

Don't Write a Novel When You Only Have Room for a Short Story

Most nonfiction videos are less than a half hour in length. It's better to develop one theme completely in a short video than to try to cram in too much and lose the flow of the video. Resist the pressure to try to make a single video that will be all things to all people. It isn't possible.

Be Cautious about Interviews

Interviews are an important part of documentary and nonfiction videos, but they can get awfully dull. And they slow down the video. A person talking will average about one hundred words per minute. But in the same minute you can show six to ten different images, if you want to, at a comfortable pace. Start with the person being interviewed, and then go to other images while the voice continues. Complementary images can reduce the number of words needed. And contradictory images can show, quickly and incontrovertibly, that the speaker is uninformed—or lying.

A Video Is Always Right Now and Right Here

The events in a video always occur in the present, because we are seeing them happen, now. Video is concrete; you have to have something to show. But it isn't literal. You can play with time and space. A man can walk out his office door and be anywhere—on the moon, in the fourteenth century, or across the country. You can cut from one location to another without a transition, as long as the difference is clearly evident.

When I started writing for films, I asked a documentary writer-director the best way to get from one scene to another.

"That's easy," he said. "Hit the return key on your typewriter twice."

You Can't Show a Negative

Because video is concrete, it's almost impossible in a video to show that something isn't there or doesn't exist. One beginning screenwriter wrote a scene where one character holds another at the point of a gun. In the stage directions he wrote, "The gun is not loaded." How do you show that in a video?

Watch Your Language

Be careful of using terms you may not completely understand. Don't write "Dissolve to . . ." unless you really understand what a dissolve is and how it is used in the conventions of video and film. Avoid terms like *pan* and *zoom*. They may sound very professional to you, but unless you use them absolutely correctly, they'll mark you as an amateur. You'll never go wrong if you simply say, "Next we see . . ."

A Client Story: The Client Who Wanted Too Much

A university wanted a video to motivate incoming freshmen to schedule their basic core courses in their first two years, rather then leaving them until close to graduation, when they caused scheduling problems and sometimes kept seniors from graduating with their class. The university said this was a serious problem, and the task force thought a video for freshmen would help. But as part of the program, they wanted to show various departments within the university in a favorable light. And they then wanted to be able to use the video as a public relations vehicle for the general public. They asked several production companies to respond with a proposal for the video.

One production company contacted me about working with them on the proposal, and I added my son, Greg, who had just graduated from the university, as co-writer. As we researched the project, we all agreed that if we truly wanted the video to motivate freshmen, it had to focus on freshmen and speak directly to them. We felt the benefit to freshmen was to learn the advantages of getting core courses out of the way early. And we planned to deliver this by having older students tell how leftover core courses had screwed them up in their junior and senior years.

But we believed it simply could not be made in such a way that it could also do P.R. for the humanities departments at the university, and we said that in our presentation. We felt that the worst thing that could happen would be for us to get the assignment and then have to try to resolve what we saw as conflicting purposes and audiences.

We didn't get the job. The client went for a producer willing to give them what they asked for, not what they needed. And that's their right. We were satisfied that we had made an honest proposal that would have handled what they said was their primary need.

Exercise: Create a Treatment

If you did an existential outline of a video as the exercise in Chapter 5, use that outline to write the treatment for a video.

If you didn't, find a short commercial video, view it several times, and then write what might have been the treatment for it. As you are writing, if you get an idea for a way to improve on the video, write that instead.

7 Writing the Script

As a scriptwriter, my job is to tell what goes into the video; not to write a manual on "How to make my movie." —GREG HAMPE, writer-producer

The script is the basic production document for the video. As such, it is also a legal description of the video that is to be produced and can be so used in court. The script is a detailed blueprint of the video for filming and for editing. It tells what is shot in each scene, how it is shot, who is in the scene, and what is said. Into the script must go everything that the client needs to know to approve the plan for production, everything the producer needs to know to do a final budget, everything the director needs to know to shoot the footage, everything the casting director needs to know to select actors, everything the actors need to know to perform credibly, and everything the editor needs to know to cut the video.

And nothing more.

A good script may at first seem a little thin on paper. That's because it's the director's job to bring the script to life, and the editor's job to organize the footage into a video.

You write the script more or less the way you described it in the treatment, but in full detail. It starts from the opening fade-in of the first scene and runs in a continuous progression of scenes to the closing fade-out. It is written in master scenes which describe all the action and speech that occur at a specific location at a given point in time. You start a new scene whenever you change the time or place.

Script Formats

The first time I tried to write a script, I wasted an inordinate amount of time trying to find out what a script should look like. There are two basic formats for scripts—the classic screenplay format and the television two column format—and it doesn't really matter very much which you use, or even whether, for some reason, you invent your own, as long as you, the client, and the production company all agree that it's the right way to script this production.

The Classic Screenplay Format

The screenplay format used for a theatrical film is typed in "tombstone" fashion—straight down the page. Figure 7-1 is an example of the classic screenplay format from the recruiting video I wrote for Cannon's International Business College of Honolulu. A portion of the treatment for this script appeared in Chapter 6.

In formatting the classic screenplay, use one inch margins top and bottom and set left and right indentations for each element as indicated below.

The elements of the classic screenplay format are:

The scene number. Scenes are numbered at the left-hand side of the page, one and a half inches from the edge of the paper.

In writing a proper Hollywood screenplay for a feature film or television movie, the scriptwriter does not number the scenes. That's because the script will go through many, many revisions before production begins. The scenes are not numbered until the script goes into production and a shooting script

FIGURE 7-1

Classic Screenplay Format: Excerpt from a Script for Cannon's International Business College

---

At Cannon's You Can *Revised Final Draft Script - 14*

42 INT. CANNON'S AT SCHOOL TIME CLOCK—DAY

Nicely dressed STUDENTS checking in or out.

MUSIC continues under.

INSTRUCTOR
(Continues off camera)
We stress punctuality and courtesy, because business expects people to be on time, and to be courteous and considerate. We're teaching success habits. That's why at Cannon's you can.

{S=:15 | RT=6:25}

43 INT. CANNON'S JOB PLACEMENT INTERVIEW CLASS—DAY

STUDENTS in class showing practice job placement interview techniques. MUSIC: Continues under.

NARRATOR
To get a job, you have to get past the job interview. Cannon's offers practice in job placement techniques—more habits of success.

MUSIC in full.

We see a practice interview, with smiling STUDENTS and a positive attitude, with THEME MUSIC in full. MALE STUDENT arrives at the door. FEMALE STUDENT meets him, checking her watch. Hands him a necktie. They make it in time. TEACHER counselling.

{S=:30 | RT=6:55}

---

is prepared. Until then, the script is said to be "in development." The sad fact is that most feature film screenplays never get out of development and into production.

A commercial video, however, is essentially in production when the script is assigned, so I number the scenes in the script. This makes it easier for the client (for whom this may be the first and possibly the only video production of his life) to follow the scene changes and gives him a clear set of landmarks for questions and revisions. If later changes add a scene after, say, scene 25, I change scene 25 to 25A and make the new scene 25B. If a scene is deleted, I keep the scene number and next to it write "Scene deleted."

The setting. The location for the scene is single-spaced, in all capital letters, beginning two inches from the left edge of the paper, and ending one inch from the right edge. This includes indicating whether the scene is an exterior (EXT.) or interior (INT.) and whether it takes place during the day or at night. This is normally in the form

21 INT. SALES OFFICE—DAY

For some commercial video scripts you may not need to indicate exterior or interior and day or night. Use them if it helps; leave them out if they just clutter the pages.

Description of action. The action in the scene, including stage directions, is single spaced, beginning two inches from the left edge of the paper and ending one inch from the right edge. Use all capital letters for the NAME or IDENTITY of a character the first time he or she appears in the video (but from then on type the name in upper- and lowercase letters). And use all caps for all SOUNDS, CAMERA DIRECTIONS, and SHOTS.

ROGER DAVIS sits with his feet on the desk, reading the paper and ignoring the insistent RINGING of the telephone. JOYCE SMITH enters through the front door, her arms full of sales materials. Awkwardly juggling the things she's carrying, she gets an arm free and picks up the receiver. PUSH IN to CU of Joyce.

Characters. Character names, typed in all capital letters (without a colon at the end), begin four inches from the left edge of the paper.

Parenthetical information. Notes telling how a line is spoken or indicating that the speaker is off camera are placed in parentheses directly below and to the left of the character name, beginning three and a half inches from the left edge of the paper and ending three inches from the right edge.

Dialogue. Narration or dialogue is single-spaced and centered below the speaker's name, beginning three inches from the left edge of the paper and ending two and a half inches from the right edge.

```
                    JOYCE
               (Annoyed)
          They've hung up. Roger!
          Didn't you hear the phone?
```

Transitions. Editing instructions, such as FADE IN or DISSOLVE, go in all capital letters at the right side of the page, beginning six and a half inches from the left edge of the paper and ending at the right margin.

```
                                   DISSOLVE TO:
```

For commercial videos I keep a running account of time in this position in the form

```
                                   {S=:07 | RT=1:50}
```

where S = the expected length of the scene and RT = the expected running time of the video to the end of the scene.

In the script, the full scene would look like this:

21 INT. SALES OFFICE—DAY

ROGER DAVIS sits with his feet on the desk, reading the paper and ignoring the insistent RINGING of the telephone. JOYCE SMITH enters through the front door, her arms full of sales materials. Awkwardly juggling the things she's carrying, she gets an arm free and picks up the receiver. PUSH IN to CU of Joyce.

JOYCE
(Annoyed)
They've hung up. Roger!
Didn't you hear the phone?

{S = :07 | RT = 1:50}

A complete script in classic screenplay format appears in Appendix 6.

The TV Two Column Format

This format splits apart audio and video much more completely than the classic screenplay. It is the standard format in live television, because the director can easily keep track of both picture and sound. It's the format normally used for television commercials.

Producers and directors who have come up through television tend to prefer this format while those who started in film generally prefer the classic screenplay format.

The example in Figure 7-2 is from a half-hour documentary entitled *Light in Art*, which I wrote for the *Spectrum Hawaii* series on Hawaii Public Television.

As you can see, in the TV two column format, picture information goes on the left, audio information on the right. In some ad agencies the audio side is typed in all capital letters. I don't do this for the simple reason that it's harder for a narrator or actor to read all caps than to read copy in upper and lower case.

Figure 7-2

TV Two Column Format: Excerpt from the Script for *Light in Art*

Light in Art - Final Draft *Page 10*

36	WS of prisms and rods from the side. Push in to CU of one prism with some color in it. (08:17:50)	NARRATOR: This sculpture on a wall in the court of the astronomy department at the University of Hawaii, is made of prisms, which catch the light of the sun . . . {S=:10 | RT= 05:14}
37	Spectrum lines on the wall (08:19:05)	and break it into the colors of the visible spectrum. Put these colors back together again and you have clear, white light. {S=:12 | RT= 05:26}
38	DISSOLVE TO: Studio: Lights set up for three color experiment.	NARRATOR: White light breaks down into the primary colors of red, blue, and green. These can be mixed to produce any color in the visible spectrum. {S=:09 | RT= 05:35}
39	TECHNICIANS putting filter gels on a light.	NARRATOR: In the studio, three lights were gelled to approximate one of the primary colors. {S=:06 | RT= 05:41}
40	Light with red gel turned on. (We see the red glow in the snoot.)	NARRATOR: Red {S=:01 | RT= 05:41}
41	We see a red circle on the wall.	{S=:02 | RT= 05:43}

Light in Art - Final Draft *Page 11*

	Video	Audio
42	Light with blue gel turned on. (We see the blue glow in the snoot.)	NARRATOR: Blue {S=:01 | RT= 05:44}
43	We see a blue circle.	{S=:02 | RT= 05:46}
44	Light with green gel turned on. (We see the green glow in the snoot.)	NARRATOR: Green {S=:01 | RT= 05:47}
45	We see a green circle.	{S=:02 | RT= 05:49}
46	Red and blue lights on. (We see the colors in the snoot.)	NARRATOR: When the red and blue lights are combined, {S=:04 | RT= 05:53}
47	See red and blue overlap.	. . . the area where they overlap is a different color . . . magenta. {S=:04 | RT= 05:57}
48	Blue and green lights on. (See the colors in the snoots.)	NARRATOR: Blue and green {S=:02 | RT= 05:59}
49	See blue and green overlap.	. . . produce cyan . . . {S=:02 | RT= 06:01}
50	Red and green lights come on. (See the colors in the snoot.)	NARRATOR: While combining red and green {S=:02.5 | RT= 06:03.5}
51	See red and green overlap.	produces the unexpected color yellow. {S=:02.5 | RT= 06:06}

Some TV scripts type the video information in all caps. I don't do that for the same reason.

Scenes are numbered. I try to follow more or less the same rules for capitalization in the two column format as in the classic screenplay: Use all caps for transitions, such as DISSOLVE TO; CHARACTERS, the first time they appear; CAMERA MOVEMENTS; and shots, such as CU (close-up), WS (wide shot), and LS (long shot).

In the sample script you'll sometimes see a set of numbers in parentheses, for example:

> Spectrum lines on the
> wall (08:19:05)

These numbers are the time code which identifies the start of that shot in the camera footage. The final draft of the script was written after much of the program had been shot. I had a window print VHS copy of the camera footage, so I was essentially writing from existing footage.

Getting It Written

I especially like the classic screenplay format for use with clients who are not accustomed to reading a script, because as they read down the page they get both the images and sound. With the TV two column format I've found that some clients read only the right-hand side of the script and either miss what is happening visually or have trouble integrating it with the sound.

Write the script the way you described it in the treatment. Write it in the simplest language you can find. Use short words and short sentences. Describe a scene briefly and tell what action takes place. Don't give any detail that isn't absolutely essential. Limit narration to information the audience needs.

Camera Directions

Most of the time, it won't be necessary to mention camera movement, camera angles, close-ups, long shots, and so on. A master scene simply describes what happens in that scene and leaves it up to the director to decide how to photograph it.

Obviously, when the sense of the scene demands it, camera directions should be written into the script.

Close-up of the two pennies
lying on the table.

or

CU of pennies on table.

If, as the writer, you want a long shot or a medium shot or a close-up, write it in. But don't for a minute think that you've given an order to the director, who will, as the French say, *realize* your script. The director may use your suggested long shot or may block the scene in a totally different way. So the point is not to get bogged down in camera directions, changing angles, reverse shots, point of view, and so on, in writing the script. Just tell the story.

Changes from the Treatment

Sometimes an idea that seemed good in the treatment just won't play in the script. Don't be afraid to change it. And sometimes you'll get a good idea that didn't occur to you when you were writing the treatment. Use it.

Yes, the treatment is the approved outline for the script. And you should follow it as closely as possible. Don't make capricious changes. But be aware that as you get deeper into the process and become more of an expert on both the subject you are writing about and the script you're writing, you're likely to find ways to make improvements. If you're sure they *are* improvements, write them into the script. The worst thing that will happen is that the client won't like them or the producer will say they will cost too much. And you'll change them back.

What if There Is No Treatment?

I like to write a treatment before I write the script for all the reasons I set forth in the previous chapter. But the truth is, I don't always write a treatment. The most common reason is that there just isn't time. The shooting schedule is set, or the video has to be finished by a certain date. Sure, there probably *is* time to write the treatment, but there probably just isn't enough time to get two sets of approvals—one for the treatment and another for the script.

If I'm writing from existing footage, the detail is so complete that a treatment would be, essentially, a script. So why not write the script and be done with it?

If you haven't done a treatment, you write the script with the same careful research and organization that would go into the treatment and with all the detail of a script.

Script Review

When you have completed the first draft script, it goes to your client for approval. If that's the production company who will produce the video, there's no problem. Deliver it and go to work on something else until they come back to you with comments.

But if you have been hired directly by the client for whom the video is being made, the situation gets a little trickier. If the production company has been selected, and especially if a budget has been set, let the producer or director have a look at your script, if possible, before it goes to the client. Without realizing it, you may have added extra scenes, set-ups, or characters not in the treatment which will add more cost than the budget can stand. Or you may have had a neat idea, such as an aerial shot of the factory, without taking into consideration how many hours of expensive helicopter time (at several hundred dollars an hour) that one shot may take.

Most of these things should have been ironed out in the treatment, but let the production company review the script anyway. You might even want to put a note on it saying something like:

> Here's the first draft script. I think I've stayed pretty close to the treatment, but I'd like you to look it over to be sure we're still within budget before it goes to the client.

Revision and Approval

Expect changes! Writing a commercial video is not an ego exercise. You're a hired gun for a paying client. You try to give your clients what they *need*, but in the last analysis, if you'd like to get paid, you're going to have to give them what they *want*. Assuming that the script has been written fairly closely to the approved treatment, the client should come back with only minor revisions. These will be word changes in dialogue or narration for the most part.

You don't have to give in automatically just because the client asks for changes. Government and business bureaucrats have a jargon of their own, and they really do think and speak in it. They may become uncomfortable with plain speech. But don't let them change your muscular Anglo-Saxon words into obtuse Latinate polysyllabics just for their own comfort. Remind them that the audience may not be familiar with "the specialized language of experts in the field."

Just as you are becoming more knowledgeable about the script as you work on it, the client also is learning more about the project with each meeting and draft. Sometimes the fully fleshed-out version of the first draft script points up something that the client really doesn't want for some reason. It may be that it was glossed over in the treatment, or that the client just didn't realize that this is what you had in mind. So you may have to change a scene or two.

But if the client comes back with a different concept from what was in the approved treatment, that's a major rewrite and you are entitled to more money.

Once you have the revisions from the client, get them made and get the final draft back as soon as possible.

Approval of the script is a progress payment milestone. Send an invoice and get paid.

A Client Story: When You Can't Live with the Changes

Because commercial scriptwriting is a work-for-hire arrangement not an artistic endeavor, the client has strong economic leverage to get his own way. Within reason, this is as it should be. The person paying the bills should be able to buy the product he or she wants. But sometimes the client is essentially a bureaucrat who works for a government agency or a nonprofit organization and administers someone else's money. Then what do you do when the client is wrong?

I stumbled onto the answer by accident. The client was a nonprofit organization working on a state contract. The person in charge of the project for which I was doing the script had dreamed it up and gotten the contract from the state. Therefore he had very definite ideas about what needed to be done, even though he knew nothing about video. We had argued interminably over strategy and tactics while I tried to teach him something about what makes good video, and I thought I was making headway with him when I got back the approved treatment. I finished the script, delivered it, and expected nothing more than word changes to come out of the review process. Instead, he came in with pages of changes he wanted made, most of them taking the script back to the kind of talky, slow, nonvisual production I thought I had talked him out of. Finally, I said to him, "I'll make these changes if you insist. But I think I'll have to take my name off the credits."

The next day he came to my office, announced that he had hardly slept that night, and reopened the discussion from a much softer position. On reflection I realized that this kind of bureaucrat spends a significant portion of his time trying to get his name put *on* projects. So when I threatened to take mine *off*, he panicked. Through a sleepless night he convinced himself that if the changes he was insisting on were so bad that I would want to *remove* my name from the credits, they must be very bad indeed. Suddenly, he was prepared to compromise on all of the most serious points. The final version, while not as good as I thought it might have been, was acceptable, and the video was well received when it was shown.

Exercise: Compare Writing in Both Formats

Write a short sequence, lasting ninety seconds, using the classic screenplay format. Time each shot with a stopwatch.

Then rewrite the same sequence using the TV two column format.

Note how the format affects the way you write the scene. Does the format affect the meaning of what you have written?

Writing Narration

> You can hardly go wrong if you'll write narration as if you were being fined $10 a word.
>
> —"WRITING WITHOUT WORDS," *PHOTOMETHODS* MAGAZINE

The purpose of narration is to tell the audience the things which they need to know and may not be able to pick up from the footage on their own. Its purpose is *not* to fill the soundtrack with meaningless words like the three guys in the booth on *Monday Night Football.*

As a documentary filmmaker, my preferred way to handle narration was, wherever possible, not to have any. Life doesn't come with narration or music—or a laugh track, for that matter. Therefore, I reasoned, a film that observes life shouldn't either. Through several films I stood on principle and avoided narration completely. The problem is that life also doesn't come with a limited running time. But films and videos do, and a few words of well chosen narration can often cover what would otherwise take several minutes of footage to explain naturalistically. So, when running time gets short, and the documentary material is rich, even the most committed cinéma vérité filmmaker can find himself typing out a narration script.

Think of narration as a precious resource. You have the potential for between one thousand and fifteen hundred words of narration in a fifteen minute video. That's all. Oh, sure, if you get one of those speed talkers, you could get it up to twenty-five hundred words. But that's still not much. And it would make a lousy video. So treat narration as a valuable asset and don't waste it.

Keep It Simple

If the footage is good, the narration can be straightforward, in easy-to-understand English. Keep the language simple and the sentences short. Be prosaic, not flowery. Yes, narration can be clever. It can be humorous. It should always be interesting. *And it should never get in the way of the pictures.*

What belongs in the narration script? The things the audience needs to know to understand your video that are not covered by the video itself. And very little else.

You don't tell the audience what they are looking at:

```
Islanders fishing in the lagoon

                    NARRATOR
          Here we see the people of
          Tula Tula fishing from their
          canoes . . .
```

unless the audience won't know what it is if you don't tell them.

```
38  EXT. ROCKY SHORES—DAY

    From the lanai atop the Reef Tank, showing the
    water tower and the Rocky Shores tanks and
    area.

                    NARRATOR
          The Rocky Shores area
          replicates the conditions of a
          shoreline intertidal zone.
          About every ninety seconds,
          six hundred gallons of water
          is dropped from this
          tower . . .

    Surge of water rushes through the exhibit.
```

NARRATOR
simulating the crash of a
wave against the rocks . . .
sending water surging into
the various tide pool tanks.

Poetic Narration

What about using poetry or lyrical prose in narration? I've only seen it work really well, once, and that was in John Grierson's classic 1930s documentary, *Night Train*. Grierson got the poet laureate of England to write the narration in blank verse *after* the film was shot.

When we write for publication, we use words to paint pictures. Our purpose is to have our readers *see* what we are describing in their mind's eye. But when we write for the screen, we are going to show the pictures to the audience as pictures. I can't say this often enough: *When language is used in narration to evoke images, it gets in the way of the images you are showing on the screen.*

When I was teaching documentary film, two of my students made an antiwar film using children's war toys and war games as images. In those days my students shot with silent film cameras and then added wild sound to the picture in editing. In class, these two showed a cut of their film, completely silent, and we all agreed that it was well made and did what they wanted. There were strong pictures of little kids playing with guns intercut with draftees being inducted into the army at the time of the Vietnam War.

In the next phase, the students selected sections from a lot of interviews they had conducted and added a narration. They also were working with a student composer from the university music department who developed a heavy, ominous score for the film. Finally, they put all the sound together with the picture. And suddenly the film was slow, ponderous, pretentious, overbearing, and worst of all, obvious. It was as if each channel—picture, voice, and music—was trying to carry the whole story. As a result, there was so much redundancy in the film that it needed to be cut way back, perhaps to half its length or less.

Illustrative Videos

People do make videos in which the pictures are there to illustrate a poem or a piece of music. These are meant to be works of art and are outside the realm of scriptwriting for commercial videos. That's because discussions of art—without a strong foundation in aesthetics and art theory—inevitably boil down to "I may not know much about art, but I know what I like." And who can argue with that?

Write Narration as Late as Possible

As a documentary writer-director, I always liked to write narration as I was editing the final cut of the documentary. By that time I had a good idea of how well the images carried the essential information and where narration would be needed. I knew how much space was available for narration, and I could make the words and pictures merge the best possible way.

Narration in the *First Night* Script

Figure 8-1 shows an excerpt from the script I wrote for *First Night*, an eight minute promotion and fundraising film for First Night Honolulu. First Night is an alcohol-free, community New Year's Eve celebration which features arts, crafts, and spectator participation. As with those documentaries I used to do, the footage for *First Night* had already been shot when I wrote the script. It had good images and quite a few on-camera sound bites. In this script, the narration tells the audience whatever they need to know that they may not know.

In scenes 84, 85, and 86, for example, people are playing with

Figure 8-1

Excerpt from the Script for *First Night*

SC NO	TAPE NO	TIME CODE HR MN SC FR	LENGTH SC FR	VIDEO	AUDIO
84	04	04:12:01:21 —07:21	06:00	Chimes overhead, pan to second and third set, man stretches to hit chime.	SOUND: Natural sound. NARRATOR: This is a musical playground. {RT = 7:44:14}
85	04	04:12:16:12 —17:04	00:22	Boy runs stick over chimes.	SOUND: Natural sound. {RT = 7:45:06}
86	04	04:10:15:07 —25:18	10:11	Woman runs mallet on chimes. Push in to see her smile. She laughs and strikes again as we see a CU of the chimes.	SOUND: Natural sound. {RT = 7:55:17}
87	06	06:11:07:00 —22:16	15:16	Slack key guitarist Ray Kane.	KANE: (Plays and sings) So you get the idea what slack key is all about. By playing the melody and accompanying yourself on the bass. {RT = 8:11:03}

SC NO	TAPE NO	TIME CODE HR MN SC FR	LENGTH SC FR	VIDEO	AUDIO
88	10	10:05:56:15 —06:04:20	08:05	Smiling woman.	WOMAN: I think I like that everybody's down here. It's really a lot of fun to have something to do that's not alcoholic, that's family, that's fun. It was great. {RT = 8:19:08}
89	04	04:06:57:08 —07:00:19	03:11	Threesome.	WOMAN: Oh, for sure . . . we're going to stay till the early hours of the morning. {RT = 8:22:19}
90	10	10:05:37:23 —41:02	03:09	Tying resolutions on Resolution Tree.	NARRATOR: This is First Night's Resolution Tree, for New Year's resolutions. {RT = 8:25:28}
91	08	08:11:41:25 —49:28	08:03	Woman at Resolution Tree.	WOMAN: (Do you know what your resolution is going to be?) To lose weight and save money. It's kind of a continuing resolution. {RT = 8:34:01}

SC NO	TAPE NO	TIME CODE HR MN SC FR	LENGTH SC FR	VIDEO	AUDIO
92	08	08:12:55:23 —57:23	02:00	Man at Resolution Tree.	MAN: To get rich. {RT = 8:36:01}
93	05	03:26:28:00 —46:13	18:13	Romeo & Juliet	SOUND: Natural sound. NARRATOR: This is an improv version of Romeo and Juliet with audience participation. SOUND: Natural sound: Then Romeo died. (Audience counts down 10, 9, 8 etc.) {RT = 8:54:14}
94	10	10:02:12:25 —16:00	03:05	Women eating, wave.	SOUND: Natural sound. {RT = 8:57:19}

musical instruments which seem be set out on a lawn. The narration informs us, "This is a musical playground." And that's all. We see the people playing. We see they are enjoying themselves. We see a woman hit a chime and smile and then hit it again and laugh out loud with joy. That doesn't have to be described.

In scenes 88 and 89 we get testimonials—no narration needed. But in scene 90 the narration is needed to set up scenes 91 and 92. The narration tells us, "This is First Night's Resolution Tree, for New Year's resolutions." That's all we need to know what's going on, so the following shots of people telling what their resolutions are will make sense and be funny.

Scene 93 comes from a long piece of video in which performers, with audience participation, do a humorous takeoff on *Romeo and Juliet*, ending with Romeo dying to an audience countdown. If I could have included the whole two minutes of tape of that scene, the viewers would have been able to figure out what was going on and would have enjoyed the ending on their own. I actually made this one of the longest scenes in the video, but it still ran only eighteen seconds. And that included the narrator setting up the gag by telling us, "This is an improv version of *Romeo and Juliet* with audience participation." Again, that's all that needed to be said, and that's all that got written.

Pictures First

As scriptwriters for commercial videos, however, we rarely have the luxury of waiting until we're editing the video before writing the narration. We usually have to complete the script—and that includes the narration—before the video goes into production.

Clients love to read the narration ahead of time. It's the one part of the script they feel they truly understand. But the commercial scriptwriter who writes the narration before fully visualizing the images to be used is borrowing trouble. In the first place, the lazy person inside all of us is likely to look at a well-

(but prematurely) written narration and select pictures to illustrate it. Which inevitably results in a talky "show-and-tell" script instead of a blueprint for an evocative video.

In the second place, images are the visual evidence of your video. They have to be able to stand on their own. Even when narration is the major element in the audio track, the rule remains, *Pictures first.* If the scene is well visualized in the initial organization and in the treatment, narration will follow picture as it should.

Narration in the *Emeralds on Black Velvet* Script

Figure 8-2 is an excerpt from a script I wrote for a sales video about a luxury condominium project on the Big Island of Hawaii. I'll call it the "Gold Coast Resort," which is not its real name.

This segment, which includes the title of the video, deals with the sales point that the developers have had the foresight and the financial resources to keep the area relatively unspoiled. To investors, aware of the effects of runaway development in Waikiki and on Maui, this is a major consideration.

Scenes 15 and 16 establish a luxury car traveling on the highway, which is a two lane road through an aging lava field. Driving along this road, one can scarcely see the green oases along the coastline which are resort developments. The narration points this out. Following the rule that you can't show a negative, it underscores the absence of a developed look with the story about the travel writer who said, "Why, there's nothing there."

In scene 17 we can see from the air the several resort enclaves along the coast, while the narration tells us that "more than two billion dollars in luxurious resorts are tucked into this twelve mile stretch of coastline . . . like emeralds on black velvet." This sets up the background for the title, EMERALDS ON BLACK VELVET.

Scene 19 continues to show the unspoiled nature of the area, while the narration explains, "The existing resorts are hard to

FIGURE 8-2

Excerpt from the Script *Emeralds on Black Velvet*

Emeralds on Black Velvet *3*

15 EXT. MAIN HIGHWAY—DAY

Mercedes, BMW, or other luxury car on the main highway.

MUSIC
(in full then under)

NARRATOR
Today you can drive from the
airport near Kailua-Kona to
the Gold Coast along a paved,
two-lane highway.
{S=:08 | RT=2:27}

16 EXT. HIGHWAY—DAY

Driving along the highway from inside the car.

NARRATOR
From the road you can
hardly see the excitement
building along the coast. A
travel writer, driving into the
area for the first time,
remarked, "Why, there's
nothing here."
{S=:09 | RT=2:36}

17 AERIAL—DAY

Aerial of the Kohala Coast (of the sort to be used in the sales office).

NARRATOR
However, more than two
billion dollars in luxurious
resorts are tucked into the
lava fields along this twelve
mile stretch of golden
coastline . . . like emeralds
on black velvet.

Emeralds on Black Velvet *4*

17 CONTINUED

Use paintbox to add emerald flashes to the three Gold Coast resorts.

Title: EMERALDS ON BLACK VELVET

MUSIC
(in full)

{S = :14 | RT = 2:43}
DISSOLVE TO

18 (SCENE DELETED)

19 AERIAL—DAY OR

EXT. GOLD COAST—DAY

Aerial of the Gold Coast, or looking at the coast from the highway.

MUSIC
(fades under)

NARRATOR
The existing resorts are hard
to spot from the road because
of careful planning.

{S = :05 | RT = 2:48}

20 EXT. GOLD COAST RESORT—DAY

Entrance to Gold Coast Resort.

NARRATOR
We keep our emeralds
hidden.
This is the jeweled setting for
the most precious gem of all
. . . the Gold Coast Resort.

{S = :08 | RT = 2:56}

21 EXT. GOLD COAST RESORT—DAY

Residences.

NARRATOR
At Gold Coast Resort, all
buildings are low rise,
blending into the landscape.

{S = :04 | RT = 3:00}

spot from the road because of careful planning." This pays off in scene 20 with the statement "We keep our emeralds hidden." Scenes 20 and 21 show the attractive entrance to the resort and the residential area. The narration focuses us on the Gold Coast Resort and underscores the way it is kept low-rise so that it blends with the landscape.

In this section of script, we have narration in every scene, but it follows and complements the visual evidence of an area being kept as close to nature as possible in spite of more than two billion dollars' worth of development.

Using an On-Camera Spokesperson

Quite often a commercial video will use a spokesperson (or "spokes") to handle many of the functions of the narrator. The spokesperson appears on camera to introduce scenes or events and usually does all of the off-camera (or "voice-over") narration, as well.

Why Use a Spokesperson?

There are several reasons for choosing to use an on-camera spokesperson:

Authority/credibility. The person you have selected as a spokesperson is a recognized authority on the topic of the video and adds credibility to the message. In a medical video, for instance, you might plan to use a well-known doctor.

Celebrity/attention. You might choose to use a celebrity as your spokesperson to draw attention to the message.

Abstract content. If the information you must present in the video does not lend itself to concrete imagery, one solution is to place a spokesperson on camera and have that person tell the audience the information.

Demonstration. An on-camera spokesperson can demonstrate a product or take the audience on a guided tour of an area.

Movement. An on-camera spokesperson can often add a sense of movement to an otherwise static video by walking or riding through the location.

Dramatic effect. Some statements are more powerful when we can see the person making the statement than they would be in voice-over narration. Especially when you don't have strong visuals to go with the strong statement, the reaction of the spokesperson to the words he or she is saying may make the most dramatic appeal to the audience.

Ego trips. Sometimes you'll find yourself having to use someone from the client as a spokesperson for no good reason except that that person wants to be in the video. When politicians are involved, for example, expect it. When working with government agencies this is always a potential problem. Some self-made business successes think they can do anything, including acting on camera. Occasionally they're right. Usually they aren't. Often you can convince the ego-trip spokespersons that acting in the video will be too time-consuming for them. Then you can shunt them into a short introductory statement or put them in a couple of scenes where they are seen and talked about but not heard.

Spokesperson in the *Hawaii Family Stress Center* Script

The Hawaii Family Stress Center had a successful program for preventing child abuse, but very little money or recognition. They wanted a video which would explain the program and help raise funds. It would premier at a fund-raising dinner and auction and then would be shown to the state legislature as part of an appeal for funding.

While the subject matter of the video—child abuse and its prevention—was certainly dramatic, both the necessity for confidentiality and the tiny budget for the production meant we could not do a reality documentary. Much of the sales pitch came in the form of statistics and social science studies which we had no easy way to turn into concrete visuals. What we did have was the availability, as a volunteer spokesperson, of Bob Seavey, who had recently retired after many years as the news anchor on the CBS affiliate in Honolulu. To people in Hawaii, Seavey had the same kind of credibility as Walter Cronkite or David Brinkley.

Use of Seavey as the spokesperson for this script gave us both the authority and the credibility of an established news anchor and the celebrity appeal of a well-known television personality. Our spokesperson could carry the points in the script where we didn't have good visual evidence and could provide dramatic effect as he delivered powerful statements about child abuse.

In his first scene on camera, I bolstered his authority with the visual evidence surrounding him, a library set where he could easily pick up textbooks and studies on child abuse.

In scenes 6, 7, and 8 the spokesperson goes to the heart of the Hawaii Family Stress Center program, identifying parents who are at risk for child abuse by using a combination of well-established risk factors. In scene 7, we see a graphic listing the risk factors and the spokesperson becomes a voice-over narrator. He returns in scene 8 to talk about the success of the Hawaii Family Stress Center program, quoting from scientific studies he picks up in the library set.

Again in scene 9 he becomes a voice-over narrator as the video returns to visual evidence within a hospital. And throughout the remainder of the video, he alternates as on-camera spokesperson and voice-over narrator, coming into the scene when needed or retreating off camera to talk about what is on the screen.

FIGURE 8-3

Excerpt from the Script *Hawaii Family Stress Center*

Hawaii Family Stress Center

6 INT. STUDIO—LIBRARY SET

Spokesman on camera.

SPOKESMAN

What kind of person would abuse or neglect a little child? Fortunately, we know the answer.

Today we can identify—with better than ninety-five percent accuracy—parents who are *at risk* for child abuse. This doesn't mean they *will* become abusive or neglectful parents. It does mean that *virtually all* abusive and neglectful parents come from this at risk group.

{S=:25 | RT=2:31}

7 GRAPHIC LISTS THE AT RISK FACTORS AS THE SPOKESMAN TALKS ABOUT THEM:

FAMILY 'AT RISK' FACTORS FOR CHILD ABUSE AND NEGLECT

Parents who were abused as children

History of mental illness and violence

Substance abuse

Rigid and unrealistic expectations

Current severe financial problems

Social isolation

Heavy continuous child care—no relief

(CONTINUED)

7 CONTINUED

SPOKESMAN
(Voice-over)
Factors putting a family at risk include:
Parents who were themselves abused or severely emotionally deprived as children.
A family history of mental illness, violence, or marital discord.
Substance abuse by either parent.
Parents with rigid and unrealistic expectations for their children.
Current severe financial problems.
Social isolation away from the extended family or some other support group.
The burden of heavy continuous child care with several small children in the family. And no relief.

{S = :35 | RT = 3:06}

8 INT. STUDIO—LIBRARY SET

Spokesman on camera

SPOKESMAN
As you might expect, people who do not do well in life, generally also do very poorly at parenting. Fortunately, today, we not only know how to find who is at risk, we now know how to *prevent* child abuse and neglect *almost completely.*
I realize that's not the sort

(CONTINUED)

8 CONTINUED

of thing you usually hear. Usually organizations like ours say, "We're making great strides . . ." or "With your help we can come closer to finding a cure . . ."

Spokesman picks up "scientific studies"

SPOKESMAN
(continues)
These are the facts: We have *virtually no cases* of child abuse among the families we have worked with.

As early as 1972, a study in Denver screened five hundred families for risk factors of child abuse. One hundred were identified as at risk. Half of these took part in a program of child abuse prevention. The other half did nothing. The Result: No child abuse was found in the four hundred families screened as low risk, and no child abuse was found in the half of the high risk families in the prevention program.

The control group—those families at risk who were identified and nothing more—had a *twenty percent* incidence of child abuse. Here in Hawaii, from 1981 to 1987, one thousand high risk families were screened and worked with by Hawaii

(CONTINUED)

Hawaii Family Stress Center *6*

8 CONTINUED

Family Stress Center, with
only one case of mild abuse.

The Healthy Start and
Neighbor Island Family
Support programs have also
served hundreds of families
in Hawaii with an extremely
low abuse rate.

{S=:1:30 | RT=4:36}

9 INT. HOSPITAL NURSE'S STATION—DAY

Nurse's station—DOCTOR OR NURSE on the telephone

SPOKESMAN
(Voice-over)
The entry point for
preventing child abuse is the
birth of a newborn baby.

The staff of Hawaii Family
Stress Center receives
referral calls from physicians
and other hospital staff
members about families of
newborns they may be
concerned are at risk for
child abuse.

{S=: 18 | RT=4:54}

The Cost of Using a Spokesperson

In this case, the use of an on-camera spokesperson was a cost-saving device because our spokesperson had volunteered his time and we could quickly shoot all his scenes in one studio location. Each on-camera shot of the spokesperson replaced a difficult location scene we now would not have to shoot.

In many cases, however, the use of a spokesperson will add

to the cost of the production. You have to pay the spokesperson as an actor. You may need a makeup artist on the crew when the spokesperson is used. You may want to use the spokesperson in several different locations, which may mean you pay the spokesperson and the makeup artist for several days of shooting. Shooting on-camera voice is usually time-consuming. If the spokesperson doesn't blow his lines, a car will start or a plane will fly overhead, ruining the sound and causing a retake. All of which adds to the cost of the production.

As a video scriptwriter you factor all this into the decision to use or not to use an on-camera spokesperson.

Write Narration for the Ear, Not the Eye

Narration is written to be heard not read. Which means that in writing you need to think about the sound of the narration.

How Does the Narrator Sound?

Is your narrator a man, a woman, or a child? Or is the narrator the characterization of an animal, such as Smokey the Bear; an abstraction, such as the Voice of Liberty; or an object, such as a school bus? I once did a safety film for elementary school children called *Stanley the Friendly School Bus*. Stanley narrated, talking directly to the children. Which brought up the question, What does a school bus sound like? Our Stanley was vaguely adolescent, the knowledgeable voice of an older brother.

The narrator's tone will usually be conversational, but there might be a good reason for it to be flip or sarcastic, or on the other hand, serious and sincere—known as a Voice of God narration.

Will you use one narrator or more than one? Most of the time one will do. But sometimes it makes sense to use two—or more. For instance, in one video where I had both a lot of technical information and a lot of warm, fuzzy feeling stuff to go in the narration, I used a male and a female narrator. And because I like to cast against stereotype, I had the female voice do the technical stuff while the male voice handled the warm fuzzies. Under other circumstances it might have made sense to use two women or two men or an adult and a child. The point is that your narrator or narrators can be whoever or whatever you need to help you do the job of informing the audience.

Listen to the Words as You Write Them

Use a short word in preference to a long one and short, simple sentences rather than long, complex ones. Your audience has to get it on the first hearing. They can't go back and reread something they find confusing. That doesn't mean narration can't be—or shouldn't be—dramatic, punchy, clever, humorous, or pointed. It can be all those things. But only if the audience can understand it on the first hearing.

Read narration aloud to yourself as you write it. I mean it, *out loud,* not in your head. If you find you are stumbling over words or phrases, change them. If you can't read the narration correctly—when you wrote it—how can you expect a narrator to read it?

Then read it aloud to other people to be sure they can follow the thoughts expressed. If they're having trouble understanding the meaning, tell them what it means, as simply as possible. *Then write that down and use it for the narration.*

Rhythm. Spoken language has its own rhythm, which makes the words easier to say and easier to understand. You'll feel it as you read out loud. Some sentences are easy to say; some aren't. If you find a passage you seem to stumble over each time you read it, the reason may be that it breaks the rhythm of the narration. Taking out a word—or adding one—may be all that is needed.

Watch out for tongue twisters. "She sells seashells down by the seashore" not only is hard to say but can easily put a lot of sibilant hissing on your sound track. And "Peter Piper picked a peck of pickled peppers" may make the microphone pop with every initial *p*. So in writing the narration make it easy for your narrator by avoiding the kinds of word constructions tongue twisters are made of. Again, reading out loud will be the tip-off that something isn't working.

Parenthetical expressions are a no-no. Narration is linear and always goes forward. Parenthetical expressions break a thought in the middle for a digression and then return to complete the thought. That's good style in print writing, but a real problem in writing for the ear. Here's an example:

NARRATOR
This program aims to make
an educational
system—designed in the
nineteenth century and not
much changed
since—compatible with the
technologies and vocational
demands of the twenty-first
century.

The parenthetical expression "—designed in the nineteenth century and not much changed since—" modifies "educational system," but breaks up the thought of the sentence. That's no problem in print, where, if you don't quite get it the first time, you can go back and read it again. But it might be better written for the ear this way:

NARRATOR
America's education system
was designed in the
nineteenth century and has
not changed much since then.
This program aims to make it
compatible with the
technologies and the
vocational requirements of
the twenty-first century.

Possessives. It has become quite fashionable (but still grammatically wrong) to throw a lone apostrophe behind virtually any noun ending in *s* to indicate the possessive.

Isn't that Chris' computer?

But if you say that out loud, it won't sound right. The rule is: In English, show possession by adding an apostrophe and an *s* to the noun.

Isn't that Chris's computer?

The single exception to the rule is: When the noun forms its plural by adding *s*, *es*, or *ies*, show the plural possessive simply by adding an apostrophe to the final *s*. Again, the reason is to make the words sound right. If we are talking about a car belonging to Mr. and Mrs. Jones, we don't say:

I rode in the Joneses's car.

That's just one *s* too many. Instead we say, and you can write:

I rode in the Joneses' car.

Write out numbers and symbols. Write out numbers the way you want them read. If you write 1,500, the narrator may read it "one thousand five hundred" or "fifteen hundred." Decide which you want and write it that way. Spell out common symbols such as dollars, cents, and percent. Write "seven million dollars" or "eighty-nine cents," not "$7 million" or "89¢." Also, when you write out numbers and symbols, you maintain the relative correspondence between the length of the passage in the script and the running time on the audio track.

Give a phonetic pronunciation to names and foreign words. In your research you've found out how to pronounce the name of the artist who is interviewed, or the correct pronunciation of a foreign phrase you have to use. So make life easy for the director and the narrator by giving the pronunciation phonetically, after the name or phrase:

10	Academy of Art Painting: *The Justice of Trajan* by Delacroix. Camera explores Chiaroscuro effect.	NARRATOR: Other painters developed the effect known as Chiaroscuro (Key are uh SKYOOR oh) in which light and shadow were used for dramatic effect . . . and to produce a sense of depth . . .

Use conjunctions. Some English teacher, somewhere, probably told you not to begin a sentence with *and* or *but*—or any other conjunction. That's because, according to grammatical rule, conjunctions connect simple sentences into compound or complex sentences. But did you know that readability formulas such as the Flesch Reading Ease Scale or Gunning's Fog Index count a conjunction as the start of a new sentence, even when it's in the middle of a compound sentence? That's because the reader or listener treats it functionally as the start of a new thought. So break up those compound sentences. And don't be afraid to start a sentence with a conjunction. It can make the thought easier to understand.

Keep reading directions to a minimum. We all have the desire to direct the narrator by remote control, but we have to fight it. You really don't need a lot of stage directions telling the narrator how to read your words. In fact, if you put them in, the narrator will ignore them anyway, and you'll just annoy the director. Certainly, at the start of the script you may want to indicate the style of narration:

NARRATOR
(light, conversational tone)

or

NARRATOR
(sincere, authoritative)

But resist the temptation to dump an adverb into the script whenever the narrator's name appears. The same goes for dialogue. Use reading directions sparingly if you hope to have them followed.

Use a stopwatch. Nothing cures overwriting like a stopwatch. Get one and time each scene. Read the narration out loud with dramatic emphasis while you time it. But don't time just the words in the narration. Visualize the action that occurs without narration and time that as well.

A Client Story: Reading the Punctuation

I produced several films for a state run education center staffed by educational administrators. They were good people, but they really didn't understand the first thing about video or film. One of the program managers—call him Mr. Fault—was notorious for finding some small item to find fault with, as evidence that he had "done his homework."

Most of the films were done as pure documentaries, working from a proposal or treatment and writing narration as the film was edited. But one of the productions required a complete script in advance. As in any bureaucracy, script review was the occasion for a meeting of everyone involved to go over my script line by line. And like most clients, they spent the most time poring over the narration, as that was the part they thought they understood. I would change a word here, strengthen a concept there, until we finally reached the end of the script without a comment from Mr. Fault. But when the director of the center looked around the table and asked if there were any other comments on the script, it was Mr. Fault's time to shine.

"Barry," he said, "in the narration in scene 58 where you have a dash, shouldn't that be a semicolon?"

Exercise: Write a Short Script from a Newspaper Article

Find a story on the front page of your newspaper and rewrite it as a short script. Make up whatever visual evidence you need. Use the text of the article as the foundation for your narration. Decide on the type of narrator and the sound of the narration, but do not use a spokesperson for this exercise. Write narration only for the information the audience needs to understand your video. See how much text can be replaced with visual evidence.

When you are finished, read the narration you've written aloud to someone else.

Writing Dialogue

> Many people worry about their dialogue; it might be awkward and stilted. It probably is. So what? . . . Writing dialogue is like learning to swim; you're going to flounder around, but the more you do the easier it gets.
>
> —Syd Field, *Screenplay: The Foundations of Screenwriting*

It's hard enough to write decent dialogue in a fiction film, where all you have to do is tell a story. But its gets even harder in a commercial video, where you can find yourself trying to put words in the mouths of actors about a product, process, or service to please a client who doesn't really *care* how people talk.

The Difference Between Conversation and Dialogue

Conversation *maintains contact* among two or more people and sometimes carries information. It is made up of incomplete ideas and fragments of sentences. The parties feel free to interrupt each other, to talk at the same time, and to change the subject capriciously.

Conversation follows social and linguistic rules. For instance, Party A to a conversation would not explain at great length something he knows Party B already understands. To do so would be a social insult. Similarly, in most social groups, people who know each other well do not call each other by name except:

1. Possibly when they meet for the first time that day (although they may simply say, "Hi!")
2. When they want to get the other person's attention, either because there are several people in the room or in the conversation or because the other person is not paying attention
3. For emphasis, usually when they are annoyed or angry with the other person

As long as the conversation is working for the parties involved, they pay little or no attention to its form. They may lace their utterances with repetitions, *y'knows,* interminable pauses, mistakes, and mispronunciations.

Dialogue, on the other hand, takes place among two or more characters for the purpose of informing a third party—the audience.

Dialogue Must Sound Real

Dialogue is artificial speech which must be accepted by an audience as believable. When the lights go down and the video comes up on the screen, you get the benefit of the doubt from what theater people call the willing suspension of disbelief. But the audience will only give you so much slack. For years, 3M ran a commercial in which someone in the family would call out, "Who's got the Scotch Brand Tape?" They used the words "Scotch Brand Tape" because they were trying to protect their brand name from becoming generic. But nobody in America—other than the actors in those commercials (and I'll bet this includes the president of 3M)—calls their tape anything but "Scotch tape." So the dialogue never rang true.

Good dialogue, therefore, has to fall comfortably between

two extremes. On one side is the stilted language of corporate, legal, and bureaucratic English—the "Who's got the Scotch Brand Tape?" utterances.

At the other extreme is the muddy sound of realspeak, full of *ums*, *uhs*, *likes*, and *y'knows*. You can learn a lot about what people really do say and how they say it by watching documentary films and listening to interviews. Or take a look at a transcript of people talking. Thoughts are not completed. Antecedents to pronouns are left out. Repetition runs rampant. Grammar is abused. And often the point of the conversation is never even stated, because the speakers already *know* what they're talking about.

But you just can't put that stuff in a script. You have to write the dialogue the way people *think* they are talking and not the way they actually speak.

Why Use Dialogue?

Why bother? If dialogue is so difficult, why not just use a narrator or a spokesperson? There are several good reasons to use dialogue in a commercial video:

To increase audience interest. Most of us would rather watch a little dramatic scene than sit still for show and tell with a narrator. Using actors to carry the information can often increase interest—if the actors are good and the dialogue is well written.

To stage a demonstration. If you want to show the audience what happens in a particular situation, you might do it with an enactment. For instance, for a workplace safety film, I showed the audience what actually could happen during an occupational safety and health inspection.

Figure 9-1 shows an excerpt from the script. We used a spokesperson both on camera and off camera as a narrator. In this scene, the spokesperson, as narrator, sets up the situation, and then the actors take over with dialogue.

FIGURE 9-1

Dialogue in the Script *Safe and Healthful Working Conditions*

Safe and Healthful Working Conditions *13*

16 INTERIOR, CONSTRUCTION TRAILER

Compliance Officer #1 enters, shows his credentials to CONSTRUCTION WORKER near door and is directed to PROJECT MANAGER. Shows his credentials. They shake hands. Informs Project Manager he's there to conduct an inspection.

SPOKESPERSON (V.O.): The compliance officer presents his credentials and seeks out the highest level of management at the work site. It's important to have top level management involved from the beginning of any compliance inspection so that the occupational safety and health program has accountability and credibility.

At this construction site the representative of top management is the project manager.

The compliance officer says he is there to conduct an inspection of the site. If this is other than a regular programmed inspection, he explains that. If the inspection is in response to a complaint, he gives the employer a copy of the complaint.

COMPLIANCE OFFICER #1: I need to conduct a brief opening conference, to go over some things before we begin the inspection walk-around. Where can we do that? Here?

PROJECT MANAGER: Sure, this is the best place.

Safe and Healthful Working Conditions 14

COMPLIANCE OFFICER #1: And I need to know . . . will you be going on the walk-around with me or will it be someone else? Because if it's someone else, then that person should be here for the opening conference.

PROJECT MANAGER: No, I'll go around with you.

COMPLIANCE OFFICER #1: Are the workers unionized?

PROJECT MANAGER: Yes.

COMPLIANCE OFFICER #1: Is there a shop steward, who will go around with us?

PROJECT MANAGER: Yes. (To construction worker near door) Jack, find Kimo for me and tell him I need him.

For credibility. Audiences understand that the narrator speaks for the client. When you want to praise the client's work or products, you might prefer to have it done by someone other than the narrator. As we saw in the last chapter, a spokesperson may be used to increase credibility. Another way is to have people who seem to represent the viewer talk about the client's work or services. Shoppers in a store, for instance, can talk credibly about the store and its products while they seem to be shopping.

To make the information easier to absorb. For some reason, most of us seem to absorb and retain information better if we receive it while apparently eavesdropping on people who are talking about it. When there's a lot of information to impart, and it's not very visual, having two or three people discuss it can often be better than using a narrator or even a spokesperson. For instance, in writing a video about employee benefits at the Bank of Hawaii, I used a young couple talking after dinner. Since the majority of the bank's employees are women, I had the wife explaining the new program to her husband. This gave the women in the audience a person they could identify with, and it was a way of implying to them that *this* wife and mother understands all this financial stuff, so you can, too.

To add human interest and humor. Scenes with actors and dialogue open up the possibilities of the script. You can bring in a piece of the outside world and use it as a reference point for your audience, as a point of human interest, or even as the focus for some humor.

Avoiding Awkward Dialogue

When I wrote the training video about employee benefits at Bank of Hawaii, I had the problem of trying to keep the dialogue natural while meeting the client's legal needs. I had the wife (Lynn) talking to her husband (Jay) at the dinner table. In the first draft I had her trying to tell him about the bank's new employee benefits in everyday language. I thought this would help make it more understandable as well as more realistic. And it almost worked, although there were sections that just didn't come across easily as family dialogue. Eventually the bank's legal department said no to that draft. Legally correct language had to be used.

So in the next draft, whenever we came to one of the sections where legal terms had to be used, I'd have Lynn start the sentence in plain language and then I'd segue to the narrator saying the same thing, who would continue the thought in its precise legal form. Figure 9-2 shows how it worked. Using this

FIGURE 9-2

Dialogue in the Bank of Hawaii Employee Benefits Video

Bank of Hawaii Script 7

Lynn goes to the kitchen for cookies, while they continue talking.

LYNN
The profit sharing plan is an
incentive to work well and
make the company profitable.

JAY
How's it work?

LYNN
O.K., first they figure out how
much money is available for
profit sharing at the end of
the year. There's a formula
that they use to determine
that. And that money is
divided among the employees
according to another formula.

JAY
Sounds complicated.

LYNN
It is, a little. But the way I
understand it, the
participating employers'
contribution . . .

Lynn's voice segues to the Announcer as we

DISSOLVE TO:

8 POST PRODUCTION—GRAPHIC

PARTICIPATING EMPLOYERS'
CONTRIBUTION

Determined by a schedule that is based on Bancorp Hawaii, Inc.'s adjusted net income and adjusted return on equity.

(CONTINUES)

8 CONTINUED

(See "Profit Sharing Contribution" in the Plan prospectus.)

MUSIC
(Theme in and under)

ANNOUNCER
(voice over, picks up the sentence Lynn started)
The participating employers' contribution is determined by a schedule that is based on Bancorp Hawaii, Inc.'s adjusted net income and adjusted return on equity. Please refer to the section titled, "Profit Sharing Contribution," in the Plan prospectus.

9 POST PRODUCTION—GRAPHIC

ELIGIBLE MEMBER'S SHARE

If you are an eligible member of the Plan, your share of the participating employers' contribution is the proportion that your base salary or wages represents of the base salary or wages of all eligible members.

ANNOUNCER
(voice over)
If you are an eligible member of the Plan, your share of the participating employers' contribution is the proportion that your base salary or wages represents of the base salary or wages of all eligible members.

Segue from announcer to Lynn as we

DISSOLVE TO:

Bank of Hawaii Script 9

10 INT. EMPLOYEE'S HOME—NIGHT

Live action continues.

LYNN
(finishes the sentence started by the announcer)
. . . of all eligible members.
In other words, if you think
of my base salary as a
percentage of all the base
salaries and wages of all the
eligible members, then that's
the percentage of the
profit-sharing that I receive.

JAY
When do we get the money? I
think it would be nice if we'd
buy a boat.

---

device, the characters remained natural and believable, while the narrator handled the "Scotch Brand Tape" statements.

Suggestions for Writing Dialogue

Decide Who the Speakers Are

Dialogue begins with characterization. Who are the people in the scene? Why are they there? What do you know about them? It may help you write better dialogue if you'll do a little back story on your characters the way screenplay writers do. This is a brief biography which you make up that tells you more about the person who is speaking. Even before you get into characterization, you'll need to decide how many of what kind of people are in the scene. Do you want a man and a woman? If so, are they strangers, lovers, friends, married? Are a man and a woman best for this scene in this video? Would it be better if you used a mother and her two daughters? How about two nine-year-old boys?

Who Says What?

Once you've decided who the people are, you have to determine what they do, what they say, and how they say it. In many dialogue scenes in a commercial video, one person has the answers and the others need to ask questions to find out what they (and the audience) want to know. Remember that it *never* occurs in real life that two people who share the information recite it to each other. That only happens in bad radio commercials:

MAN
I think it would be nice to
plant roses this year.

WOMAN
Then you should head down
to the Garden Center. All
their roses are forty percent
off through Sunday.

MAN
Say, that's right. And the
Garden Center has all the
plant food, fertilizer, and
tools I'll need, too.

WOMAN
Sure, and if your order's too
big to fit in the car, the
Garden Center delivers.

That's a conversation that never took place between real people, anywhere in the world, ever. But I can hear dialogue like that every day on the radio.

Keep It Short

Good video dialogue tends to consist of short speeches that bounce comfortably back and forth among the characters. A long speech by any character is a monologue and the character becomes a spokesperson—while all the other characters in the scene slowly die of nothing to do while the camera is on them.

Keep in Mind the Suggestions for Narration

Many of the suggestions for writing narration will apply equally to dialogue. What do the characters sound like? Use short words and short sentences. Read the dialogue aloud as you write it. Find the appropriate rhythm for the speech. Avoid tongue-twister sentences. Never, ever, use a parenthetical expression in dialogue. Watch how you write possessive constructions. Write out numbers and symbols. Spell names and foreign words phonetically. Use conjunctions to start sentences. Keep reading directions to a minimum. Time each scene with a stopwatch.

Say a Name Once and Move On

You identify characters by name, and the way the audience knows what the names are is for each character either to introduce himself or be called by name by another character. Inexperienced dialogue writers keep tucking the names into dialogue, either for emphasis ("Well, Joe, this is serious . . .") or because they are afraid the audience didn't get the name the first time it was said. In a short commercial video the names usually aren't very important, anyway. So mention them once and move on.

Watch Your Grammar

You write prose for print in complete, grammatical sentences and well-crafted paragraphs. But almost nobody talks that way. Don't let the rules of grammar drag down your dialogue. Use sentence fragments. Use one word sentences. Start a thought with one character and let another complete it. When in doubt, follow social rule rather than grammatical rule. In print I might actually find an opportunity to write "It is I." In dialogue I would always use "It's me," unless I wanted to use overly correct grammar for characterization.

Understate

On stage, actors project their voices so they can be heard in the last row. And when stage actors come to video or film they have to learn to understate, to speak softly for the microphone. Similarly, the best language for video and film dialogue will be simple words in simple form. Simplify, simplify!

Don't Say What You Can Show

Just as you don't use narration to describe what the audience can see is happening, you don't use dialogue to talk about something you can just as easily show.

Give Your Characters Something to Do

You don't just stick two or three people on an empty sound stage and have them talk. Get them busy doing something that relates to the video, and they'll have something to talk about. If you reach the point where your characters don't have anything to do, you may want to ask yourself whether a dialogue video is the right way to go.

A Client Story: Don't Write Dumb Scenes

This isn't about one of my clients. It's about a training film made for the Navy that I saw when I was in flight training, and saw again and again during my time in the service. The film was made to show radar controllers how to guide pilots through a radar controlled approach to an airport runway. And rather than make another film on the same subject for pilots, they just showed us the same movie. Mostly it was pretty good, except for one dumb scene.

The narration in that scene suggested that as a way of increasing the pilot's confidence in the radar controller, the controller should tell the pilot some information that the pilot could check for himself in the cockpit. Cut to a controller on the radio to a plane, telling the pilots that the runway they would be landing on was eight thousand feet long and three hundred feet wide. Cut to the cockpit of the plane. The co-pilot checks this information in the navigation guide and gives the pilot a big smile and a thumbs up.

To someone at the film production company, that scene made sense. And obviously it didn't bother the Navy supply officer or whoever had to approve the script and film and authorize payment. But to a pilot, the fact that the controller knew the length and width of the runway was no more reassuring than that he knew the earth was round.

Dumb scene.

Exercise: Analyze Dialogue in Commercials

Watch TV spots and listen to radio commercials with dialogue in them. Make a note of one or two that seem silly or unrealistic. Try to analyze why. If you can, tape them and go over them several times. Then pick one and rewrite it so it makes sense and still does its job.

At the same time, note any spots with particularly good dialogue. Analyze these spots and try to develop a theory about what makes their dialogue work.

10 Music and Sounds

Extraordinary how potent cheap music is.
—Noël Coward, *Private Lives*

What about music? The theme music for the video you are writing is your concern, but not your responsibility. The director—or the music director with the director's approval—will select the music to be used when the video is produced.

Music and the Writer

Only in a very rare instance will you be directly involved in planning the use of music in the video. Usually this will be when the client has a jingle or piece of music already identified with it or has commissioned an original song for the video. Then you might find yourself trying to write the video to match the music rather than writing the script visually and letting the score complement the visual evidence.

In the script examples I've included in previous chapters, there have been oblique references to music:

MUSIC
(Theme in)

or

MUSIC
(Continues under)

You may want to indicate a musical style or a mood in your description:

MUSIC
(Light, upbeat theme.)

or

MUSIC
(Band music of the sort heard
at football games.)

A video may have more than one theme, and you'll want to distinguish the themes in your description:

MUSIC
(Segues to a soft, romantic theme.)

Notes of this sort are useful whether the producer will be using themes from a stock music library or will be having music specially composed for the video. It gives the producer, director, or music director a sense of what you have in mind. But the final decision about music will normally be out of your hands.

Using Popular Music

There is always the temptation to score the video out of your own collection of popular music. Don't. It isn't legal, and you might get the client all excited about something the producer won't be able to deliver.

"Why not?" you ask. "I see it all the time on TV. Sports especially. They do a visual essay scored with a popular song."

Sure. Frank Sinatra sings, "Here's to the Winners," while

football players do high fives in slow motion. Television networks and TV stations can do that because they pay a hefty annual fee for a blanket clearance to use recorded music. They can, because they're broadcasters. You can't. At least not without spending a lot of time and a lot of money. Actually, if you have plenty of both, you can secure the rights to virtually any recorded music. But it requires several different clearances. And for a current hit song, the fee will be high—probably more than the total budget for the video you're writing.

Stock Music

Audio studios maintain a library of stock music, which is updated every few months. This will often have soundalike themes which are similar to current popular music or to the soundtrack scores of hit movies. These themes are not exactly the same as the popular music, but they are in the same style.

Stock music libraries also contain a wide range of generic themes which can be used to score videos and films. The catalog lists categories, titles, and brief descriptive notes which suggest what the music will be like. But someone has to listen to it to decide whether it is appropriate for the video. If you are good at music, that someone might be you—at an additional fee.

Figure 10-1 reproduces a page from the catalog of Associated Production Music, a stock music library in Los Angeles. Each of the titles represents a CD with anywhere from twenty to forty cuts of varying lengths recorded on it. Each CD represents a major category. If you were the music director selecting music for a video for children, you'd want to check out APM 2: Children. You might find something there that suits your purpose. I don't know what's on that particular CD, but it could be anything from the sound of a music box playing nursery rhymes to a full orchestra playing "The Teddy Bears' Picnic." It might also turn out that the person who set up this category had an idea that children's music should be cute, or sweet, or sentimental, which might not be what you want at all. So you would listen to APM 2, but you might also check out APM 10: Happy/

FIGURE 10-1

Excerpt from a Stock Music Catalog

Library	Title	Composer	Description
	AMERICANA		
APM 1	**AMERICANA**	Various	
KPM 6	**TRADEWINDS**	G. DeWilde/M. Dalton	Pastoral, pleasant acoustic guitar and piano enhanced by lush orchestra.
KPM 33	**PIONEERS**	M. Emney	Positive grand scale themes along with lyrical cues.
KPM 39 ▲	**ATMOSPHERIC JOURNEYS 2**	G. DeWilde	Sounds of Africa, Eastern Europe, the Orient and the Mediterranean.
KPM 71	**AROUND THE WORLD IN 80 MINUTES (2)**	Various	Music of the USA, West Indies, Hawaii, and South America.
KPM 89	**RED, WHITE AND BLUE**	G. DeWilde	Traditional music of Great Britain and the U.S.
KPM 95	**USA**	G. Preskett	A musical portrait of Americana from hoedown to orchestral panorama.
BRR 34	**CAJUN/COUNTRY MUSIC**	Various	Louisiana! New Orleans! Nashville! A lively musical guide to these regions.
SCD 076 ▲	**MAGNIFICENT WESTERN**	Various	Full orchestral scores in the great Western film tradition.
	CHILDREN		
APM 2	**CHILDREN**	Various	
KPM 87	**WHIMSY**	D. Walter	A wry, reflective and gently humorous look at life. Scored for small ensemble.
KPM 130	**STORYTELLERS**	P. Kingsland	Imaginative themes depicting the lyrical, dramaticand humorous aspects of fantasy.
KPM 147 ▲	**CHILDREN'S HOUR**	Various	Gentle, charming and playful sounds for the very young.
BRE 5 ▲	**CHILDREN/ANIMATION**	J. Hodge	Lighthearted electronics for fun and games.
SCD 075 ▲	**STRICTLY FOR CHILDREN**	Various	Charming and amusing, includes well-known folk tunes.
TIM 20 ▲	**CHILD'S PLAY**	P. Gosling	Comedy, mystery, chase, hi-tech and light-hearted.
	COMEDY/ANIMATION		
APM 3	**COMEDY/ANIMATION**	Various	
KPM 43 ▲	**PERSONAL GLIMPSES**	G. Preskett	Thematic suites: classical, ragtime, comedy and light interest.
KPM 87	**WHIMSY**	D. Walter	A wry, reflective and gently humorous look at life. Scored for small ensemble.
KPM 131	**COMEDY CLASSICS - 1**	Various	A naughty celebration of discomfort, slapstick and the absurd.
KPM 132	**COMEDY CLASSICS - 2**	D. Farnon/P. Gerrard	A comedy collection suitable for animation, children's programs, archive films or just silly bits and pieces.
BRF 8 ▲	**COMIC CUTS**	J. Hodge	A collection of comedy capers in convenient commercial cuts.
BRF 9 ▲	**JUST FOR LAUGHS**	C. Marshall	Funny stuff.
BRF 10	**LOONY TUNES**	Various	A compilation of favorite funnies from the BRF series.
SCD 033	**COMIC CUTS**	Various	Effects, gags, stings, links and bridges.
SCD 074 ▲	**COMIC COLLECTION 1**	Various	From silly to sillier, traditional funny stuff.
TIM 12	**SERENDIPITY**	B. Morgan	Africa-styled jazz and quirky mechanical tracks.
TIM 13	**SERENDIPITY RIDES AGAIN**	B. Morgan	From mysterious to New Age to humorous.
	COUNTRY/WESTERN		
APM 4	**COUNTRY/WESTERN**	Various	
KPM 71	**AROUND THE WORLD IN 80 MINUTES (2)**		Music of the USA, West Indies, Hawaii, and South America.
KPM 95	**USA**	G. Preskett	A musical portrait of Americana from hoedown to orchestral panorama.
KPM 121 ▲	**FREEWHEELIN'**	G. Preskett	Optimistic and bright with a touch of country.
BRR 27 ▲	**VISIONS OF COUNTRY**	C. Marshall/R. Matthews	Country-Western and Country-Rock,includes vocals.
BRR 34	**CAJUN/COUNTRY MUSIC**	Various	Louisiana! New Orleans! Nashville! A lively musical guide to these regions.
TIM 4	**GUITAR SKETCHES**	S. Grossman	Compositions for solo acoustic guitar featuring twelve string, bottle neck and six string.
	DOCUMENTARY: CURRENT AFFAIRS		
APM 5	**DOCUMENTARY: CURRENT AFFAIRS**	Various	
KPM 2	**CLASSICAL FUSION 1 & 2**	G. DeWilde	Classical and contemporary styles for sports and industry.
KPM 3	**CLASSICAL FUSION 3**	G. DeWilde	Classical and contemporary styles for sports and industry.

Light Interest, APM 11: Holidays & Special Occasions, maybe APM 15: Jazz and APM 20: Piano.

If you were looking for music for an industrial video, you'd want to listen to some of the cuts on APM 12: Industry. The catalog listing for this CD is shown in Figure 10-2. It shows the

Figure 10-2

Stock Music Listing—Industrial Theme

APM 12
Industry

INDUSTRY
Music for business and industry

	Title / Composer	Time	*Notes*
1	BUSINESS WORLD K. MANSFIELD	2:10	SERIOUS, DELIBERATE
2	PLANNING FOR PEOPLE A. MC CRORIE-SHAND, A. SEAR	2:16	SUBDUED INTENSITY
3	ROUGH BREED (THE) K. MANSFIELD	2:05	DETERMINED
4	QUALITY CONTROL FRANK RICOTTI	3:03	MECHANICAL
5	PROVING GROUND RAY RUSSELL	3:48	HEAVY MOVEMENT
6	ARC OF ELECTRICITY A. DUTT	3:50	MECHANICAL
7	A TIME OF CHANGE K. MANSFIELD	2:33	RESTLESS
8	UPDATE REPORT K. MANSFIELD	1:55	PROGRESSIVE
9	CUTTING EDGE PAUL KEOGH	2:19	DELIBERATE
10	TECHNOCRAFT A. JACKMAN, G. JACKMAN, K. MC ALEA	1:12	HEAVY ACTIVITY
11	SOFT FOCUS RAY RUSSELL	2:46	SMOOTH MOVEMENT
12	TELEGRAPHICS RAY RUSSELL	3:02	SMOOTH MOVEMENT
13	HIGH PERFORMANCE WARREN BENNETT	2:50	MECHANICAL
14	TURBO TREVOR BASTOW	2:02	UPTEMPO
15	ACTION REPORT TREVOR BASTOW	2:38	FAST, MOVEMENT
16	HEART OF THE MACHINE (THE) D. MACKAY	3:24	PROPULSIVE
17	HERE AND NOW K. MANSFIELD	3:10	SERIOUS, PROPULSIVE
18	FUTURE POSITIVE K. MANSFIELD	2:34	URGENT
19	FREIGHTWAYS G. DE WILDE	2:54	DYNAMIC
20	ENTERPRISE ZONE G. DE WILDE	3:44	BUILDING
21	FOREFRONT PAUL KEOGH	3:19	SLOW INTRO, ACTIVE
22	TIME KEEPS MOVING W. BENNETT	2:13	HEAVY BEAT
23	HI-TECH P. WILSON	2:30	MECHANICAL
24	FLYING PAST P. WILSON	2:25	DRIVING, ACTION
25	NEW RANGE (THE) G. DE WILDE	2:44	FAST, MOVEMENT
26	LIGHT DRIVE D. MACKAY	3:10	FAST, FLUENT

number and title of each cut on the CD, the running time of the cut in minutes and seconds, and offers one or two adjectives to describe the mood of the music. The name of the composer or arranger is shown beneath the title.

Stock libraries often include classical music which is in the public domain. Figure 10-3 shows the catalog listing for APM 19: Period: Classical. This includes themes by Bach, Vivaldi, Handel, Mozart, Beethoven, and Dvorak, and other themes described in the notes as "in the style of" Mahler, Prokofiev, Shostakovich, and Stravinsky.

Sounds and Sound Effects

In addition to the use of a musical theme, you can enrich a video by adding other sounds. Audio studios also have stock libraries of sound effects. So you can write into your script the sounds of a ticking clock, a car or a plane, a fog horn, a cash register, or just about anything you need.

Quite often footage shot in news style with a shotgun microphone on the camera may have inadequate sound. For instance, if the camera is aimed at the speaker at a podium, it may pick up the audience applause very weakly or not at all. If that's the client's CEO at the podium, you don't want it to sound like only three people are clapping. Use a sound effect:

9 INT. AUDITORIUM—DAY

MC introduces company CEO. Sound of APPLAUSE as CEO is introduced.

If you have an outdoor scene, but the audio track is picking up the cars on the freeway just out of sight, replace the track with a sound effect:

19 EXT. FOREST—DAY

Establishing shot of peaceful stream in the woods. Sound of WATER IN STREAM. Birds CHIRPING.

Figure 10-4 reproduces a page from the catalog for the APM sound effects library with an alphabetical listing of sounds. Just

Figure 10-3

Stock Music Listing—Classical Theme

APM 19*
Period: Classical

PERIOD: CLASSICAL

Classical music through the ages

1	BENEDICTUS R. MYHILL	1:27	MONASTIC CHANT
2	TAVERN TALES DAVID SNELL	1:32	MEDIEVAL, DANCE
3	SIR RICHARD'S PLEASURE RICHARD MYHILL	1:20	RENAISSANCE, AIR
4	LARKRISE RICHARD HARVEY	1:24	RENAISSANCE, HARPSICHORD & RECORDER
5	QUEEN'S CONSORT (THE) G. DE WILDE	1:18	BAROQUE, STYLE OF HANDEL
6	RONDEAU (PURCELL) F. TRENCH	0:59	BAROQUE
7	INVENTION #8 (BACH) F. TRENCH	1:59	BAROQUE, PIANO & ORCHESTRA
8	BRANDENBURG #3 (BACH) F. TRENCH	0:59	BAROQUE, 1ST MOVEMENT
9	ARIA (PASQUINI) F. TRENCH	0:59	BAROQUE
10	FOUR SEASONS (VIVALDI) F. TRENCH	0:59	BAROQUE, "SPRING", 1ST MVT.
11	WATER MUSIC (HANDEL) F. TRENCH	0:59	BAROQUE, HORNPIPE
12	PHYSICK GARDEN (THE) G. DE WILDE	2:00	BAROQUE, STYLE OF HANDEL
13	SYMPHONY #40 (MOZART) F. TRENCH	0:59	CLASSICAL, 1ST MOVEMENT
14	SERENADE, EINE KLEINE NACHTMUSIK F. TRENCH	0:59	CLASSICAL, MOZART
15	MINUET (BOCCHERINI) F. TRENCH	0:59	CLASSICAL, STRING QUARTET IN E
16	PASTORAL SYMPHONY (BEETHOVEN) F. TRENCH	0:59	CLASSICAL, 1ST MOVEMENT
17	BY THE STREAM ALEC GOULD	1:45	CLASSICAL, STYLE OF MOZART
18	ETUDE #1 A. GOULD	2:05	STRING QUARTET, ALLEGRO
19	ETUDE #4 A. GOULD	2:14	STRING QUARTET, MINUET
20	ETUDE #5 A. GOULD	2:53	STRING QUARTET, LENTO
21	YESTERDAYS G. DE WILDE	2:45	19TH CENTURY, DARK
22	ON THE STEPPES D. SNELL	1:26	19TH CENTURY, RUSSIAN STYLE
23	NOCTURNE (BORODIN) F. TRENCH	0:59	19TH CENTURY, STRING QUARTET #2
24	NEW WORLD SYMPHONY (DVORAK) F. TRENCH	0:59	19TH CENTURY, LARGO
25	FLIGHT OF THE BUMBLEBEE F. TRENCH	0:59	19TH CENTURY, RIMSKY-KORSAKOV
26	ADAGIO A. GOULD	1:57	19TH CENTURY, STYLE OF MAHLER
27	FINAL APPROACH (THE) G. DE WILDE	3:31	20TH CENTURY, BOLERO
28	OLYMPUS R. HARVEY	1:46	20TH CENTURY, FUTURISTIC FANFARE
29	TRANS SIBERIAN EXPRESS D. SNELL	2:06	20TH CENTURY, STYLE OF PROKOFIEV
30	RED PATROL D. SNELL	1:52	20TH CENTURY, STYLE OF SHOSTAKOVICH
31	PAGAN RITE J. CAMERON	2:24	20TH CENTURY, STYLE OF STRAVINSKY

FIGURE 10-4

Excerpt from a Sound Effects Catalog

Compressed air tool, loosening	SFX 008 - 22
Compressed air tool, tightening	SFX 008 - 23
Compressed air tool, paint spray	SFX 008 - 24
Compressed air tools	SFX 008 - 25
Drill	SFX 008 - 2
Gas pump	SFX 008 - 15
Grinding (metal)	SFX 008 - 6
Grinding (wood)	SFX 008 - 11
Lathe, metal	SFX 008 - 1
Plane, wood	SFX 008 - 14
Sand blasting	SFX 008 - 7
Trolley jack	SFX 008 - 20
Welding, electric arc	SFX 008 - 4
Welding, gas	SFX 008 - 3
Wheel balancing unit	SFX 008 - 21
Microwave oven	SFX 004 - 37
Military	
English Civil War	SFX 007 - 38
Modern Battle	SFX 007 - 39
Monorail	SFX 006 - 27
Motorcycle	
Harley	SFX 006 - 1
Yamaha	SFX 006 - 3
Gangs	SFX 006 - 2
NNNNNNNNNNNNNNNNNNNNNNNNNNNNNNNNNNNNNNNNNNNNNNNNNNN	
Night-time atmosphere	SFX 007 - 35
OOOOOOOOOOOOOOOOOOOOOOOOOOOOOOOOOOOOOOOOOOOOOOOOOOO	
Office	
Air Conditioning	SFX 007 - 24 & 25
Background	SFX 003 - 32
Basement Boiler Room/Air Conditioner	SFX 007 - 27
Computer Room	SFX 007 - 19
Electronic Dealing Console	SFX 007 - 20
Electronic Share Dealing Room	SFX 007 - 20 & 21
Futures Market Dealing Floor	SFX 007 - 23
Large Office	SFX 007 - 26
Office Equipment	
Computer plotter	SFX 008 - 33
Fax machine	SFX 008 - 32
Golf Ball printer	SFX 008 - 31
Mailing machine	SFX 008 - 36
Personal computer	SFX 008 - 30
Photocopier	SFX 008 - 34
Teletype terminal	SFX 008 - 37
Typewriter, electric	SFX 008 - 29
Typewriter, manual	SFX 008 - 26, 27, 28
Oven door	SFX 004 - 36
PPPPPPPPPPPPPPPPPPPPPPPPPPPPPPPPPPPPPPPPPPPPPPPPPPP	
Pager	SFX 008 - 42 & 43
Pigs	SFX 002 - 44
Ping Pong (Table Tennis)	SFX 005 - 11
Photocopier	SFX 004 - 57
Plane, wood	SFX 008 - 14
Pool/Snooker	SFX 005 - 13
Potter's Wheel, manual	SFX 008 - 59

on this one page, you can find a variety of machinery noises, sounds of a microwave oven, office noises and office equipment, an oven door, pigs, and a pool table.

A Client Story: Orchestrated Shop Noise

Years ago, when I was a one man film production unit for an education center, I wrote and produced two films for the Burlington County, New Jersey, vocational-technical high school. In one of the films I had to show scenes from something like twenty-five or thirty vocational-technical shops in less than twenty minutes. To get them all in, I even filmed students in the print shop producing the opening titles and students in the commercial art shop drawing the closing titles. In recording the audio to go with picture, I was struck by the range and variety of sounds in each of the shops.

Later, when I was editing the film, I had the idea that it could be truly interesting and exciting to compose those sounds into a score for the film. Alas, synthesizer technology was in its infancy, and I lacked the musical ability to do the job. Also there was deadline pressure, and I was, after all, just one person trying to emulate an entire production unit. So I didn't do it. I still think it's a neat idea. And I give it to you.

Exercise: Visit an Audio Recording Studio

Look in the Yellow Pages under Recording Service—Sound and Video. Go through the listings and advertisements to see what is offered in your area. Call one or more of the audio studios and ask if you may visit to become familiar with their facilities. If you are able to visit at a time when they are not busy, ask if you can listen to a few cuts of stock music and sound effects. Most studios will be glad to do this *when they are not busy,* because they consider it good marketing. But if they are very busy, on deadline, with clients backed up and growing impatient, they won't even have time to say hello. So call, make an appointment, and call again on the day of the appointment to confirm that it's still a good time to visit.

Other Forms and Formats

Scripts follow a particular form, just as any plan is drawn up within a set of rules accepted by the people who must understand that plan before they can put it into action.

—Joseph Gillis, *The Screen Writer's Guide*

Your responsibility as the scriptwriter is generally limited to researching and writing the treatment and the video script. But there are a number of other forms and formats which you should be aware of. These include shooting scripts, narration scripts, editing scripts, and storyboards.

The Shooting Script

I once had a film student who claimed she had never realized that a film was shot out of order in bits and pieces and then edited together. But that's the way it is done. It is more efficient (and cost-effective) to shoot, for example, all the airport footage while you have the cast and crew at the airport. So a shooting script is prepared which lumps together all the scenes from the same location—or featuring the same players—so that they can be shot at the same time, regardless of where they appear in the original script.

The Director Organizes the Shooting Script

The shooting script is the director's responsibility, not the scriptwriter's. That should be obvious, because it is the director's responsibility to block out each day's shooting, determining where, when, what, and who for the day. However, if it's relatively easy for you to go into your word processor and reorganize the scenes by location, then you may end up doing the shooting script.

If you are a computer-savvy scriptwriter, this might be a service you can offer your clients. Back when I was both writing and directing, I actually wrote several scripts in a computer database program so creating the shooting script would be easy. By using database codes, I could break scenes out by location, by normal sequence, or by character. Several of the script formatting programs in Appendix 1 will do this.

Priorities

There are no hard and fast rules about how a shooting script should be organized. The main thing is to save time and money. Therefore, a shooting script tries to find the most economical way to organize the production.

Because weather can complicate outside shooting, most producers try to shoot exteriors early in the production, with some kind of interior alternative planned in case the weather goes bad.

If there's a particular person, such as the company president or a celebrity spokesperson, available for a limited time, then all of that person's scenes may be clustered together, regardless of location, even if that means extra running around or backtracking.

Similarly, if there are a lot of people in some scenes, and only a few in others, the producer will want to try to get all the crowd scenes out of the way at the same time.

In Appendix 3 I've shown a portion of the shooting script

from a retail video I wrote about Sea Life Park at Makapuu Point on Oahu. In addition to writing the script, I was hired by the production company as assistant director. And my first job was to break down the script I had written into a shooting script organized by locations. This excerpt shows two locations. The first is the park's education department and the second is the Ocean Science Theater, where sea animals train and perform before an audience.

Following that are a few pages from the original video script with the scenes in their proper order. This fragment includes scenes in the education department and in the Ocean Science Theater, so you can see how the scenes in the shooting script fit into the continuity of the video script.

Editing Script

When you write a script from existing footage, you're actually doing a paper edit of the video. The resulting script may be just like any other. But, quite often, it becomes a specific blueprint for editing the video—an editing script.

The editing script organizes the material, times out the scenes, tells where each element comes from, and provides for new elements such as narration, sound effects, titles, supers, and so on.

As the scriptwriter, you review the footage and make your own log of what's there. Then you organize it, just as you would any other script, add any scenes which you feel must be in the program that are *not* in the footage, and write the script.

The *First Night* Editing Script

The excerpt from the *First Night* script, Figure 8-1 in Chapter 8, is one example of an editing script. It formally organizes the material in columns. The first column is the scene number. The next is the number of the tape reel on which the scene is found. The next column has the beginning and ending time code for the scene. The next shows the length of the scene in seconds and frames. Only after all this do we finally get to something which looks like script information—the video and audio. If, in addition, there existed interviews or wild sound which would be used with the video, that might have a column of its own, also.

The *First Night* script is a complete blueprint for editing. It is understood, however, that in any paper edit, a few cuts may not work exactly as written. No cut from one scene to the next is final until the editor has physically spliced the film or electronically joined the video images—*and then looked at the result*. Sometimes, what seems like a neat idea on paper just doesn't work in practice. However, Pete Dawson, who cut the *First Night* video, told me, "Anytime you need a testimonial, I'll give you one. I don't think any of my cuts were more than a few frames different from the way you wrote them."

The Kentucky Fried Chicken Editing Script

Figure 11-1 is an excerpt from the script for a video chronicling a special day for the Kentucky Fried Chicken restaurants in Hawaii. Most of the footage was shot in a single day using two cameras operating independently, although some footage of a planning session for the big day had been shot in advance. There was no script and, as far as I can tell, no treatment had been written prior to shooting. As a result, some elements which needed to be in the show did not exist on video.

The production company supplied me with VHS copies of all the camera footage with time code window-printed directly onto the picture. I logged the footage and went through the same research and organizing process as I would for any script, talking with the client and collecting everything written about Kentucky Fried Chicken Celebration Day in Hawaii.

The resulting script looks much like any other classic screenplay format video script. Where I used existing footage, the reel number or name and the time code at the start of the scene are shown in brackets { }. Some additional scenes had to be in-

FIGURE 11-1

Excerpt from the Editing Script for *Operation Breakthrough*

Script, Operation Breakthrough *Page - 4*

13 INT. STUDIO—DAY

Close-up Area Manager #1

AREA MANAGER #1
We needed to show the public
. . . and our own Kentucky
Fried Chicken family . . . that
KFC is keeping up with the
times!
{S = :07.5 | RT = 1:48}

14 EXT. WAIKIKI/KALAKAUA AVE. KENTUCKY FRIED CHICKEN—DAY

Banner above the Restaurant: "Celebration Day"
{R 11:13:16}

MUSIC
(Dixieland Band music)

MALE NARRATOR
Celebration Day started
bright and early . . .
{S = :02 | RT = 1:50}

15 EXT. HAWAII KAI KENTUCKY FRIED CHICKEN—DAY

EMPLOYEE cleaning the window. Through the window we can see the decorations that have been put up.
{R 10:14:19}

MUSIC
(Continues)

MALE NARRATOR
Each of the restaurants had
been professionally decorated
for the big day . . .
{S = :04 | RT = 1:54}

Script, Operation Breakthrough *Page - 5*

16 EXT. HAWAII KAI KENTUCKY FRIED CHICKEN—DAY

Cleaning in front of the restaurant. {R 10:09:46}

MUSIC
(Continues)

MALE NARRATOR
(continues)
. . . but there was still lots to
do.

MUSIC
(in full)

{S = :02 | RT = 1:56}

17 POST-EDITING—GETTING READY MONTAGE

Montage: Fast cut shots of things happening to get ready for Celebration Day. This is edited for speed and excitement, (Some shots may be a second or less) and is backed with the full sound of the Dixieland band:

Hawaii Kai—putting juice or milk shake equipment together. {R 10:01:15}

KFC Villa—Woman blowing up balloon. {R 01:04:26}

KFC Villa—Bus, stretch out (snap up) banner reading, "Colonel's Cavalcade" {R 01:03:30}

KFC Villa—Man blowing up balloon. {R 01:04:04}

Kapiolani—Chauffeurs wiping down the limo. {R 04:12:31}

Hawaii Kai—Man working on carousel. {R 10:04:25}

KFC Villa—Side of bus, hand pushed balloon out the window. {R 01:07:09}

Hawaii Kai—CU inflating helium balloon. {R 10:04:44}

Hawaii Kai—CU putting "Cross the Road" sign on the counter. {R 10:07:25}

KFC Villa—Dixieland Band gets on bus. {R :01:09:16} {R 01:10:54}

Hawaii Kai—Wheeling out the statue of Colonel Sanders. {R 10:07:48}

Hawaii Kai—Employee prepping chicken in flour, etc. {R 10:02:35} cluded. Because there was a very limited budget for pickup shooting, I wrote the scenes which were needed so that they could be done quickly in the studio or in some cases by using a graphics camera during editing.

For example, scene 13 is a pickup, to be shot in the studio. Scene 14 is from existing footage. The notation in brackets {R 11:13:16} means in this case that it came from reel 11, and the scene begins at time code 11 hours, 13 minutes, and 16 seconds. Remember that while time code *may* reflect the actual clock time at the moment of shooting, usually it is just an arbitrary reference code for locating scenes in the footage. Many directors set the hour in the time code to reflect the reel number of the tape being shot, which is why this is reel 11 and starts at 11 hours on the time code.

Scene 17 is a montage of things happening to get ready for Celebration Day. Here, I told the editor what I thought ought to happen, and then gave him a list of shots to draw on. It's editor's choice as to exactly which shots to use, for how long, in what order. But the shots to work from are all listed. He didn't have to go into the footage and find them.

In short, an editing script is just like any other script, only a trifle more technical. Incidentally, I write a very tight editing script, because I've paid my dues as both a video and a film editor. If you're not comfortable with this kind of fine-cut editing blueprint, don't do it. Just find the scenes you want in the existing footage, describe the picture and sound, and indicate about where each scene should start. Make it clear to the editor that he or she has plenty of leeway in cutting the scenes together as long as the essential information is included.

Narration Script

When the narration is recorded in the audio recording studio, there's no need for all the visual information, stage directions, and other items that are part of a finished script. The director wants the narrator to be able to read easily, comfortably, and conversationally.

So a narration script is prepared which includes only those scenes with narration. The narration script may show just the audio portion, or it may include a brief note about what is happening visually and any critical timing in the scene. Again, this is not really your problem as scriptwriter. But you may be asked if you can pull out the narration from your word processor fairly easily. If you say yes, you'll be asked to do it. Some of the script formatting software listed in Appendix 1 will let you do this quite easily.

Figure 11-2 shows the narration script for the excerpt from *Light in Art*, which appeared as Figure 7-2 in Chapter 7.

The scene numbers provide a reference for the narrator, the director, and the audio engineer. The director can quickly cross-reference to the full video script to refresh his memory about what occurs visually in the scene. The narrator may want to ask about the reading of scene 46 or 52. And the audio engineer will use the scene numbers to cue the tape at the start of a new take. Or when the narrator muffs a line, the director will say, "Let's start again at scene 39."

Storyboards

A storyboard is always helpful if the video concept is hard to visualize from a written description. A storyboard lets you show little drawings of the pictures you intend for the video and write in the narration, the dialogue, or a description of what is heard next to each image. Directors use storyboards to block the scene, define the space they are working in, and set their camera angles.

But storyboards simply are not your problem. They're the director's responsibility. They also represent an additional expense on the production budget, which is a concern for the producer. So the decision to use storyboards will be made by the production company, although, as the writer, you may be asked to work with the storyboard artist to be sure the artist's boards convey the intent of your script.

If you want to play with storyboards, you can buy storyboard

FIGURE 11-2

Excerpt from the Narration Script for *Light in Art*

Narration Script, *Light in Art* *Page - 4*

35 This is another work of art which makes pure light an artistic element. This sculpture on a wall in the court of the Astronomy Department at the University of Hawaii, is made of prisms, which catch the light of the sun . . . and break it into the colors of the visible spectrum. Put these colors back together again and you have clear, white light.

38 White light breaks down into the primary colors of red, blue, and green. These can be mixed to produce any color in the visible spectrum.

39 In the studio, three lights were gelled to approximate one of the primary colors.

40 Red

42 Blue

44 Green

46 When the red and blue lights are combined, . . . the area where they overlap is a different color . . . magenta.

48 Blue and green . . . produce cyan . . .

50 While combining red and green produces the unexpected color . . . yellow.

52 When all three primaries are mixed . . . the color of the light produced in this studio test is close to white.

Narration Script, *Light in Art* *Page - 5*

54 The dancer's arm interferes with the light from the three sources and casts many different shadows. Where it blocks the light from each of the primary sources, we see a secondary color . . . yellow, magenta, or cyan. Where it blocks the light from two of the primary sources you can see the third primary color . . . red, blue, or green. And where it blocks the light from all three, you can see the complete absence of light . . . a black shadow.

---

forms in a graphic arts supply store. Or if you have a computer set up for desktop publishing—with stored clip art or the ability to scan images into the computer—you can create your own storyboard system. Figure 11-3 shows a sample storyboard form.

A Client Story: Words into Pictures

My first job out of college was as the circulation promotion copywriter for the Philadelphia *Evening and Sunday Bulletin*. The client naturally was my boss, who, although he was an excellent still photographer, seemed to be very poor at translating the words describing images in a script into a mental picture of what the video would look like. I'd give him the script for a commercial, and he'd say, "No! It's no good. You don't even mention the *Bulletin* until the end of the spot."

Not true. I opened the spot with a close-up of the *Sunday Bulletin* and showed close-ups of the various sections of the paper (with the *Bulletin* logo prominently displayed) all through the spot. But he hadn't noticed that. Finally, I realized

FIGURE 11-3

Sample Storyboard Form

Scene ______

Scene ______

Scene ______

he was only reading the right-hand side of the script. I learned that if I wanted to get my boss to approve a script, I had to have pictures represent the pictures.

From then on, for him, I always did storyboards.

Exercise: Make a Shooting Script

Create a shooting script. Take one of the scripts you've worked on in prior exercises and break it down into a shooting script. Write a paragraph explaining why you organized it the way you did.

Or take a video you have (or have taped off the air) and make a running log of the scenes and characters. Then break this out into a shooting script. (Don't use a situation comedy, as these have three or four standing sets and do almost all production within those sets, shooting the scenes in order in front of a studio audience.) State in a paragraph why you chose to organize the shooting script the way you did.

12 Traps and Pitfalls

> Wisdom consists in being able to distinguish among dangers and make a choice of the least harmful.
>
> —MACHIAVELLI, *The Prince*

There are any number of things that you, as an inexperienced scriptwriter, can do in the process of developing a script that will cause problems for your client and eventually for you. In the early stages of your scriptwriting career you can get so focused on wanting to get the first paid assignment and seeing your work translated into video that you'll believe everything and agree to anything. This chapter will point out some of the ways things can go wrong and tell you how to play defense.

Don't Write Dialogue for Non-Actors

A non-actor is anyone in the vast majority of the population who has never studied how to say a writer's words on stage or on camera. Non-actors can include the CEO of the client company, the research director of the lab you're featuring in the video, the coach of the little league team, the mother of the student who got an award—in short, anyone who wasn't selected by a casting director and sent over for an audition. Non-actors don't know how to relax on camera, don't know how to walk so it looks natural, and are no good at memorizing dialogue.

I never write dialogue for non-actors unless I am ordered to by my client. What I know from my years of experience directing and editing documentaries is that most people have no problem talking on camera *as long as you don't tell them what to say or how to say it.*

When you write dialogue for a non-actor, you risk turning him into a *bad* actor. Most people will be themselves on camera, if you'll let them. But if you try to turn them into actors when they're not trained for it, what you'll get are bad acting and an unacceptable performance. Where real people are used in the video, I simply suggest what they can be expected to say and leave it up to the director to elicit the information from them. Sometimes I may include a question designed to evoke the necessary comments.

For example, in the highway video shown in Chapter 6, there was a section where we wanted specific comments from residents and business people in the construction area. In the treatment and in the script I suggested who they would be and what they would say and let the director take it from there.

28 EXT. DIFFERENT PRIVATE HOME—DAY

Spokesman with RESIDENT #2.

SPOKESMAN
(Introduces resident and
asks:) How do you feel about
the project?

RESIDENT #2
(Expresses concern about
inconvenience.)

29 EXT. BUSINESS ALONG THE HIGHWAY—DAY

Spokesman with a BUSINESS PERSON.

SPOKESMAN
(Introduces business person
and asks:) What do you think
the highway project will
mean for business?

BUSINESS PERSON
(Expresses concern that the project may cut into business.)

"Can't We Use a Teleprompter?"

Even after you've said you don't want to write dialogue for people who are not trained as actors, someone will ask if it isn't possible to use a Teleprompter or cue card, so the person can read the dialogue they still want you to write. Sure. And no. Sure, it's possible. But except for a news anchor person sitting at a desk and looking straight into the camera, hardly anyone really looks natural reading from a Teleprompter. Their head moves, their hands gesture, but the eyes never stray from the written word. And that's the best you get when the person is trained to do it. With a non-actor it just gets worse.

If you are required to write dialogue for non-actors, do it. But never volunteer it.

Avoid Extra Locations

Once you've been on location, you'll get a feel for just how much work it takes to make a scene look natural on video. The director of photography may set anywhere from two or three to twenty or more lights just to get the scene to look as if no lights at all are being used. And every one of those lights, with its associated grip equipment, stand, and cables, has to be brought off the truck and set up. The camera, tripod, microphones, and various other equipment such as a dolly and dolly rails, window gels, microphone boom stands, and a hundred and one other things, also have to be brought out and set up. And when shooting is finished at that location it all has to be packed up and put back on the truck, taken to the next location, and brought out and set up all over again.

So if you write a five second scene in a new location, there may be an hour or two of setup time and an hour of breakdown time required in addition to travel and whatever time is needed to get an acceptable take of your five second scene. That doesn't mean you should put the whole video in one location and leave it there. It does mean that you should be aware of what it costs the producer and crew each time you add a new location to the script.

"Don't Worry about Pictures; We've Got Lots of Slides"

The first time I heard the one about the client having lots of slides to use as visuals, I was taken in. For some reason I visualized professional photographs, properly lit and artistically composed. What I got was box after box of tiny 110 Instamatic slides shot by somebody's relative, and I had to try to make a professional program out of amateur snapshots.

When the client tells you there are lots of slides, get a look at them before you agree to use them. And get the director or video editor from the production company to look also. Then draw straws to see who is tactfully going to explain to the client why these slides won't do the job.

"We've Got Plenty of Video"

Same song, different verse. One of the worst traps you can find yourself in is trying to write a script using existing footage that was shot for some other purpose. You may find that you've got hours of close-ups of a product that means nothing to the program you're writing. And that every time the camera gets close to the stuff you're interested in, it moves on to something else, *because what you are interested in was not the purpose for which the footage was shot.*

Be cautious in accepting an assignment of this sort. Make it conditional on the footage being usable, because the client may not have any idea what is there. He just knows there's five hours of videotape in the vault that he paid several thousand dollars to have shot.

Explain that the footage may not work, or that additional scenes may have to be shot. Then get a look at it and see if you can salvage a show from it. Be sure you'll get paid for looking, whether the footage is usable or not.

There's No Such Thing as a "Simple Update"

Clients *always* seem to think that revising and updating an existing video is a simple job. Don't you believe it. Unless you wrote the original script, already have it stored in your computer, and are going to change just a few words in the narration, an update is a new script and a new program. Here's why:

If you did not write the original script, you have to view the existing program with the client to find out what is there and what has to be changed. If you are lucky, the client has a copy of the script from which the existing program was made. If not, you'll have to go back and log a scene-by-scene summary of it so you will know exactly what is there when you go to write. Then you need to research and organize the new material so that it fits with that part of the existing script which is being kept. In essence, you are creating a new video by combining elements of the old program with new material. Expect it to take you longer than writing a new script from scratch.

Client Contact

Usually your client will be a production company or an advertising or P.R. agency, while the client will be a company or organization which wants a video made. As the scriptwriter, you may have quite a bit of contact with the client, often on your own. If you always keep in mind that you represent your client and remember to be businesslike, be loyal, and be discreet, you shouldn't have any problems. Otherwise, there are several traps to fall into.

Represent Your Client Well

Your client got you this job, so show your gratitude by doing a good job of representing him. Be on time to meetings, dress properly, and be respectful to the client. Don't gossip about your client, and never badmouth your client to the client. It could happen that the client will tell you that he doesn't like one of your client's producers or directors and hopes that person won't be working on this video. Be noncommittal about it—it's not your decision—and immediately carry the information back to your client.

If it should happen that you simply can't get along with the client, avoid a confrontation. Go back to your client, explain the problem, and resign from the job.

Stay Within Budget

The fear of every producer is that the scriptwriter will get into a meeting with the client, have a creative brainstorm, and get the client all enthused about a great idea that can't possibly be done within the existing budget. Remember that a big part of what you get paid for is being able to execute a satisfactory solution to the client's communication need at the price he is willing to pay.

Don't Bypass Your Client

The dumbest thing any freelancer can do is to try to bypass the production company or agency which sent him out on this job and try to solicit future work for himself. First off, the client may have a long and friendly relationship with your client. In which case he'll probably call your client and ask, "What's with this freelancer you sent me who is trying to cut you out?" When that happens, you not only lose the future work but may lose the script you're working on.

If your client is a production company and the client wants a brochure to go along with the script, your client probably will not object to you writing it. Your client may just say, "Go ahead on your own," or he may want to bill the work through his company. Whichever he wants to do, it's his right. The client is his client, and you don't know how much time and effort has gone into developing the relationship that you are benefitting from.

If your client is an ad agency, and the client talks to you about doing a brochure to go along with the script, you say, "Yes, *we* can do that." Then you go back to the agency and say that the client wants a brochure. You'll probably be hired to write it, and your client will produce it. And everybody stays friendly.

Don't Talk about Your Client's Business

If you are any good at video scriptwriting, you can find yourself working for more than one production company and more than one advertising or P.R. agency. While you are working with your clients, you are going to hear things about their business: changes in personnel, new equipment, new business they are pitching, and so on. It should be obvious that *what you hear in one client's office should never be repeated in another*. Get a reputation as a gossip and you'll next get a reputation as a writer no one will hire.

Know When to Let Go of the Project

Once you have delivered the script and been paid for your services, you're out of it. It's up to the producer and director to make the video. Most of the time, what you see on the screen will be different from what you saw in your head when you were writing the script. Usually the differences won't matter. They'll simply be alternatives to the images you had in mind. Occasionally they'll be better than anything you thought of. Sometimes they'll be worse. In any case, *it's no longer your problem.*

I've had scripts I loved messed up by poor directing, bad casting, and uninspired editing. I just had to let them go. You do, too. If you weren't hired to direct principal photography or to edit the footage, you have absolutely no say in how either should be done—unless you are *asked* by the person who hired you.

If you have ambitions to be a director, keep your mouth shut and learn from the obvious mistakes of the fool who is ruining your script. When you finally get the chance to direct, you'll find out that it takes an incredible amount of work even to do a bad job.

A Client Story: Smoothing the English

One of my clients is an advertising agency in Honolulu which markets to Japanese visitors to Hawaii. Usually I get a call to research and write something which will then be translated into Japanese. So I was a little surprised when my friend at the agency called me to do a rewrite from Japanese to English of the narration script for a condominium sales video. He said, "I have an English translation of the Japanese script, but it needs to be smoothed out."

For a simple "smoothing" of the translation, I quoted him a day of my time. He provided me with a copy of the video in Japanese and an English translation of the narration. Unfortunately, the translation was not cued to picture. It was in proper sequence, so most of the time I could guess where it should start, but not always. So to prepare for the smoothing, I first had to log the video and try to match picture to sound to translation. Next, I realized that Japanese social values lead to a different selling approach than the style that works with Americans. For instance, Japanese tourists seem to feel more comfortable going where they know others have gone before. When you show a beach scene to the Japanese, you want to fill it with lots of Japanese having a good time. When you show a beach scene to an American, the beach should be empty. His idea of a great place—at least in fantasy—is to be the only person there. Finally, the video ended with a series of scenes of bathroom fixtures for which there was no English narration. I never found out what this was about, but I knew it was no way to end a sales video for Americans.

At that point, I called the client and said, "This is more than just smoothing out the translator's English. This is a complete rewrite." I doubled my original quote, explained why, and to his everlasting credit, he agreed. I was able to hold most of the video as it was, while altering the narration to fit an American audience. And I did suggest some scene changes, such as getting rid of the bathrooms in the final scene.

Exercise: Do a Client Loyalty Check

The trickiest pitfall is disloyalty to your client, whether intentional or unintentional. List a dozen hypothetical situations that could come up in your dealings with your client, the client, and other clients. Identify the loyal act and the disloyal act in each situation.

13 Learning about Video and Film

Any sufficiently advanced technology is indistinguishable from magic.

—Arthur C. Clarke,
The Lost Worlds of 2001

A lot of fairly technical things happen between the time you come up with an idea for a video or film and the day you stand in the back of a darkened room while an audience views the finished product. It is certainly not essential that you, as a scriptwriter, master all forms of video technology. But you'll be a better scriptwriter if you know how things work.

The production process for a video might take only a day or two, or as long as several years. It can cost a few hundred dollars, or many, many thousands. It can be a marvelously exciting experience, or an incredibly frustrating one. Video and film are corporate media with many people doing a lot of different technical specialties. And if all you know about production is what you've learned from watching TV shows and movies about making TV shows and movies, you can end up with a lot of false assumptions that could be costly when your script goes into production.

Therefore, this chapter will be a fast overview of video and film production activities and terms. The two media are quite different in their technology, although the recording and playback processes are very similar. Film is a chemical/mechanical medium, while video is electronic. In what follows, where the production process is similar in both media, I'll treat them the same. Where the differences in the media lead to different processes, I'll distinguish them for you.

So, let's see what has to be done to make a commercial video happen.

Pre-Production

Pre-production encompasses all the work on the production prior to actual filming. This is where you live as the scriptwriter.

Concept

Every production starts with a concept. It tells what the video will be about, and what effect it is expected to have on an audience. In most cases the concept for a commercial video will come from your client. It may be as simple as "XYZ Corporation needs a new sales video for their laserware line," from which you'll need to flesh out the details. Or it may be a fairly complete idea. In general, the concept for a commercial video should be able to be stated in not more than a hundred words.

Treatment and Script Preparation and Approval

We've dealt with the scripting process in detail in Chapters 2 through 10. Nothing has changed.

Budget

The production budget details the cost of the video. It may be a *given* at the concept stage. That is, the client says, "I want to make a video about X and I expect to spend about $15,000." That's it. You have to write a video which can be produced from start to finish for that amount. Or the client may say to the production company, "This is what I want. How much will it cost?" A budget estimate can be developed from a good treatment.

The budget normally includes the cost of pre-production, including research and writing, and the cost of post production editing and completion of the video. It usually specifies delivery of a master tape or negative and one release-quality print. The cost of additional prints for distribution is normally outside the production budget.

Forget about $1,000/minute. There is no truth whatever to the notion that a video or film should cost so many dollars per minute. Popular wisdom often comes up with the rule of thumb of $1,000 per minute. The fact is, that figure was first talked about for 35mm industrial filmmaking in the 1930s, when you could get a steak dinner for a quarter and buy a new Buick for under $1,000. And it was no more accurate then than it is now. The cost of producing a video or film *always* depends entirely on what is to be shot, how many days it will take to shoot it, how large a crew is required, what equipment will be used, and the cost of actors, props, makeup, special effects, and special items such as original music. Sure, there's an average, and at the moment I have no idea what it is. About 1980 I did a study of the production budgets of award-winning industrial films, and the cost per minute of running time ranged from a low of $400 per minute to a high of over $4,000.

The writer and the budget. The production budget is important to the writer for several reasons. One is in establishing your fee for writing the script. You want to know that there is enough money to cover your time and costs. And you want to know that you are being adequately compensated. Another, of course, is that you may have to write the script to fit a preset budget. Finally, you may have a potential client tell you that he or she is thinking about having a video produced. This statement is *always* followed immediately by the question, How much do you think it will cost? Unless you are an experienced producer, *do not answer with a dollar figure.* Just say that the cost can vary widely, and you'll be glad to introduce the client to one or more of the production companies you work with. If you state a number, you're stuck with it. It could be insufficient to cover the actual cost of production, and you may find your writing fee shrinking as production costs mount. Or, almost as bad, it could be *less* than the client is willing to spend. So get the client to a producer and let the producer talk cost (with the clear understanding in advance that if a production results, you write the script).

Scouting

Scouting is necessary if the video is to be shot on location. The director needs to know about the places where he will be filming: what they look like, what the light and sound levels will be, and whether there are going to be any constraints on shooting. As the writer, you may have done your own scout of the shooting situation as part of your research phase.

Casting

The director needs to audition the actors—or the non-actors, such as company executives and employees—who will be appearing in the video. To help with this, the director may use a casting director, who is familiar with the talent available and will handle the details of setting up auditions. This is not normally your problem as the writer. In reality, by the time auditions are held, you may well have gone on to another project. The director or casting director may, however, ask you for more detailed notes on the characters in the script to help with casting the parts.

Rehearsals

If the video requires actors to create a scene and believable characters, the director will probably schedule some rehearsal time prior to principal photography.

Most commercial videos, however, are usually produced the way advertising commercials are. That is, they are shot in very short takes of a few seconds to a minute. The actors are expected to arrive knowing their lines, and rehearsals amount to one or two run-throughs during which the camera may actually be running. When I was directing, if I was working with non-actors, I always recorded rehearsals. That's because non-actors are likely to be better when they think the camera isn't on. Also, non-actors usually get worse with repetition rather than better, so the first try may well be the best.

Planning

Either the producer or the director is responsible for preparing a shooting script (or having one done) and developing a production schedule which will make the most efficient and effective use of time, money, people, and equipment. They will select a production crew to work on the project. While it is possible to shoot a video with just a camera operator, the normal *minimum* crew for a commercial video will include a director, engineer, camera operator, and grip or production assistant. More complex videos will require additional people, such as a makeup artist, Teleprompter operator, sound recordist, camera assistant, and more grips. The producer may or may not be a part of the crew. Some producers go on the shoot. Some stay in the office and organize the next production. Some are producer-directors, in which case the producer has to go wherever the director goes, and vice versa.

The appropriate videotape or filmstock has to be selected and ordered. And the appropriate production equipment has to be chosen and reserved or rented.

Production

Then the video or film goes into production.

Principal Photography

Principal photography is the actual shooting of the videotape or film footage and recording of the sound—in the studio and on location. Scenes are photographed in master shots in which all the action is recorded. Then the scene is reshot, getting close-ups of action or from the point of view of one or more of the characters. Each time the scene is shot is a take, and the take may be slated visually and audibly. Once the camera is up to speed, a grip or the camera assistant steps in front of the camera, holding a board called a slate on which is written the production information, and announces, "Scene thirty-four, take three."

Normally, far more footage is shot than can be used in the final version. This allows for retakes, changes in camera position or camera angle, and some risk taking—filming of scenes or events that could be great if they work out, or could be nothing. The relationship of the amount of footage shot to that used in the final print is the shooting ratio. Most commercial videos will have a shooting ratio of at least 10:1. That means the director will record ten minutes of tape for every minute of final running time. Some may be less; others may run 20:1, or even 50:1 or 100:1. It all depends on what is being shot.

MOS and sync footage. *MOS* is the industry term for silent footage, derived, so the story goes, from a German director in Hollywood in the thirties who is supposed to have said, "Ve vill zhoot zis scene Mit Out Sound."

Sync or *lip sync* footage refers to film shot with picture and sound synchronized together. This is usually done *double-system,* where the film is exposed in the camera and the sound is recorded on a separate audio recorder. When the scene is slated, a clapper is slapped together to establish sync between the film in the camera and the tape in the recorder. There is also *single-system* sound sync, in which the audio is recorded directly onto the film in the camera, either as an optical track within the film or onto a magnetic strip bonded to the film. Single-system sound is hardly ever used today. And *lip sync* now often means the post-production technique of recording a voice synchronized to lip movements on film. This is also known as *post sync*.

Videotape, of course, records both picture and sound on the same piece of tape.

Laboratory Processing and Sound Transfer for Film

If the production is shot on film, then during principal photography, the camera original filmstock is sent off to the film processing laboratory to be developed. The film exposed in the camera is called *original* rather than *negative* because, while it may be a negative, it may just as easily be a reversal original (like slide film), which yields a positive rather than a negative image when developed.

A work print is usually made. This is a low-cost film print made from the original for use in editing. The film original is carefully stored—often in a vault at the lab—until it is needed to make the final print of the film.

At the same time, the sound that has been recorded on audio tape is transferred at a sound laboratory to magnetic film. This is a filmstock base that has been coated with a magnetic emulsion for recording. The "mag film" is used to synchronize sound to picture and create the sound track in editing and post-production.

Film-to-video transfer. Today, there are more videotape players than projectors in businesses, schools, and organizations. As a result, even though the production may be shot on film, the plan will often be to complete it as a video. Therefore, it is quite common, today, to have the film and sound transfered directly to videotape for editing. When this happens, the rest of post production is a videotape process rather than a film process.

Post Production

Editing is the heart of the production process. We talk joyfully about *shooting* a video or film. But after all that footage is shot, the real work begins. Most of what gets shot is never used. Only a little bit—one foot in ten or less—is ever seen by the audience. What the audience sees is the video or film which is created during post production.

Editing to Rough Cut

The footage, whether video or film, is logged for later reference, and the takes which will probably be used in the video are noted, as are the takes that are no good. The editor pays careful attention to logging and labeling *everything*, so that any take can be identified and found at any time. This is especially critical in editing film, which is physically cut and gets broken down from the camera rolls into smaller and smaller rolls for use in editing. Because videotape is not cut and spliced, but is rerecorded in editing, all the scenes remain intact on the original videotape reel.

The good takes are then organized into a rough cut, which is the first edited version of the video. The rough cut is made to see how things go together. Since the editing may not be much more than putting the takes together, the rough cut will usually be longer than the intended final length of the video. Such refinements as music, narration, titles, and special effects may only be suggested.

Video editing. The rough cut stage in videotape editing is referred to as an "off-line edit." A video rough cut can be edited tighter than a film rough cut because nothing is actually cut away. Video editing equipment is computer-based, with the computer remembering each edit which is made. Generally, the computer decision list from off-line editing can be used in the final assembly, or "on-line edit."

Film editing. Once the work print and mag film come back from their labs, the first job of the editor is to synchronize picture and sound, log the footage for later reference, and select the takes that will be used in the rough cut (eliminating those that won't). A film rough cut will be looser than a video off-line, because the film is physically cut and spliced. The editor leaves a few extra frames at the head and tail of each scene, to have material to work with when it's time for the fine cut.

Approval. Approval of the rough cut by the client is approval of the overall organization of the video; it gives the producer the right to go ahead with further editing.

Titles, Opticals, Music, Narration

Some film and sound elements are not normally produced during principal photography, because what they will be like usually depends on how the video comes together in editing.

Titles and optical effects. The producer should provide the sponsor or client with a written list of titles for approval as early as possible. For film, the titles, along with special animation and optical effects if required, are shot during post production. Since videotape is edited by rerecording, titles and effects may be put in as the video is edited in off-line or may be held out until the on-line edit.

Music and narration. Music, if it is to be used, is selected, transferred, and scored to the edited work print. If there is to be a narration, it is recorded and transferred at this point. For video, music and narration usually can be edited into the production well toward the end of the editing process.

Editing to Fine Cut

The fine cut is very close to the finished product. It includes all the elements of the finished print except those which cannot be added until the film is printed or the video master is created in on-line editing.

Video fine cut. The video fine cut is a continuation of the rough cut process, tightening the edits and adding titles, other graphic elements, music, and narration.

Film fine cut. The work print is edited into a template for the final print. Corrections and changes suggested by the rough cut are made. Titles and optical effects are added to the work print, music and narration tracks are added to the sound, and the film is cut to its proper running length. The fine cut is an analog of what the finished film will be like, but there are still some steps to go through.

Film interlock—review and approval. Interlock is the showing of the film fine cut with the edited work print and the mixed sound tracks synchronized together. It is a critical formal step, because approval by the client at interlock gives the filmmaker the right to cut the original, mix the sound, and have a print made—all of which are expensive. It is the last point at which changes can be made inexpensively. If the client should request changes after giving approval at interlock, they have to be made at the client's expense.

Video approval. The video fine cut is shown to the client for approval. Although for videotape this is not quite as critical a production point as a film interlock—since it does not involve cutting the original—it is still the final point for corrections and changes prior to the creation of the finished video master during on-line editing, which is considerably more expensive than off-line.

The Sound Mix

In film production, the sound mix is the point at which the filmmaker takes the edited fine cut work print and all the various edited sound tracks (there may be several) to a sound lab for rerecording. The tracks are skillfully blended into a composite magnetic track—a single roll of 16mm or 35mm magnetic film—in perfect sync with the picture. Then the sound is transferred from the "comp mag" to an optical track, which is used in making the print of the film.

Until recently there has been no comparable stage in video production to the film sound mix, and video sound suffered in comparison to film sound. Today, however, it is possible to synchronize an edited fine cut videotape with a multitrack audio recorder—either analog or digital. This eliminates the two track limitation of videotape sound and opens video to the same sound potential as film. Sounds can be separated into various tracks, wild sounds can be added, music can segue comfortably from one selection to another, and all the sound for the video can be precisely layered into a single composite track. This is referred to as *sound sweetening*, which is the blending of the sound tracks in the audio lab, and *layback*, which is the process of rerecording the sweetened audio track onto the video master.

Video On-Line; Creating the Video Master

Depending on the editing system used, the video fine cut may be the video master, or the master may be created in a final stage of video post production, on-line editing. For example, if the off-line is done using three-quarter inch or BetaCam videotape original, the on-line may rerecord the original to one inch videotape.

An on-line editing suite bears a striking resemblance to the command deck of the Starship *Enterprise*. There are a lot of inputs, a lot of video displays, and a fairly sophisticated computer running the whole thing. In the on-line, *everything* that goes into the video is included. When a video on-line is complete, the video is ready to show or to have copies dubbed from it.

Laboratory Post Production for Film

Following interlock and the sound mix, there are still several steps to go through before a film is completed. This assumes that the film is being posted as film, not as videotape, and that a film release print will result.

Conforming Original

The camera original is taken out of the vault and sent with the edited work print to a conforming editor. Conforming original is the most critical technical step in post production, since it involves cutting and splicing the original to match the work print frame for frame.

The original is usually conformed into A and B rolls, using edge numbers printed on the original and on the work print as a guide. Edge numbers are the film equivalent of time code in video. Indeed, today the edge numbers may be expressed as time code. All the odd-numbered scenes in the film are placed in one printing roll, called the A roll, and all the even-numbered scenes are placed on the other, the B roll. (In conforming, a "scene" is a single strip of film running from one splice to the next.) Both rolls are spaced out with black leader between each scene, so they match the work print in length. Without going into technical details, it's enough to know that A and B rolls make it easier to control the final printing of the film. Note that the film original is physically cut in the creation of A and B rolls. In theory, the original could be re-edited for other use. In practice, once the original has been conformed, this is rarely done.

Printing the Film

Now the preprint materials—the A and B rolls, the optical track, the edited work print, and a scene-by-scene log of the work print—go to the processing laboratory. The original is timed, which means estimating the correct printing exposure for each scene, and color-corrected, which means determining the color composition of the light on the film printer to give each scene the best color.

Timing and color-correction are estimates, although extremely accurate ones, at most labs. The real test lies in the first print made: the answer print, which answers the question, How close did we get? The answer print is also sometimes called a check print. It is for internal use for checking and correcting the printing estimates. It is not a print to be shown to the public. Filmmakers expect to make some minor timing and color changes after viewing the answer print. If major changes are required, however, the lab should provide a new answer print.

Correction and Printing of Release Print

The filmmaker goes over the answer print and notes any scenes that are too light or too dark, or are off in color. The synchronization of the sound track with the picture is checked. Then the answer print is returned to the lab, the changes are made, and a release print is struck. This should be the first perfect print of the film and is the one shown to the public.

Distribution

The point to the exercise is to be able to manufacture as many copies of the video or film as are needed. If this is a retail video and you own a piece, you hope the demand will be tremendous and will go on forever. If it's an industrial for a corporate client, enough copies will be made to service the client's departments and branch offices. Each time the mastering materials go through the film printer or across the video tape heads, however, a minuscule amount is worn away, and eventually the prints don't look so good. Therefore, the film A and B rolls or the first video master will be used to make a film printing negative or a duplicate video master from which prints in quantity can be struck. As these wear out, new printing masters can be made from the original masters.

Manufacture of a Film Printing Negative

For ease and economy in printing, and to protect the original on the A and B rolls, a printing negative is usually made. This is a single strand of negative from which prints in quantity can be struck. In making the printing negative, the film can be blown up from 16mm to 35mm for theater use, or printed down from 35mm to 16mm or even to Super-8mm. If the film is to be released on videotape or video cassette, a video master will be made from a clean release print (which is often interlocked with the composite magnetic track for the best possible sound).

Manufacture of a Duplicate Video Master

A duplicate video master may be made from the on-line master for making copies, or a second on-line master can be created for this purpose.

It is possible to do a tape-to-film transfer from videotape, resulting in a film printing negative and sound track from which prints on motion picture film can be made. This is an expensive process. Good quality prints can be made from high quality broadcast videotape onto 16mm color film. Acceptable prints can be made from small format videotape, but there will be a noticeable loss in picture quality.

Manufacture of Prints in Quantity

Film. An answer print is made from the printing negative, in case any minor timing or color corrections have to be made. On approval of the answer print, an order can be placed for the total number of prints desired. Generally, the larger the order, the lower the cost per print.

Video. Video prints are made by dubbing or rerecording from the master. The production company can make a limited number of copies but may not be set up to do dubs in quantity. Some production companies, however, have invested in duplicating equipment and offer prints in quantity at a reasonable price. Otherwise, for a large number of copies, it may be more cost-effective, and result in better quality, to send the video master to a video laboratory which specializes in making dubs.

Word of Caution

After approval of the video fine cut or the film at interlock, there's a human tendency to want to rush out prints so they can be seen by others. As soon as the client has given approval, he or she will immediately think of several dozen emergency uses which need a print right now—regardless of the delivery date in the contract. For video, this is not too terrible, because after the on-line, what you see is what you dub. But for film it could be a disaster, and producers should try to fight it until they've got a perfect print that everyone will be satisfied with.

A Client Story: What the Wrong Director Can Do to Your Script

I got the job of writing the video for the Hilton Hawaiian Village (outlined in the treatment in Figure 6-1 in Chapter 6) by convincing my client, Dennis Burns at Pacific Focus, that all my years of doing documentaries had given me a good ear for writing believable dialogue. He'd already sold the Hilton on the concept of three different couples getting together on the last day of their vacations to chat about their experience. This sort of thing would be deadly if it wasn't credible. But if the characters played their parts believably, the audience would eavesdrop on something quite interesting.

When I completed the first draft, both my client and the marketing people at the Hilton Hawaiian Village were very pleased. The Hilton people asked for a few word changes, but otherwise they loved the script. At this point the production was turned over to a staff director, who engaged a casting director to find actors to play the parts. I met with the director and casting director once to give them some notes on the characters as I saw them, and then I moved on to another project. I did hear that they were considering an actress for the part of Ginny who I thought was wrong, but it was no longer my concern. The video went into production and then into post.

And then I got a call from my client. Dennis told me there was a problem. The client had loved the script but was not at all happy with two of the characters as they appeared in the video. Would I come over and take a look and see what could be done?

Of course.

I saw immediately that the problem was that Steve and Ginny DeAngelo hadn't been cast as I had written them.

> STEVE and GINNY DEANGELO are in their forties—middle Americans from Minnesota, where he is middle management and she teaches school. He wears Sears slacks and a plain color sport shirt. She wears shorts and a top.

I had seen the DeAngelos as the salt of the earth—nice people who had saved up for a vacation in Hawaii, brought the kids, and were enjoying themselves. Steve was an accountant or an engineer, a pipe smoker who liked facts and became the source of factual information about the Village. Ginny was a teacher and a nice person, having the time of her life in a new environment about which she didn't know very much. They weren't as sophisticated as the world traveler couple or as rich as the Yuppies, but all three couples had to be likable. People viewing the tape had to be able to identify with one of them.

The director, unfortunately, saw them as comic figures. He cast a heavyset, loud-talking actor as Steve, and instead of dressing him in subdued slacks and a knit shirt, he put him in the worst sort of tourist crap, noisy Bermuda shorts and the sort of Hawaiian shirt worn only by tourists in movies. Instead of playing Ginny as ingenuous, he turned her into an airhead.

My client didn't want to spend the money to recast and reshoot all the scenes with the DeAngelos, and asked me if I could rewrite the script so that they would be seen less, and we'd use a narrator instead of their grating voices to give the audience the information that would otherwise have come from Steve and Ginny. The other two couples would continue to be seen and heard.

I did a rewrite. A narration was recorded. The editor did a recut. And the client still hated it.

Back to the word processor for the third time. This time, the script used a straight narration over pretty pictures, which could have been done to begin with much more cheaply. The client accepted the third version. I was paid for two rewrites. The video won a Telly Award. But the client, my client, and I all knew that a director with a bad idea had taken away something we thought we were going to like much better.

Exercise: Take a Production Field Trip

Set yourself the goal of checking out each step in video production. If you are lucky enough to live where there is film production going on, investigate that as well.

In the Yellow Pages, find the names of the production companies in your area. They should be listed under one or more of the following headings:

Motion Picture Producers & Studios
Television Films—Producers & Distributors
Television Program Producers
Television Stations & Broadcasting Companies
Video Production Services
Video Tape Editing

If these are not the correct subject headings for your area, find the ones that are. Then make contact with a production company. Tell them you are studying scriptwriting and want to get more familiar with the production process. Try to visit the set of a video in production. Promise that you'll keep quiet and stay out of the way. Don't offer to help. Unless you know so much about production that you don't need this chapter, you don't know enough to be useful. Take notes so you can ask questions later. Don't bother the production people when they are working.

If you've behaved yourself on the set, they'll probably trust you to sit in the back of the room while the video is edited. Again, observe, take notes, and ask questions later.

14 Getting Started

A journey of a thousand miles must begin with a single step. —LAO-TZU, *Tao Te Ching*

And requires about two million more if you're going to get there. —BARRY HAMPE

In the magazine world, you can send off a query letter, and if the editor likes the idea for the article, you can get a go-ahead to write it. If you lack experience, you may be asked if you are willing to write the piece on spec, where the magazine is not committed to buy the finished article. You write it the best you can, and if the editor likes it, you get published and eventually paid. If the editor doesn't like the finished article, you've had a learning experience.

The Catch-22 of commercial scriptwriting is that it is almost impossible to get an assignment to write a script until you can demonstrate that you *can* write a script. Production assignments come with deadlines, and a production company is not usually willing to take a chance on a would-be scriptwriter with no experience. The financial risk is just too great.

There are exceptions, of course. You may be reading this book because you researched a topic and wrote a terrific article about it, and now a producer has given you an assignment to write the script for a video on the same topic. Or you're a writer at a P.R. firm and one of your clients wants a video.

Getting Your First Scriptwriting Assignment

If you already have the assignment, congratulations. For most writers, however, to get work as a scriptwriter, unless you have a lot of experience in production, you need a demonstration script. Without one, the receptionist at any of the production companies you call on has a better chance of getting a scriptwriting assignment than you do.

Even after many years in the business, with a list of credits as long as your arm, I still have to show samples of my work when I'm talking to a new prospect. And that's as it should be. The only time I *don't* show samples is when the prospect has been pre-sold. If I go in for an interview and the prospect says, "So-and-so says you're the person to write this video for me," and then goes right into discussing his project, I don't take the samples out of my bag unless they're asked for. Why take a chance on showing the prospect something that might turn him off? If he's sold, let him stay that way.

Creating a Demonstration Script

The demonstration script shows your prospective clients

- that you know how a script goes together,
- that you can think and write visually,
- that you know how to pace a script to maintain a good ratio between images and talk,
- that you can write words for the ear,
- and that you know how to organize the material for presentation to an audience with a good beginning, a solid ending, and a middle which flows seamlessly between them.

How do you get a demonstration script? You're going to have to write it. And you are probably going to have to do it on spec.

Here are several different ways to create your demonstration script:

Pick a topic and write a script. You could just decide that you want to do a script on some subject, much the same as you would do a magazine article on spec. You pick the topic, research it, organize the material, and write it. There are two drawbacks to this approach. The first is that a critical element in commercial scriptwriting is the writer's interaction with the clients—the production company and the client for the video. This approach misses out on that. The second is that this process doesn't help you market yourself as a scriptwriter. You're writing, but you are not demonstrating what you can do to someone who might hire you.

Find a producer with a pet project. Most production companies are client driven. The work comes in from their clients, the production company assigns a crew, and the video gets made. And when client work is slow, management would like to have something to keep the crews and equipment working. In most production companies there are a couple of projects being talked about for this purpose. One could be a video about a local landmark or historic event. Or it might be a music video or some kind of pretty pictures presentation. One such idea that I was involved with was called video postcards. All the production company needs to get going is a script.

And that's where you come in. Offer to research and write it on spec as a learning experience. Get an agreement that if you produce an acceptable script, you'll be paid for it. This way the production company gets a script for their pet project, without spending money in front. If they like what you do, they also get a writer they can use in the future. You get the chance to research and write a real script, which will be produced if you are successful. You also get a working relation with a production company. And in the end you get a demonstration script.

Help out a charitable organization. There are lots of nonprofit organizations in your area. Most of them would like to have a video to tell about what they do. Find one you like and offer to write the script for them. Again, you get to write the script for a real project. You have the experience of dealing with a client. And you end up with a demonstration script. When you have either a treatment or a first draft of the script completed, try to find a producer at a production company to critique your work. This will give you the production company input.

Try low-budget broadcast. The proliferation of independent and cable television channels in most areas has resulted in a raft of low-budget shows. For instance, many markets now have one or more real estate programs which show houses that are for sale. Someone has to write everything that is said. It's not the most exciting scriptwriting, but it can get you some production credits and could lead to something better.

Investigate community access cable television. Cable systems have a community access channel. A lot of bad TV gets produced there. But there usually are a few dedicated people who are trying to make a difference with cable programming. See if you can help—and at the same time end up with a demonstration script.

Check out advertising and public relations associations. Contact the advertising and public relations associations in your area. They often get requests for freebies and usually have trouble finding people to do them. National headquarters for several such organizations are listed in Appendix 5.

Take a course and write a script. You might sign up for a course in scriptwriting at a nearby college and work on your demonstration script as class work.

Should You Show a Sample Video?

As the scriptwriter, you're responsible for the blueprint, not the building. The video which is produced is someone else's execution of your script. Certainly, if the video is unquestionably first rate, or if you also produced or directed—and you're proud of the result—get some copies made to show. But if the video that results from your demonstration script is obviously low quality, poorly executed, badly acted, technically poor, or in other ways not up to industry standards, don't even mention it. Production people would *rather* look at a sample reel than read a script. Partly that's because they can tell in an instant if a video is not up to their standards. So they only have to watch the ones that they like all the way through. But if they hire you, they're going to have to stand or fall on what's written in your script, not on what some director somewhere else created from your work. There's more than one script I like very much that isn't on my sample reel, because I'm not happy with the way the director executed it.

Yes, I do have a sample reel. It contains five carefully chosen videos made over the last few years. When I'm looking for clients, I send the sample reel out along with copies of the first draft scripts for each video on it. I send the first draft script because that is the best example of *my* work. It shows what the client received from me. Later drafts can include changes from many sources, which may not have improved the script. I recall one script I did for a state agency in which the bureaucrats kept changing my short, simple words into long, jargonish phrases. I wouldn't want to show anyone the final draft of that one.

Getting Your First Paid Assignment

Andrew Dintenfass, who is now a Hollywood cinematographer, is my model for the way to market your services in the video and film business. When I was doing documentaries in Philadelphia in the early 1970s, I had a terrific cameraman, Jack Behr, who had done several documentaries with me. Then Jack left for the West Coast, where he has become a successful screenwriter, and I got involved in running a theater. In those days, Andy was a highly successful freelance cameraman and director of photography. When I first knew him, he could—and often did—work seven days a week, traveling all over the country to shoot documentary and industrial films. One reason he was so successful was that he paid attention to marketing himself.

After Jack left, I got a call from Andy. He'd gotten my name from someone and wanted to come by and show me his reel. I said I didn't have anything in production or scheduled right then, so it would just be a waste of time for both of us, but I'd be glad to keep him in mind if anything came up. From then on, for more than a year, I got a call from Andy every couple of months—"just checking." Then I was hired to produce and direct the documentary on mental patients that I wrote about in Chapter 3. I immediately thought of Andy. I called him, looked at his reel, which was great, and hired him to shoot the film. He got the job because he was an excellent cameraman. But he got the call because he had kept in touch with me, even when I didn't need a camera operator.

Creating a Prospect List

The first step in getting a scriptwriting assignment is to let people know you write scripts. To do this, you need to define your prospects. The people who are potential prospects include:

- Video and film production companies
- Advertising agencies
- Public relations agencies
- Television stations and cable TV operators
- Corporate in-house video production departments

Don't they have their own writers? you might ask. Some do, and they can be downright churlish when you call. Others don't. Some production companies have a large enough volume of work to justify having a writer on staff. But even they may need to use a freelance scriptwriter if they get really busy.

Others depend completely on freelancers. Some advertising and public relations agencies will have their in-house copywriters do the scripts for videos. But many agencies consider producing a video nothing but an annoyance. It takes a lot of time, doesn't pay the agency very well, and doesn't generate any additional billing. They'd rather do a TV commercial, where the production budget for a thirty second spot may actually be more than the budget for a fifteen minute video. And once the commercial is produced, it's a cash cow, because the agency buys the TV time for it to run and receives a 15 percent commission on the cost of the time. Such agencies are good prospects, because they'd rather hire a freelance scriptwriter than tie up their in-house copywriters on what they consider a low-priority, collateral project.

TV stations often do not carry a writer on staff, unless it's a writer-producer or writer-director. Even if they have a writer, he or she is likely to be swamped with work most of the time. So you want to let them know you're available. And corporate in-house video departments usually have a very small staff, which may be just one person who is always overworked. This person could be really glad to know about you. One way to meet the corporate communicators is to join and attend meetings of their associations. The video people will probably belong to ITVA, the International Television Association, which has chapters in most major cities. The corporate communicators may belong to the International Association of Business Communicators or to a local public relations association.

Making Contact

Your objective is to get as many potential clients as possible to think of you when they need a script. They won't need one every day. Some may never use a freelancer. Some may not need one for a year or more. One or two might even be looking for a scriptwriter on the day you call. But don't count on it. So get out the Yellow Pages and start making phone calls.

Whom to ask for. Your prospect—the person you want to talk with—may have one of several different titles. If you are calling a production company, he or she may be the head of production or may be called executive producer, producer, or even creative director. If you are calling an advertising agency or public relations firm, your prospect could be the copy chief, creative director, or agency producer. At a TV station your prospect may be the head of production, executive producer, or program director. I've found it never hurts to be frank with the person who answers the phone about why I'm calling and whom I want to speak with. I say I'm a freelance scriptwriter and ask for the person likely to be assigning scripts. If that elicits a name, I'm on my way. If not, I'll prompt with the various titles that apply.

Be clear about what you want. This is what you are trying to accomplish with the phone call:

1. Get the name and title of the person at the company you are calling most likely to hire a freelance scriptwriter.
2. Talk with this person if possible.
3. Make an appointment to meet the person and show your demonstration script.

If your prospect is busy—and half the time they will be—you can call back later or send a letter introducing yourself and asking for an appointment. You can leave your name and phone number as a courtesy, but don't expect the prospect to call you back. Some may. Most won't. The reason is that the person in this position almost always has more phone calls to return than time to return them.

What to say. How you open the conversation may determine whether you get an appointment or get the runaround. If you are tentative or hesitant or beat around the bush and waste your prospect's time, you'll mark yourself as an amateur and probably get a polite brush-off. So once you get on the phone with the prospect, you have to get to the point and get what you called for. Don't waste time with small talk; you don't know the prospect and he doesn't know you. Introduce yourself and state your business. Tell the prospect you're a freelance scriptwriter and you'd like to set up an appointment to show your work. Make sure the person you're talking with is the person who actually deals with freelancers. If not, ask to speak to the appropriate person.

Even if you've got the right person, your prospect is going to be cautious at first. If your prospect really doesn't use freelance writing, he'll probably say so and end the conversation, either by asking you to send him your résumé and samples for his files, or by saying, frankly, that he really can't use you and meeting would be a waste of time for both of you. In either case, you thank him and send a follow-up letter.

However, if he does use freelancers at all, then he should be interested in knowing more about you. He may ask, "What sort of things have you done?" He wants to know what you've done professionally. At the moment, he doesn't care where you went to college or how many video and film courses you've taken. Almost everyone who calls him studied video or film somewhere. What jumps you out of that crowd is professional accomplishment.

Even if you have written four hundred published magazine articles and only one demonstration script, start with the script. That's where your prospect lives. Let him know you have written for video. Then bolster your credibility with your background as a journalist. If the demonstration script is all you've got, make the most of it. Tell him what the client's reaction was to the script or something about an interesting challenge in writing it. What you don't do is say, "I'm just starting out," or "This is the only script I've ever written," or "I don't have much of a background as a scriptwriter." You want to tell the prospect, "I've just written a script. I pleased the client. And I understand about writing in pictures."

By this time, he ought to want to see you. Make an appointment. If he's too busy to see you right now, make an appointment for when you ought to call back to set an appointment to meet.

What about your college courses? I don't know any real professionals who care much at all about where you went to college or what courses in video and film you've taken. Talking about your courses marks you as either (1) an inexperienced beginner who has just graduated and is trying to break into the field or (2) even worse, a person who hasn't racked up any professional credits since graduating. There will be time to talk about where you went to college and whom you studied with at the interview (if it seems relevant to bring it up).

Send a follow-up letter. Immediately after speaking with a prospect, send a follow-up letter. If you have a business card identifying you as a writer or scriptwriter, include it. The letter should be very brief, because its primary purpose is to have the prospect start a file on you, in which will be your name, address, and phone number. Its secondary purpose is to reinforce your phone conversation. If you have set an appointment for an interview, mention that you look forward to seeing the prospect at the stated time and place. If the prospect has asked you to call back next week or next month to set an interview, say that you look forward to speaking with him again at that time. And if the prospect has said there's no point to meeting, just say thanks for taking time to talk with me, and if your situation changes in the future I'll be glad to meet with you.

The Maytag Model of Marketing

Your situation in marketing yourself as a freelance scriptwriter is similar to that of the people of Maytag. They are selling a big ticket item that their customers buy only once every ten years or more. The thrust of their marketing is to have their prospects think *Maytag* at the moment they decide they need a major appliance. Maytag doesn't know when that moment will be. So they keep their name continually in front of their prospects.

That's what you have to do. Your phone calls will result in a list of prospects. Now you have to meet them and impress them that you can do the job when they need a script. And, like Andy Dintenfass, keep calling back.

Making the Rounds

You must know what you expect to get out of each appointment you have with a prospect. Don't, for example, expect an immediate assignment. A producer or creative director is not the same as a magazine editor to whom you can pitch an idea and get a go-ahead for an article. Your prospect's business is client driven. He won't have a job for you until some client has a job for him that needs a script.

In a first meeting you want to accomplish the following:

- Meet the person responsible for contracting for freelance scripts.
- Impress the prospect that you are seriously interested in scriptwriting on a freelance basis and that you know enough about video scriptwriting to do a good job.
- Get some idea of how frequently they use freelance writers.
- Get some idea of their need for an additional freelancer.
- Show the prospect your demonstration script.
- Get additional leads, if possible.

Why you need a meeting. People are reluctant to do business with someone they don't know. You want to become more than a name and a call-back phone number to your prospect. Your goal is to have the prospect think of you favorably both as a person and as an asset who can be called on when needed.

Qualify the prospect. An interview of this sort is a two-way street. You get to ask questions as well as answer them. You want to know how good this prospect is. You'll have gotten some idea from your phone call. Now you want to know if this prospect uses freelance writers frequently, occasionally, or rarely. And you want to know if the prospect has one or more freelancers they're happy with, or if there's a real need for a new person, such as you. Ask.

Show your samples. Get your demonstration script into the prospect's hands during the meeting. If you're lucky, the prospect will browse through it. This may be your best chance to have it read. Be prepared to answer questions about the script. If there are some things you're particularly proud of in it, point them out. Have a copy you can leave with the prospect. If you have a résumé which is relevant to your goal of freelance scriptwriting, offer a copy of that as well.

Try for additional leads. There may be other people within the prospect's organization who also hire freelancers. You can tactfully ask if the prospect is the only person who hires freelancers or if there is anyone else there whom you should meet. The prospect may also ask you what other companies you've talked with. There's no harm in volunteering one or two names—after which you can ask if the prospect can suggest anyone else. Understand that freelancers are important to most video production communities. Production companies have a vested interest in seeing that good freelancers have enough work that they will stay in business and be available when that production company needs them. If the production company had enough work of its own to support a freelancer, they would probably hire someone full time.

What if you're offered a full-time job? It happens. More than once, when I've been marketing myself as a freelancer, the prospect has asked if I would be interested in coming aboard full time. You should think about the possibility ahead of time, so you have an answer if the question comes up. Only you know if you would prefer to freelance or if you would rather be part of a team. Two points in favor of going on staff are (1) it's a way to gain a lot of experience and build up a good set of samples without having to wait for freelance jobs to come in, and (2) it's a way to meet others in the industry on a peer level.

Send a follow-up letter. After the interview, get off a timely letter to the prospect. Follow up on any suggestions or comments made during the meeting.

Call again. Call back in a few weeks. If you've done a script in the meantime, let the prospect know that. If you've followed up a lead the prospect gave you, thank him for it. If the prospect mentioned a project that might be coming in for which a freelancer would be needed, ask how that is developing. Keep the call short and friendly. You just want to make contact and keep your name in the prospect's mind.

Be Businesslike

This is for those of you who are new to selling yourself as a freelancer. Your prospect is in business and serves clients who are in business. Because you've called to sell your services, the prospect assumes you are in business also. Don't disappoint him.

Don't be late. Be a few minutes early for your appointment. Video production is a time-bound endeavor, and while promptness won't necessarily get you a job, arriving late will count against you. Bring along a book or magazine, or something to work on. While the prospect expects you to be on time, he or she will be late to the meeting about half the time, because of a call from a client, a shoot that's running long, or an emergency in the edit bay. It's the way the business works.

Dress for business. Your prospect may show up for the meeting in jeans and a T-shirt, but you shouldn't. Wear whatever is appropriate for city office workers in your area. Video production is not a three piece suit business, but it will be comforting to your prospect to know that if he or she takes you along to the client's office for a script conference, you'll know how to dress appropriately.

Show pristine samples. If you are presenting samples, deliver a correctly spelled, perfectly typed, sparkling clean manuscript. I present scripts in a report cover that costs about a dollar. It shows that I value my stuff and that I value the chance to show it to the prospect.

Don't expect a critique. The prospect is not running a school or a consulting service for would-be scriptwriters. Do not expect the prospect to critique your work beyond saying either, "I like it," or "No, it doesn't work for me." If you are showing your stuff to prospects but not getting a very positive response, you may want to think about taking a writing course or joining a writers' group, where you may get some helpful criticism.

A Client Story: Sample Specific

I got a call from the in-house producer for a department store chain. Their personnel department wanted to do an employee benefits video, so I included the script I did for Bank of Hawaii and the video which was produced from it. The producer and the communications director were quite happy with that and were pleased that it was so close to what they wanted. But they told me later that the manager within the company who had asked for the benefits video said, "Yes, but doesn't he have something specifically on 401-K benefits? That's what we're doing here."

A postscript to this: they had a budget cut and did the whole job in-house, including writing. But the producer liked my work so much that when he got an outside assignment for a high budget, two-minute commercial, he hired me to write it—at a very handsome fee.

Exercise: Start Your Demonstration Script

Get started on your demonstration script. Start making calls as outlined in this chapter until you find somebody willing to take a chance on you. Then follow up and do the best job you possibly can.

15 The Business of Scriptwriting

Drive thy business; let it not drive thee.

—Benjamin Franklin,
Poor Richard's Almanac

At last, the phone rings, and one of your prospects wants a script. Now what do you do? You know how to research and write it, but how do you cut the deal?

Setting the Price

Generally, the script for a commercial video is written for a fixed price. An offer of work will usually come with either a dollar sign or a question mark. That is, your client will either say, "I need a script for a ten minute video about XYZ, and I can pay a thousand dollars," or "How much would you charge to do a script about XYZ?" *Don't rush to answer.* You don't have enough information to give your client a price. Ask for details.

What's the Production Budget?

For years, *Writer's Market* has suggested that one way of pricing a script is to charge 10 percent of the gross production budget. If you know the budget, you have a ballpark figure for pricing the script. That doesn't mean that if the production budget is $5,000, you have to accept $500 and no more. If you can show that the job will take a week of your time, then you should receive a fee based on a week of work at your normal rate. Nor does it mean that if the budget is $100,000, you're going to get $10,000, although that certainly gives you the room to ask for a substantial fee.

What Needs to Be Done and How Long Will It Take?

I calculate the minimum fee I'm willing to accept by establishing the work that has to be done, estimating how long each task will take, and multiplying the total time by my normal hourly or daily rate. How much research has to be done? Whom do you need to talk with? Do you have to travel somewhere? How much paperwork must you slog through and organize? Is there existing footage you'll need to view and log? Each of these adds to the time you'll spend on the job—time you deserve to be paid for. Then, how long will it take you to organize the material and write a treatment? Remember to allow time for a treatment meeting and a rewrite. Finally, how long will it take to write the first draft script and the final revision? In the beginning, you'll probably underestimate the time it will actually take to do each job, but as you gain experience and keep good records of your time, you'll be able to estimate a project quite accurately.

In very rare instances, when neither you nor the client really knows how much time it's going to take to do the script, you may agree on a hourly fee, usually with a total dollar ceiling. That means you'll bill the client for the hours you spend, up to a total of X. For instance, if you bill your time at $40 an hour, you might set up the agreement to bill at $40 an hour up to a total of $1,600. That gives you forty hours in which to research, organize, and write the script. If you get the job done in thirty-five hours, you bill the client $1,400. If it actually takes forty-three hours, you'll probably bill the client $1,600. However, if you arrive at forty hours and have only completed the treatment, then you'll try to renegotiate. But spare your client unpleasant surprises. If you've spent thirty hours on research, let him know that, and tell him, "It's going to take most of the rest of the forty hours just to organize the material and write the treatment. Then I expect it will take another twelve to sixteen hours to write the script." In that way, you'll probably get the total bumped up above the $1,600 ceiling, although you may not get all the way to $2,240 (which would be forty hours plus another sixteen hours times your rate of $40 an hour). You may. Or you and your client may agree on $2,000 or $1,850.

Deadlines

Do you have a reasonable amount of time to research, organize, and write the treatment and script? Or is this one of those hurry-up deals, where your client needs an approved script to shoot on Monday, and today is Friday? There's nothing wrong with taking on an assignment with very tight deadlines if (1) you're sure you can complete the job acceptably in the time available, and (2) the fee you're being paid is commensurate with the long hours and pressure involved in doing such a script.

If there's not enough time to get the script written properly, *don't take the job*. Tell your client, "I'm sorry, the earliest I could deliver this script would be Wednesday morning." Remember this: if you accept the assignment and don't deliver on time, or deliver a poorly written script because you didn't have time to do a proper job of it, your client will consider it to be *your fault. You didn't deliver*.

If the money isn't adequate for the time and aggravation

involved, I recommend that *you don't take the job*. I made this mistake for years. Clients would come to me at the last minute and say, "I need this right away, but I only have this much money. Can you do it?" The fact is that I could. And I hate to say no to people. Until it dawned on me that I was teaching these clients that it was all right to treat me that way. A few days before I left on a business trip, I got a call from a client who wanted a sequel to a script I had written the year before. I told him I was getting ready to go out of town and said I could do a treatment before I left, but could I hold up on the script for two weeks until after I got back. He said, no, he'd need the whole job before I left. I decided that sleep was for wimps and said I guessed I could get it done. He offered me $2,000, which is what he would have paid if I'd done the job normally over a couple of weeks. But I was going to have to write the script, literally, overnight. I thought that was worth a premium for overtime and aggravation. I said "I can't do this job, that fast, for that amount. Make it $2,500." He did.

Be Clear about Who Does What

Suppose the script is going to involve archival photos of a historic event or site. Whose job is it to search for and find those? Can you write a description of the sort of photo needed into the script so that a production assistant can go to the archives and search for appropriate photos? Or as part of your script research are you expected to find the pictures that will be used? Beware of statements such as "We can get lots of pictures to go in this part." When you hear that, an alarm should go off and keep clanging away in the back of your mind until you've gotten a satisfactory answer to the question, Who will get the pictures?

Some clients have the idea that they only have to pay you for the time you spend actually writing—by which they mean typing. They simply never consider that the time you spend traveling, or talking to sources, or looking at existing footage, or even talking concept with the client is billable time. Sometimes you have to teach them. You may need to explain it, when you submit your estimate. "It's a day to travel to the laboratory and interview people there, a half day looking for photos in the state archives, twenty hours to log the existing footage," and so on.

Contracts

The only way to protect yourself when a project starts to go bad is to have a contract. And quite often a written agreement will keep things from going wrong, because it spells out each party's responsibility. I have a simple one page fill-in-the-blanks letter of agreement which I use with clients. I'm not going to reproduce it, because I'm not here to give legal advice. Have your attorney draw up a form for you.

These are the things my letter of agreement includes:

Who the Parties Are

It states that this is a letter of agreement between my company and the client's company, tells where we are located, and says that this letter confirms our earlier verbal agreement.

What the Project Is

This is the job that the client wants done, e.g., "CLIENT has asked WRITER to write the script for a ten minute sales video on the XYZ process using information and material to be supplied by CLIENT."

The Work Process

In the next section, I spell out the process envisioned in the agreement. This includes each general task with a deadline for its completion. For instance:

1. Research and interviews about the XYZ process and writing a first draft treatment outline for the script to be completed by (date).

2. Review of the first draft treatment by CLIENT to be completed by (date).

3. Writing the second draft treatment incorporating changes and revisions from CLIENT to be completed by (date).

4. Review of the second draft treatment by CLIENT to be completed by (date).

5. Writing the first draft script based on approved treatment to be completed by (date).

6. Review of the first draft script by CLIENT to be completed by (date).

7. Writing and delivery of final draft script incorporating changes and revision from CLIENT to be completed by (date).

This tells the client that we are going through all these stages in order to get the script written. It says that the client will have the opportunity to review and approve the work at each stage in the process. It not only puts a responsibility on the writer to deliver the manuscript on time but it puts a responsibility on the client to complete the review process expeditiously. And some of the dates will become progress payment milestones.

Payment

Next, the writer agrees to take on the project and the client agrees to pay the writer whatever the total amount is, plus normal expenses and applicable taxes. A schedule of progress payments is set up. I usually ask for one-third of the total upon signing the agreement, one-third on approval of the treatment, and one-third on delivery of the final draft script. The contract states that time is an important part of the agreement, and that if any progress payment is not made by the time it is due, all work stops immediately and all delivery dates are cancelled until renegotiated. It also states that normal expenses include travel and living expenses when away from home, that such travel will not be taken without prior approval from the client, and that expenses shall be paid within fifteen days of submission of an itemized expense account.

Rewriting

The process says that once the treatment is approved, then the script will be written to match the approved treatment. But there are clients who change their minds. And suddenly you find that they want you to throw out half the script, even though it was approved in the treatment, and put in something else. No problem. But it costs extra. This section of the agreement says that if substantial changes in the concept or content of the script are requested by the client after approval of the script treatment, client agrees to pay for these at my hourly rate.

Completion

Some clients can sit on the final approval, seemingly forever, while you wait for them to sign off so you can get paid. Because my final script is written from a first draft script which was reviewed by the client, and which itself was written from a treatment approved by the client, I really don't expect the client to need very much time to make sure I've included the revisions that were requested. Therefore, the agreement states that the script will be presumed to be accepted so many days after the date of its delivery unless the client has notified me in writing that it was not accepted, setting forth the reasons why it was not accepted. This is a way of saying to the client, If you're going to reject this after approving the treatment and reviewing the first draft, you'd better have a good reason, and you have to put it in writing so we can show it to a judge, if necessary.

The agreement also says that regardless of notification, the script will be presumed to be accepted if the client goes ahead and produces the video substantially in accordance with the script. In other words, the client can't reject the final draft script and refuse to make the final progress payment, because he doesn't like the wording of some of the narration, and then change the words himself and go ahead and produce the video. If the video that is made is essentially the video you described in your script, the client has accepted the script and owes you the final payment.

Ownership

In the next paragraph, I say that once all the payments have been made, ownership in the work passes from the writer to the client. This reminds the client that he doesn't own what he hasn't paid for, and it makes it clear who owns the final product.

Production Credits

Some commercial videos have no credits at all other than the name of the sponsoring company. Others list the names of the people who made the video. The letter of agreement should state that the credit "Written by (writer's name)" will appear in the titles of the production and on the packaging for the production wherever production credits for the producer, director, and/or production company appear, and in the same size and style of type. That says, if the producer, director, and production company aren't taking a credit, you'll waive yours.

But if they get listed, so do you—and in the same location in the video and on the package, and in the same type. That's fair.

Additional Conditions

If there are any special conditions attached to the project, they would be listed here. For example, if you need access to certain people or projects in order to do your research, and the client has said, "No problem, I can get that," you may want to note in this section that getting you access to these things is the client's responsibility, not yours. Then when the client later says, "Here's their phone number; call and make an appointment," you can point out that that is not the deal.

Notices and Arbitration

Notices under the agreement and changes and amendments to the agreement must be made in writing. And because I don't want to spend a long time hassling over disputes at the end of the project, and I don't want to bear the cost of going to court, I include a paragraph that says disputes which cannot be settled within thirty days shall be submitted for binding arbitration to the local office of the American Arbitration Association.

Signatures

Finally, both sides agree to be legally bound by the agreement, sign it, and date their signatures.

Accelerated Schedule

"Hey, that's fine," you say, "all those milestones and progress payments. But you just told us we might be asked to do the whole job over a weekend. What then?"

Okay, get a signed agreement and get as much money as you can before you start: 50 or 60 percent in advance, with the balance due on delivery of the script. That's all you can do. Again, I think that if the client is asking you to go out of your way for him, he should be willing to do a little extra for you—like cutting the company red tape to get you a check for the advance before you start.

Milestones

When you hit a milestone, such as approval of the treatment, get the client to sign off on it—in writing. Don't expect the client to pay you automatically. He'll wait until you bill him. So send an invoice. Right away.

But I Won't Be Your Lawyer

I've included details from my letter of agreement because over thirty years I've learned some of the things that can go wrong in the writer-client relationship. These can become a checklist for your attorney in drawing up an agreement for you to use. If you write your own, you're on your own.

Writing on Spec

At the very start of your career as a scriptwriter you not only may have to write one or two scripts on spec, you may want to. You may be very happy to have the learning experience of working with a professional producer and director and an established production company while you create your demonstration script. Once you have a body of work to show, there is no more reason for you to work on spec than for the director, the editor, or the members of the crew to do so. You're able to show what you can do, and you are entitled to be paid for your work.

You'll Be Asked

The world is full of people with enough gall to be divided into three parts. Some of them will find out that you write scripts, and they will call you and ask you to write a script now, for the hope of payment later. They will try to make it sound as if you will have a vastly enriching learning experience if you "become a part of the team" (for no pay). They will say that they need to get this video completed to satisfy their boss, and unfortunately they don't have any money to pay for it, but their next project, already in the planning stages, has a terrific budget, and you'll be their writer. The last time I did one of these—for the P.R. director of a hospital—the freebie won an award, the P.R. guy was offered a better job in another town, and the big budget video was subsequently written and produced by an ad agency that was tight with his replacement. I got nothing.

They will tell you that they are developing a program for nationwide cable television, and, although they can't pay you now, when the project sells, we'll all be rich. They will say the same thing about creating a video for retail sale. They will send you a Request for Proposal, asking you to bid on writing the script for a proposed video. Part of your proposal, of course, is your creative concept for the script. While it may not look like it, this, too, is working on spec. You're coming up with the concept for a video with no guarantee of payment. I went through this exercise twice with an architectural firm in my city, and each time (surprise!) they eventually decided to do the job in house—incorporating my ideas and those of whomever else they had solicited. Neat way to get creative work for nothing.

When I Will and When I Won't

When I get calls about working on spec, I tell the caller no, I have books and scripts of my own to write on spec, and I no longer invest my time in some other guy's fantasy.

Co-venture a proposal. However, I will work on spec from time to time with a trusted producer or production company to develop a proposal for a bid. I'll do this when the potential income from the job justifies the investment. I consider this marketing, just the same as if I spent that time writing letters and making phone calls to sell my services. Even if we don't get the job we're bidding on—and it's always a crapshoot—I usually make out in other ways. That producer will call me for the next paid job he has. And if he doesn't, he'll never get another spec proposal out of me.

Retail video. And I'll jump at the chance to write a video for retail sale for a percentage. This is not exactly writing on spec, but it is doing the work in the hope that the video will sell. More on this in the next chapter.

A Client Story: When Free Wasn't Enough

This client, call him "Gus Greedy," saw the potential in cable television and developed several grandiose plans to cash in on it. He and his partners, of course, had no money, so they looked to the state or to private investors to give them twenty million dollars. Or at least a couple of million. Or a few hundred thousand. The plan Gus had come up with was just plausible enough that I got involved. I thought there was an outside chance that he might actually pull it off. So I rewrote his business plan and did treatments for a couple of cable shows in return for a small percentage in the company. As far as I was concerned, it was like betting a long shot. It didn't cost much to play, and if it came in I'd make some serious bucks.

Then Gus came up with an idea for a televised series from Hawaii. He told me he had had another writer working on it, but she was gone and he didn't have any of the stuff she'd written. He did have a "treatment" he'd done. When he faxed that to me, it turned out to be a list of characters with two or three lines of description about them. Things were slow, and I thought he might have a winner, so I agreed to whip this into a six to ten page outline with which he could go look for development money. I liked the basic idea enough that I even took a couple of characters and a concept out of notes I had done for a novel and threw those into the outline.

He loved it. He assured me that when the project was funded, I would be head writer. I said I'd like to have an agreement. He waffled on that. I said, If I don't have an agreement, I'll have to take back everything I wrote, and you'll have to start over again. He said put it in writing and fax it over. I did. In the agreement I asked that I be paid for the work I had done to date at not less than Writers Guild of America minimums, to be negotiated with my agent. And I asked to reserve the novel rights to any story ideas I came up with, so that even if the series was never produced, I'd be able to take the ideas, and the writing which I was doing for nothing, and turn them into a novel—if I wanted to.

And that's where we hit the wall. He was so convinced that this would be hugely successful that he didn't want to give me the novel rights. His producer's mind saw these as a profit center. He could hire any hack writer to do a novelization from the script and make a lot of money from the paperback sale. My final fax reminded him that he could not sell what he had not paid for and that I was withdrawing myself and all my contributions from his project. It hasn't gone anywhere since. Maybe it never would have gotten off the ground. All I know is that if Gus hadn't been so greedy, he could have continued to have a damn good writer working on his project for nothing.

Maybe I won this one.

Exercise: Make a Pricing Checklist

Develop a checklist to help you set a price for writing a video script. List all the tasks that have to be done with space to estimate the time for each task. Make a list of questions about the job to ask the client. Then do a dry run. Get someone to role-play the client and propose a project. Based on what they tell you, come up with a price for the script.

16 Writing Retail Videos

> Have your credit card ready or send twenty-nine ninety-five plus four fifty for postage and handling to . . .
>
> —CABLE TV COMMERCIAL FOR A RETAIL VIDEO

Several years ago I wrote the script for a half-hour video about a helicopter tour of the island of Kauai, on spec, for a percentage. Had I billed for my time, I would have been paid about $3,000 for the treatment and script. Instead, I make fifty cents on every videocassette sold. Over the years, that's added up to considerably more than the flat fee. And it's still going on. Every three months, I get a royalty statement.

Retail Videos

Retail videos are another growing market for commercial scriptwriters. The most common kinds of retail videos are entertainment, sports, instructional, travel, and self-improvement. But the field is growing so fast that almost any concept that can be handled visually and has a potential market is a possibility. I've written videos on Hawaii's volcanoes, Sea Life Park, hula, a preventive maintenance guide for new home buyers, how to play better golf, and the Honolulu Marathon.

Entertainment Videos

This is a growing field. It can include any kind of performance from comedy to music to dance. It also includes any kind of video you watch just for the fun of it. This would include some travel videos showing places you probably will never go but enjoy seeing. Adventure videos about skydiving or jumping off a bridge with a bungee cord attached to your ankle fit in this category, also.

Sports Videos

Sports videos are a special category of entertainment videos. These can include season highlights for a team or league, unique events such as a marathon or a fishing tournament, and any video that focuses on enjoyment of a sport. I wrote and directed several shows for a series called *Fairways of Hawaii,* which showed a celebrity and a golf pro playing some of Hawaii's beautiful resort courses.

Instructional Videos

I also wrote and directed a series of golf tips called *Play Better Golf with Rip Collins,* which aired originally as five minute television drop-ins, which were re-edited into a retail video. Cooking videos are very popular, as are home improvement programs telling how to do various plumbing, carpentry, and electrical jobs around the house. And the home computer and specialized software market has created a market for computer videos. In short, if pictures will help you understand how to do it, it can become an instructional video.

Travel Videos

Videos about Hawaii have become a mini-industry for producers in the islands. At one time I counted more than seventy-five Hawaii videos for sale. Travel videos may offer travelers a preview of a place they'd like to visit. They may show exotic locations that most people will never get to. And they can be video memory books, giving tourists a visual reminder of their trip as well as something to show the folks back home.

Self-Improvement Videos

The big hits in the area of self-improvement are exercise and aerobics videos. Initially done by aerobics instructors, they've been taken over by attractive female stars such as Jane Fonda, Victoria Principal, and Cher. But there's also a Disney exercise video for kids, and Angela Lansbury has one for the maturely active. Others include the use of self-hypnosis to get rid of bad habits and meditation to lower stress. But almost anything that comes under the heading of self-improvement from assertiveness training to zodiac sign analysis could become a video.

Writing a Retail Video

The writing process is exactly the same as that for any other commercial video: research, plan, organize, and write. The difference is that instead of having to satisfy a commercial client, your job is to make the program enjoyable to an audience. Keep it visual, keep it moving, and don't talk it to death.

I've included the complete treatment for a retail video, *The Hawaiian Volcanoes, A Force for Creation*, in Appendix 3 and the script written from the treatment in Appendix 4.

Collaborating with a Producer

A producer may hire you to write the script for a retail video for a flat fee. Or you may be asked to write it on spec for *points*. Points are a percentage of income. One point represents one percent. You may be offered a percentage of the profits, which is not necessarily a good deal, or a percentage of the gross, which is much better.

Bad points and good ones. The reason a percentage of profits is not a good deal is that the producer will charge off all his costs including overhead, and all his sales and distribution costs, such as advertising, dubbing copies, and so on before there is any profit to share. In other words, he gets back everything he invested in the project before you get anything. A percentage of the gross will be smaller, but you start getting paid with the first sale.

Marketing decisions. To decide whether you want to participate on points is really a marketing decision. In your opinion, is the video something people will want to buy? If so, how many? The potential market needs to be in the thousands. How will the video get to the potential buyers? Will it be sold in stores or advertised at mail order? What will the video sell for? If it's going at retail, your producer will have to wholesale it at about 50 percent of the retail price. Your percentage will then be based on the wholesale price. If it is sold through mail order, the producer receives the full price but has advertising and fulfillment costs which may be deducted.

If the numbers aren't there, you may want to hold out for a flat fee for the script. Or you may be willing to take a chance and write the script in your spare time.

Do it for your demo script. Obviously, writing the script for a retail video on spec is one way to get your demonstration script written. And a retail video should make a nice-looking start for your sample reel.

A Client Story: The Wannabe Scriptwriter

This client was a friend who put together a limited partnership to produce a retail video about one of the major tourist attractions on the island of Oahu. He had always wanted to write a script, and since he was the producer, he assigned the task to himself. Although he had a background as a working journalist and print writer, he had very limited experience with video and film. As a hedge, he asked me to be his script consultant. I agreed.

And then both the director and I waited for something in writing—while months passed. I offered to write the script for him for points, just to get it done, but he wanted to do it himself. Finally I received a document that was half treatment, half script. It wasn't that it was terrible; it was just amateurish. There were some good individual scenes. But overall it suffered from wandering structure and lacked focus, a point of view, and a sense of internal cohesiveness.

Instead of just pointing all this out, I took it upon myself to rip his work apart and reorganize it into a new treatment as an example for him to work from. He read it and had the good sense to recognize the big difference between wanting to be a scriptwriter and being one. The would-be scriptwriter inside him may have been disappointed. But the marketing man in his head knew he wanted a good product to sell and hired me to turn my treatment into a finished script.

Exercise: Conduct Retail Video Market Research

Visit bookstores and other retail outlets in your area that offer retail videos for sale. Make a survey of what is being offered. Talk with the store manager or video buyer about what sells and what doesn't.

Make a list of five topics for potential retail videos that you could write.

17 Producers and Directors Talk about Scriptwriters

The job of the producer . . . is to get the film made.

—Syd Field, *Selling a Screenplay: The Screenwriter's Guide to Hollywood*

Up to this point we've talked about how you, as a video scriptwriter, will deal with clients and production companies. But I thought it would be instructive for you to learn what producers and directors have to say about scriptwriters. So I talked with producers and directors in eleven cities across the country about their dealings with freelance scriptwriters.

These are people who have the day-to-day responsibility to see that their clients' videos are researched, written, produced, and delivered to the satisfaction of the clients—on time and within budget. It is not surprising, therefore, that they view scriptwriters primarily as a necessary part of their business operation. They want you to help them serve their clients so their production companies can make money and stay in business. As a result, they talked about trust and being on time for meetings and presenting yourself well rather than imaginativeness, about client service rather than inspiration, about professionalism rather than creativity. On the other hand, if a scriptwriter was willing to take care of business, they were quite willing to give him or her a great deal of latitude. In most cases, the producer or director would help set the general direction for the video and then leave the writer alone to deal with the client and come up with a completed script.

Where Do They Find Scriptwriters?

They don't advertise for scriptwriters. They find them almost completely through networking and referral and by writers marketing themselves with creativity and persistence. "The people I've used the most in the past are those I've found myself or through other directors," said Bill McCarthy, a video producer in White Bear Lake, Minnesota, serving the Twin Cities area. "One of the writers I've used is a former competitor. When he left behind the world of producing and directing and started sending me mailing pieces as a scriptwriter, I paid attention."

Most of these video professionals get a lot of calls and see a lot of résumés from would-be scriptwriters. Ron Kemp, director of broadcast services for North Carolina State University, felt he was in a buyer's market. "There are a lot of writers within thirty to forty minutes of here," he said. But, while there are many people calling themselves scriptwriters, "there's always room for talent," said Tony Bond, president of Take One, Inc., in Las Vegas. As a result, all of the professionals I talked with said they were willing to look at new writers. "If they call me cold and sound like they have their head on straight," Kemp said, "I'll ask them to send a résumé and a sample of their work, so I can sort out the flakes."

It's a two-stage process: first, make a good impression on the phone or in your contact letter and, second, send a good sample which shows you actually know how to write a script. How important is the demonstration script? "I don't see how you would hire somebody unless you had an example of their work," said Verle Peterson, president of Envision Communications, Inc., in Omaha.

What Producers Look For

Without exception, the first thing they look for in a script is the writer's ability to visualize the scene. "I used to get a lot of print writers with real good narrative and no sense of the visual," McCarthy said. "I look for a strong visual sense, not an audio brochure."

They look for a properly formatted script, to show that you know what you are doing, but not for a lot of video or film talk, blocking, and camera directions. What they want in a script is the ability to organize ideas and communicate clearly and simply. "Give me clarity, not a mixed message," said Phil Schulman of Phil Schulman Productions in Philadelphia. "Keep a very singular focus so that everything you're bringing to it is clear."

They also want to know about you—not just what you've written, but what you do when you're not writing, what you're interested in. "I once hired a writer because he mentioned he was into water sports—fishing, waterskiing, and boating," said Alan Foral, general manager of CMC Video, near Milwaukee. "I needed a script for a boat company about a boat for waterskiing."

And they want to know how you'll do in providing client service. How accessible are you? Will you be available for meetings with the client? Do you have good people skills to work with the client? "My clients are less than wonderful in communicating what they want the piece to accomplish or communicate," said Jacqueline Albarella, president of Avid Productions in Buffalo. "Sometimes clients do not have a clear vision of what they want. You have to talk to the client and listen carefully. In many cases you have to take the client and lead them by the hand through a discovery process to find out what they want to accomplish and who the final audience is."

Hints for Scriptwriters

Again, the number one response is to be visual. "Just concentrate on the verbs," said Chuck Neff of Neff Productions in St. Louis. "Don't get too complex. Keep it simple and let the pictures work. We'll often go twenty seconds or more with no narration to let the pictures breathe."

"Get a look at what the producer likes by asking for a copy of a script he considers to be a good one," suggested Bill McCarthy.

Tim Bradley, president of Tim Bradley Productions in Honolulu, suggested that as a beginning scriptwriter you should not be afraid to imitate good work that you've seen. "There's a lot to learn. If you want to be rich, hang out with rich people, not poor people. If you want to be good, study with a master, and if you can't do that, study the master's work. Ask yourself why you like it from a writing standpoint. What's in there that you can emulate? Don't be afraid to try it, especially in the beginning. You may be following the style and structure of something you like, but if you are any good, what you write will still be yours."

"Just write as much as you can," Albarella offered. "Get hooked up with a local cable access channel to keep writing. If you spend your time working at something that is not writing, you get out of the habit. If you're not used to working against those deadlines, you'll panic when a job comes along."

Pet Peeves of Producers and Directors

The number one pet peeve is having to work with a writer who does not understand video and film. "I sometimes have to work with a scriptwriter the client has hired because he loves his work in print," Bond said. "The writer doesn't understand video and produces a script that is totally inappropriate."

Missing deadlines and being late to meetings come next. And

producers and directors working on commercial videos for clients absolutely don't want to deal with the writer's ego. When they ask for rewrites, they want rewrites, not an argument. "Writers can get too attached to their own words," Bradley said. "I just went through this with an ad agency where the writer was one of the owners of the agency, and he was far too attached to what he had written."

Another peeve is the writer who goes off in a new direction, after he and the producer have already agreed on the thrust of the script. "He says, 'I came up with this, what do you think?' " Schulman said. "I say, 'That's nice, but what about this other that we agreed on?' If the writer did both, that's great. Or if the writer calls and says, 'I have this idea,' we can discuss it."

Then there's the question of loyalty. "Producers want a writer who won't take their client away," said Jim Dotson of Take One Productions, New Orleans. "We build business based on the loyalty factor."

And to this list I'll add my own pet peeve, which is people who call themselves writers who do not understand how their language works. Grammar, diction, and the connotation and denotation of words are the technical tools a writer works with. If you haven't mastered them, you're like a carpenter trying to build a house with lumber and nails, but no tool kit.

A Client Story: Don't Let This Be You

Up to now, I've told you client stories from the point of view of the scriptwriter. This is a story Alan Foral of CMC Video told me about a freelance writer he hired.

His production company had gotten the chance to do a video for a new client. This was important, not only for the job at hand, but because this client commissioned a lot of video projects. The client had been using another production company and another writer. If CMC did a good job on this project, it had the potential to develop into a lot of business. To ensure success, they had hired a writer who was considered to be very knowledgeable about automation and computer controls, which was the subject of the video. Unfortunately, things started to go bad right from the start.

"First, we had a scheduling problem," Foral said. "The writer wasn't available when the client meeting was scheduled and we had to reschedule. The client needed a seven to ten minute video. Somehow the writer didn't hear that. The client wanted to spend fifteen to twenty thousand dollars. The writer didn't hear that either. Probably because in the meeting the writer would interrupt the client and correct him on technical points. Needless to say, when we left the first meeting, the client wasn't feeling very warm and comfy about us.

"Then the writer delivered the first draft. We ran it through our budget process and came out with a thirty-two thousand dollar budget. The script ran thirty-seven minutes long and went into details the client didn't want to deal with. The ultimate goal of the video—a flashy marketing piece—was completely missing. It looked like a documentary from a university.

"Our next meeting with the client was very short. The client said, 'You guys don't know what you're doing. You didn't listen to me.' Then he threw the script down on the desk and walked out. And that was the end of the project."

Exercise: Step into the Producer's Shoes

Based on what you've learned about producers and directors in this chapter, take a look at yourself through the eyes of a producer-director at a production company. What are your strengths? What do you have to offer? What specialties and interests can you bring to an interview? Do you have sample materials? How will they look to a working professional? Is there anything you should do to make them better? What are your weak points? What do you need to do to fix them?

Do it.

Appendix 1

Scriptwriting with a Computer

Scriptwriting is easiest when you work with a computer and a word processing program. As you've seen, scripts require lots of tricky formatting, which has traditionally been a royal pain on a typewriter but is just a matter of a couple of keystrokes on a computer. And scripts routinely go through several revisions. Working on a computer you simply make the changes that are needed, hit a couple of keys, and the computer prints out the new draft while you go have coffee. Plus, all the prior drafts can be saved in the computer's memory and printed out at any time if you need them again.

With today's powerful, small laptop and notebook computers, you can carry your computer and the whole project around in your attaché case. Take it in the field for interviews or to your client's office to do revisions on the spot. And with a modem, you can send and receive changes and drafts from your computer to your client's computer electronically, over the phone lines.

Chances are, if you are a writer today, you're already working with a personal computer, either an IBM type or a Macintosh. In which case you know your equipment. If you're new to computers, they may seem mysterious, but they really aren't. I'm not going to pose as a computer expert or try to tell you everything you need to know to get started using a computer. There are already plenty of books on that subject. I just want to point out that if you aren't using a computer for scriptwriting—indeed for all your writing—you're making things hard for yourself. You can write poetry or a novel with a quill pen or a charcoal stick if that's what works for you. But if you are going to write scripts for clients, you'll be using a computer within the next couple of years, or you'll be out of business as a freelance writer.

The Hardware You Need

The basic needs are a central processing unit, or CPU; a monitor—either color or monochrome; a keyboard; and a printer. Laptop computers incorporate all these features, except the printer, in a package that will fit in an attaché case. Your printer should be able to produce letter quality or "near letter quality" typing.

Size, Speed, and Memory

Since the early 1980s, personal computers have added memory storage and become faster and smaller. The only practical limitation is that the screen must not be too small to read and the keyboard needs to fit your hands. I like a small battery-powered laptop (that also can run continuously on alternating current) that can be carried with me wherever I choose to work. It should have a minimum 20 megabyte hard disk drive, more if it is your only computer. If it is an IBM type, it should have at least the speed of an 80286 chip and preferably an 80386 chip. Laptops tend to come with one or two megabytes of random access memory. If you want to do things with graphics you'll need more. It is nice if it has a graphics capability and a modem. If it is one of the new Macintosh notebook laptops (other than the most basic PowerBook 100) it will come with speed, power, memory, and graphics.

Processing speed is not critical when you're writing. Virtually any computer can keep up with your typing speed. Power is important when you want to do things to the text you've written, such as run it through a spelling checker to look for typos and misspelled words. Then the more power your computer has, the faster that goes.

My recommendation is to buy all the power and all the memory you can afford. The reason is that software designers keep coming up with good ideas that require faster processing and ever larger memory capacity.

Low Budget Computing

While the ideal may be to get a fast 80386 laptop or Macintosh PowerBook, it's not essential. You don't have to buy a BMW or Jaguar for basic transportation. And to get started in word processing, all you need is a basic computer. The old IBM PC/XT with a monochrome monitor and a minimum 20 megabyte hard disk drive is adequate. I have one, and I still use it. It's a little slow, but it gets the job done. You should be able to buy one of these, secondhand, for almost nothing. The reason is that there's no resale market. Most people want the newer and faster models. And now, as more people want the new, powerful laptops, the price on new, powerful desktops is dropping. Shop around.

Word Processing Software

You also need some word processing software. This is the program which tells your computer to act like a typewriter with a memory. To do scripts, you need a word processing program that is WYSIWYG—pronounced "Whiz-ee-wig"—which stands for "What You See Is What You Get." Most major word processors are WYSIWYG, but there may be some low-priced programs around that aren't. What it means is that on the screen you see what you've typed exactly as it will print out. So if you are working in left and right columns, you will see left and right columns on the screen. If you've underlined or italicized, or boldfaced a word, it will appear that way on the screen.

Microsoft Word and WordPerfect

When I got my first computer, in 1984, I tried several word processing programs before settling on Microsoft Word, and I've been using Word ever since. Word is one of the two best selling word processors. The other is WordPerfect. Either will do fine. Both are WYSIWYG. Both let you handle script formatting with a couple of keystrokes. Both offer spelling checkers. Both run on IBM-type and Macintosh computers. And both work with a variety of other programs designed specifically for scriptwriting.

Spell Checker

Both Word and WordPerfect contain their own spelling checkers with a large basic dictionary to which you can add other words and names. I use the spelling checker constantly because, although I'm an A+ speller, I'm a C− typist. The spelling checker runs through the manuscript and stops at any word it doesn't have in its memory. So if I'm trying to type *form* but actually type *forn*, it will stop at *forn* and report, "WORD NOT FOUND." Unfortunately, if I scramble the inside letters so that I type *from* instead of *form*, the spelling checker will recognize *from* as a legitimate word and won't question it, even though it's wrong in context. So until we get really good context editors, you still have to proofread the final copy.

Grammatik 5

I also have a program called Grammatik 5, which will run through the text much as the spelling checker does and compare usage with a set of grammar rules in its memory. Most such programs—and there are several—are primarily diction checkers rather than grammar checkers. They have a list of words that are consistently misused, and they flag those whenever they appear, to ask if you've used them appropriately. They'll catch some punctuation errors and actually will question some grammatical usage. They also ask a lot of dumb questions, because the rules aren't tight enough, or because there isn't enough memory to write in all the subset rules necessary to do a real job of grammar editing. With each version, however, Grammatik gets a little closer to actual grammar checking. It's a valuable utility if only because it walks me through the manuscript, asking questions about usage as we go.

Norton Utilities

On the hard disk of my IBM computer, I keep the latest version of a set of programs called the Norton Utilities. These do a lot of nifty stuff, ranging from starting and stopping a timer to keep track of the time I work on a client's script to making it possible to retrieve a computer file that has been erased in error. Definitely worth the investment.

Déjà View

Déjà View is another program I keep on my hard disk and start up when I start the computer. Every five minutes or five hundred keystrokes, it saves to a file on my hard disk an exact image of everything in random access memory. Random access memory (RAM) lives only as long as there is power to the computer. If there is a power outage everything in RAM is lost. Or if something goes wrong in the program you're running, the program locks up, and you have to reboot (restart) the computer to unlock it, everything in RAM is lost. With Déjà View in operation, when that happens you can recreate what was in RAM at the time of the last save. At most you only lose a few minutes of work.

Microsoft Word, WordPerfect, Grammatik 5, the Norton Utilities, and Déjà View should be available through most computer stores and mail order houses.

Script Formatting Programs

There are a number of programs which work by themselves or with a word processor to format a script. I have only used one of these programs for any length of time, although I have played with a couple of the others. I include them here for your information. My experience is that for most scriptwriting, a powerful word processor such as Microsoft Word or WordPerfect is all you need. However, these scriptwriting programs offer some advantages in terms of formatting. Occasionally a client may require that you use one of them.

The programs listed here are not the only ones available, and more will almost certainly have been released by the time this book is published, but these will give you an idea of what's out there.

Scriptor

Scriptor provides a screenplay formatting system which works with several word processors including Microsoft Word. You type the script in your word processor according to a standard format. When you are done, you can run the script through Scriptor and come out with the scenes and pages numbered, and scenes broken automatically and properly at the bottom of the page. Scriptor also lets you indicate changes as they are made.

Scriptor is available from:

Screenplay Systems
150 East Olive Avenue, #203
Burbank, CA 91502
(818) 843-6557
Fax (818) 843-8364

ShowScape

ShowScape provides a left and right side format which can include a clip art or scanned art storyboard that can be printed on Lake Compuframes storyboard forms. ShowScape rides on the back of WordPerfect version 5.0 or greater for DOS or version 2.0 or greater for the Macintosh. One of the advantages of ShowScape is that it can provide individualized notes on each scene for up to ten different members of the crew. These could be notes for the director, for each of three or four camera operators, for the floor manager, for the videotape operator, and so on.

ShowScape comes from:

Lake Compuframes, Inc.
P.O. Box 890
Briarcliff, NY 10510-0314
(914) 941-1998
Fax (914) 941-2043

SuperScript

SuperScript works with WordPerfect to create a classic screenplay format or the slightly different television sitcom format. Using two or three keystrokes it will format each line appropriately, including capitalizing the setting line and the character name before dialogue. It will break pages appropriately and put in CONTINUEDS and MORES at the bottom of the page when needed. This is a slow program on a basic PC. It will run much better on a 286 DOS machine or on a Mac.

SuperScript is released by:

Inherit the Earth Technologies
1800 South Robertson Blvd., Suite 326
Los Angeles, CA 90035
(310) 559-3814

Script Master

Script Master provides a multicolumn, side-by-side format of up to four columns, with provision to add explanatory notes to the script. It will let you save the audio column as a separate narration script. It includes a spell checker and will generate a scene breakdown including a list of characters with speaking parts in the scene.

Movie Master

Movie Master is a screenplay word processor which produces the classic screenplay format as well as the slightly different television format. It breaks pages appropriately and generates scene breakdowns including the length of the scene and a list of characters with speaking parts in the scene. Movie Master has an optional spelling checker.

Script Master and Movie Master are available from:

Comprehensive Video Supply Corporation
148 Veterans Drive
Northvale, NJ 07647
(800) 526-0242, (201) 767-7990

It's Your Choice

There may well be a variety of other script formatting programs available. I worked with Scriptor for a couple of years until I decided I could get everything that I needed for video scriptwriting from Microsoft Word. Which word processor you use and whether you use a script formatting program depend on what you feel comfortable with.

Take a Test Drive

Give any word processor a good test at real work before you invest several hundred dollars in it. When I bought my first system, I ordered a word processor that I was assured was a big hit in offices all across the country. It may well have been. But it was a system designed for typists in offices, not for writers doing creative work. It simply did not have the flexibility necessary to the creative process. Working with it was incredibly frustrating, and I finally took it back to the computer store and asked for an exchange. Fortunately, I was able to get one.

Pick the System Your Clients Use

If all your clients are using Macintosh computers, then that's probably what you ought to use. However, if you already own an IBM, there are some conversion utilities you can get that will let you transfer IBM files to a Mac, and vice versa. And every year the two systems get closer together.

If most of your clients are using a specific word processor, then you may want to select that for your use. But, again, there are conversion programs which will let you convert a manuscript done in Microsoft Word to WordPerfect—or whatever. So you actually can pick the system you like best and still deliver the script on a disk formatted for the system your client prefers.

Remember the Learning Curve

If you are new to computers and word processing, realize that it can take two or three months to make the transition from the typewriter to the word processor. You're learning a whole new technology, and you won't be able to use it well until you've made it your own. A good way to start is with a course on the equipment and word processing software you will be using. These are offered by many computer stores and by community colleges and adult education programs.

Appendix 2

Excerpts from the Original Treatment for a Video for the State Department of Transportation and from the Resulting Script

The Treatment

A. CONTENT

1. The video opens with cars traveling through the construction area during construction time. We see barricades, large equipment, cones, signage, etc.

    a) NARRATOR:

    (1) Says that construction has been going on for some time. The Department of Transportation and the contractor have gained experience with the construction project. And motorists and residents have come to expect the construction activity. It's a good time for an update on what is going on and why.

The Script Which Resulted

1 THE VIDEO OPENS WITH CARS TRAVELING THROUGH THE CONSTRUCTION AREA DURING CONSTRUCTION TIME.

We see barricades, large equipment, cones, signage, etc.

NARRATOR
Construction to widen
Kalanianaole Highway has
been going on for some time.
By now, the Department of
Transportation and the
contractor have gained
experience with the project.
And motorists and
residents—well, if you
haven't gotten used to the
construction activity, you at
least have come to expect it.
So this is a good time for an
update on what is going on
and why.

2. Title: "KALANIANAOLE HIGHWAY CONSTRUCTION PROGRESS REPORT—PHASE I"

3. Introduce Edward Y. Hirata, Director, Department of Transportation. If possible, we might see him in two or three shots inspecting the construction site, while we hear his voice, then see him on camera as he continues speaking.

   a) MR. HIRATA:

      (1) Talks briefly about the phase one construction, stressing the benefits.

2 TITLE: KALANIANAOLE HIGHWAY CONSTRUCTION PROGRESS REPORT —PHASE I

MUSIC
Theme in

3 INTRODUCE EDWARD Y. HIRATA, DIRECTOR, DEPARTMENT OF TRANSPORTATION.

If possible, we might see him in two or three shots inspecting the construction site, while we hear his voice, then see him on camera as he continues speaking.

MR. HIRATA
We know that the construction project causes inconvenience for you. And we're trying to do everything we can to minimize problems.

Show samples of public information materials.

MR. HIRATA
(voice-over)
We've established a hot line you can call for information or to report problems. We've put Capt. Irwin in the air to report traffic conditions on ______ radio stations. We have radio public service announcements telling you about lane closures and times to try to avoid being on the highway. We're trying to keep you informed through our newsletter and ads in the paper and on TV.

Mr. Hirata on Camera

MR. HIRATA
And we've met with community groups and neighborhood boards for two way communication about the

4. Show drawings or actual finished sections if available to see the improvements.

    a) MR. HIRATA:

        (1) Talks about these improvements—new sidewalks, bike lanes, a new median strip and a safer road wide enough to accommodate East Oahu traffic. He says that it takes a lot of work and some inconvenience to accomplish this. This video will show you how the job is being accomplished.

5. Map shows the highway in Phase I broken into two sections: Wailupe Circle to West Hind Drive and West Hind Drive to East Halemaumau Street.

    a) NARRATOR:

        (1) Says this shows construction Phase I, which has two distinct sections.

project. Incidentally, we've incorporated many of your suggestions into our plans. For instance, we designed the bike lanes to accommodate suggestions from the Hawaii Bicycling League. And in the ______ area, we took out a planned pedestrian overpass and put in cross-walks, instead, after hearing from the community that that's what they wanted.

4 SHOW DRAWINGS OF COMPLETED CONSTRUCTION OR ACTUAL FINISHED SECTIONS IF AVAILABLE TO SEE THE IMPROVEMENTS.

MR. HIRATA

(voice-over)

And this is what we'll have when the work is done—new sidewalks, new, wider bike lanes, a new median strip and a much safer road that is wide enough to accommodate East Oahu traffic. It's taking a lot of work and some inconvenience to accomplish these.

This video will show you how the job is being accomplished.

5 MAP SHOWS THE HIGHWAY IN PHASE I.

Broken into two sections: Wailupe Circle to West Hind Drive and West Hind Drive to East Halemaumau Street.

NARRATOR

This shows construction Phase I, which has two distinct sections—from Wailupe Circle to West Hind Drive and from West Hind Drive to East Halemaumau Street.

6. Highway in front of Aina Haina shopping center.

   a) NARRATOR:

      (1) Says that in the first section the highway is already six lanes wide, so why is construction needed? Explains about adding new drainage system, concrete bike lanes, sidewalks and a redesigned median.

7. Construction activity on the shoulders with at least one outside lane closed. We see good working shots of culvert excavation, huge culverts being set in place, workmen close to traffic, protected only by the concrete barricades.

   a) NARRATOR:

      (1) In order to do this and to have room for construction equipment and to provide safety for the crews, one or more outside lanes must be closed.

6 HIGHWAY IN FRONT OF AINA HAINA SHOPPING CENTER.

NARRATOR
In the first section—from Wailupe Circle to West Hind Drive—the highway is already six lanes wide, so some people may ask why construction is needed here.

Rendering or video of completed section

NARRATOR
Because there is much more to the project than just widening the highway. We're putting in sidewalks, concrete bike lanes, and a redesigned median strip. At the same time adding a new drainage system and putting all the utilities underground.

7 CONSTRUCTION ACTIVITY ON THE SHOULDERS

At least one outside lane closed. We see good working shots of culvert excavation, huge culverts being set in place, workmen close to traffic, protected only by the concrete barricades.

NARRATOR
In order to do this and to have room for construction equipment and to provide safety for the crews, one or more outside lanes must be closed.

8. Shot of finished section, showing a storm drain, the bike lane, and sidewalk.

   a) NARRATOR:

      (1) This is the result. Work on this section of Phase I is scheduled for completion in December of 1991. The highway will be resurfaced with lane stripes for its final configuration.

9. Heavy equipment working in the second section—West Hind Drive to East Halemaumau Street.

   a) NARRATOR:

      (1) Says that much more extensive work is taking place in the second section between West Hind Drive and East Halemaumau Street, where the roadway is actually being widened from four lanes to six with a median barrier separating inbound and outbound traffic.

10. Map of section two (as seen in Newsletter) showing where the lanes are widened makai and mauka of the highway.

    a) NARRATOR:

       (1) Says that construction in this section will add to the highway on the makai side between East Hind Drive and Hawaii Loa Street and on the mauka side from Hawaii Loa Street to East Halemaumau Street.

8 SHOT OF FINISHED SECTION

Showing a storm drain, the bike lane, and sidewalk.

NARRATOR
This is the result. Work on this section—between Wailupe Circle and West Hind Drive—is scheduled for completion in ______.

9 SECOND SECTION—WEST HIND DRIVE TO EAST HALEMAUMAU STREET.

Heavy equipment working.

NARRATOR
Much more extensive work is taking place in the second section between West Hind Drive and East Halemaumau Street, where the roadway is actually being widened from four lanes to six with a median barrier separating inbound and outbound traffic.

10 MAP OF SECTION TWO (AS SEEN IN NEWSLETTER)

Showing where the lanes are widened makai and mauka of the highway. Highlight as each part is mentioned.

NARRATOR
Construction in this section will add to the highway on the makai side between East Hind Drive and Hawaii Loa Street and on the mauka side from Hawaii Loa Street to East Halemaumau Street.

Appendix 3

Excerpts from the Shooting Script for a Video for Sea Life Park and from the Video Script

Shooting Script

Location: Education Department

164 INT. EDUCATION DEPARTMENT—DAY

Simulated docent training session

AUDIO
(natural sound)

NARRATOR
Sea Life Park provides the docents thorough training through a comprehensive training and instructional workshop held once a year. College credit may be obtained for participation in the program.

{S=:11 | RT=20:42}

170 EXT. EDUCATION DEPARTMENT—DAY

MARILYN LEE OR MARY PICKETT

SUPER: (Name)/(Title)

MARILYN OR MARY
(Answers the question,
"What's the best thing about
the Education Program at Sea
Life Park?")
{S = :25 | RT = 23:05}

Location: Ocean Science Theater

24 INT. OCEAN SCIENCE THEATER—DAY

Dolphin swimming underwater inside the glass tank

MUSIC
(Continues)
{S = :05 | RT = 2:33}

86 INT. OCEAN SCIENCE THEATER—DAY

Continue montage: CU Fat Freddy gets a fish.

MUSIC
(Continues)
{S = :01 | RT = 10:28}

103 INT. OCEAN SCIENCE THEATER—DAY

CU Dolphin receives a fish. Pull back to see this is a training session and the fish is a reward. As we watch, the trainer gives a signal, and the dolphin obeys.

MUSIC
(Segues to)

AUDIO
(natural sound)

NARRATOR
This is a training session in
the Ocean Science Theater.
{S = :15 | RT = 12:30}

104 INT. OCEAN SCIENCE THEATER—DAY

TRAINER on camera.

TRAINER
(from interview)
(Tells briefly the process used in training.)

{S=:15 | RT=12:45}

106 INT. OCEAN SCIENCE THEATER—DAY

Trainer on camera.

TRAINER
(from interview)
(Explains that the animal is first conditioned to accept reward for some natural behavior. "You did something, so you get a fish.")

{S=:15 | RT=13:10}

107 INT. OCEAN SCIENCE THEATER—DAY

Animal learning behavior on cue.

TRAINER
(Voice-over, from interview)
(Next the principle is "Do what I ask, and then you get a fish.")

{S=:15 | RT=13:25}

108 INT. OCEAN SCIENCE THEATER—DAY

Trainer working with animal. Shows visual, auditory, and underwater cues.

TRAINER
(Voice-over, from interview)
(Explains how the cues work)

{S=:20 | RT=13:45}

DISSOLVE TO:

166 INT. OCEAN SCIENCE THEATER—DAY

STUDENT VOLUNTEER carrying something or doing volunteer work.

AUDIO
(natural sound)

NARRATOR
Sea Life Park also has a volunteer student program which gives students from the age of fifteen to senior citizens practical experience in various marine fields. Students volunteer approximately four hours a week over a four month period, and may receive high school or college credit.

{S=:15 | RT=21:27}

167 INT. OCEAN SCIENCE THEATER—DAY

Medium shot of volunteer student

SUPER: (Student's Name)/Volunteer Student

STUDENT
(Answers the question, "Why did you become a volunteer?")

{S=:20 | RT=21:47}

174 INT. OCEAN SCIENCE THEATER—DAY

CAROL working with animals and assistants before the show.

SUPER: (Name)/(Title)

CAROL
(Answers the question, "What is the purpose of the Ocean Science Theater and the show here?")

{S=:30 | RT=24:40}

175 INT. OCEAN SCIENCE THEATER—DAY

From the "stage" side looking at the audience.

AUDIO
(natural sound)

NARRATOR
And now it is show time in
the Ocean Science Theater.

Excerpt from the Sea Life Park Script

163 EXT. TOUCH TANK—DAY

Touch tank sequence: Focus on docent.

AUDIO
(natural sound)

NARRATOR
The docents at Sea Life Park are all volunteers. Their work makes possible the school and community education programs.

{S=:08 | RT=20:31}

164 INT. EDUCATION DEPARTMENT—DAY

Simulated docent training session

AUDIO
(natural sound)

NARRATOR
Sea Life Park provides the docents thorough training through a comprehensive training and instructional workshop held once a year. College credit may be obtained for participation in the program.

{S=:11 | RT=20:42}

165 EXT. SEA LIFE PARK—DAY

Medium Shot of BOB MOORE with the Park in the background.

SUPER: BOB MOORE/GENERAL MANAGER/SEA LIFE PARK

BOB
(Talks positively about the volunteer program.)

{S=:30 | RT=21:12}

166 INT. OCEAN SCIENCE THEATER—DAY

Student Volunteer carrying something or doing volunteer work.

AUDIO
(natural sound)

NARRATOR
Sea Life Park also has a volunteer student program which gives students from the age of fifteen to senior citizens practical experience in various marine fields. Students volunteer approximately four hours a week over a four month period and may receive high school or college credit.
{S = :15 | RT = 21:27}

167 INT. OCEAN SCIENCE THEATER—DAY

Medium shot of VOLUNTEER STUDENT

SUPER: MARY CLARK/STUDENT VOLUNTEER

MARY CLARK
(Answers the question, "Why did you become a volunteer?")
{S = :20 | RT = 21:47}

168 EXT. WHALER'S COVE—DAY

On board the *Essex*. Talking with the GIRL in the show.

SUPER: "Koleka"
Dorothy Wandee Toni
Swimmer

NARRATOR
This is "Koleka," who rides the whale in the Whaler's Cove show. We asked her how she became a part of Sea Life Park.

GIRL
(Answers the question, "Why do you choose to ride a whale several times a day?"
{S=:23 | RT=22:10}

169 EXT. A TRAINING AREA—DAY

(SCENE DELETED)

170 EXT. ROCKY SHORES—DAY

MARILYN LEE

SUPER: (Name)/(Title)

MARILYN
(Answers the question, "What's the best thing about the Education Program at Sea Life Park?")
{S=:25 | RT=23:05}

171 EXT. A TRAINING AREA—DAY

INGRID teaching the sea lion to ride a golf cart.

SUPER: (Name)/(Title)

INGRID
(Answers the question, "Why do you spend time training animals to do things they never thought of doing before?")
{S=:25 | RT=23:30}

172 EXT. SEA LIFE PARK—DAY

GRADUATE STUDENTS doing cooperative research.

SUPER: Adam Pack/Kathy Mardon
Graduate Students, Univ. of Hawaii
Kewalo Basin Marine Mammal Lab

GRADUATE STUDENTS
(Discuss their work at Sea Life Park)

{S=:20 | RT=23:50}

173 INT. REEF TANK—DAY

Lanai above the tank. ALEXIS, the girl diver who was feeding the fish, emerges and takes off mask.

SUPER: Alexis Freeman/Aquarist/Diver

ALEXIS
(Answers the question, "What do you do at Sea Life Park, and why are you doing it?")

{S=:20 | RT=24:10}

174 INT. OCEAN SCIENCE THEATER—DAY

CAROL working with animals and assistants before the show.

SUPER: (Name)/(Title)

CAROL
(Answers the question, "What is the purpose of the Ocean Science Theater and the show here?")

{S=:30 | RT=24:40}

175 INT. OCEAN SCIENCE THEATER—DAY

From the "stage" side looking at the audience.

AUDIO
(natural sound)

NARRATOR
And now it is show time in the Ocean Science Theater.

Tilt down to see Kamoana swimming underwater.

NARRATOR
The stars are ready . . .
{S=:06 | RT=24:46}

176 INT. OCEAN SCIENCE THEATER—DAY

MC scooping up penguins and putting them into their place on stage.

AUDIO
(natural sound)

NARRATOR
or almost ready . . . and
here's the show.
{S=:05 | RT=24:51}

Appendix 4

Complete Script Treatment, Recruiting Video for Cannon's International Business College of Honolulu

A. **PURPOSE**

1. The video will show and explain the opportunities at Cannon's International Business College of Honolulu. It will show the attractive features of the school. And it will demonstrate the value of the school.

2. The video will provide a visual introduction to the opportunities at Cannon's International Business College of Honolulu for potential students and their families. It will be shown:

   a) To people who come to the school for information.

   b) During recruiting visits to secondary schools.

   c) And to people from the neighbor islands or the mainland who may not have a chance to visit the school before matriculating.

3. The goal is to motivate the viewer to want to come in to Cannon's and talk about going to school there.

B. STYLE

1. The video will be relatively short—not less than ten minutes, nor more than about fifteen minutes.
2. It will be more visual than talk, and will be backed with a solid contemporary musical theme. The photographic style will emphasize motion. Editing will use quick cuts and dissolves on action. The visual style should approach that of a music video. The people, and the message of the video, should dance across the screen, flowing with the music.
3. Students, and others who appear in the video, will be well made up and dressed for success in terms of their peer group.
4. Testimonial statements from students and graduates will be short and to the point. This is a long commercial, not a short documentary.

C. TREATMENT

1. Fade up on establishing shot of downtown Honolulu business buildings. Strong musical theme fades in.
2. Cut to an armored car making a delivery. We may see guards carrying bags of money.
3. Dissolve to a big rotary change sorter in a bank or store. The natural sound of the change, swishing around, overpowers the music momentarily.
4. Music continues as we see shots of money being handled in a bank, a store, a restaurant.
5. Tilt down from skyscraper to see three or four students, dressed for success, in Tamarind Square. They are smiling and moving forward, confidently, with the music.
   a) A voice says, "It's their first day in the world of business . . . and they're ready . . . because they are Cannon people."

6. Dissolve to interior of Cannon's International Business College of Honolulu; see the logo.

7. Placement person by the logo (name and title on the screen) says

    a) "98.5% of all Cannon's graduates are working in the field we trained them for."

8. Graduate on screen. (With all speakers, the name and identifying title or "student" or "graduate" will be superimposed on the screen.)

    a) "Cannon's gets you ready for the world of work."

9. Student:

    a) "We're learning that what makes a successful employee is both knowledge and good work habits."

10. Different graduate:

    a) "The habits I learned at Cannon's made going to work easier. You've got it, when you get out there."

11. Another graduate:

    a) "From my own experience, what I'd say is, whatever you want to do, 'at Cannon's you can.' "

12. Exterior of Cannon's International Business College of Honolulu. We see students carrying books arriving and going into the building.

13. Superimpose the title:

AT CANNON'S YOU CAN

Cannon's
International Business College
of Honolulu

14. Dissolve to the interior of the school. The voice tells us

    a) That Cannon's International Business College of Honolulu was established in 1917 and is the only private junior college in Hawaii. That it is conveniently located on Kapiolani Blvd., close to Ala Moana Center.

15. As we see:

16. An elevator door open and smiling students flow out, moving to the music.

17. A classroom with modern AV equipment in use.

18. Room 302. Close-up of a hand moving swiftly on a 10-key.

19. More shots of active, smiling, purposeful students as the voice says:

    a) "If you're like the typical Cannon's student, you're a hard worker, with strong goals . . . and you're seeking a program for success."

20. Male student in a typing room.

    a) "People think a business college is a typing school."

21. Student's voice continues as we see a very fast typist speed typing on an electric typewriter:

    a) "Sure, everyone here learns to type . . . You need to."

22. See the male student, as he continues:

    a) "It's a skill, like reading. If you can't type, you're locked out of the modern business world."

23. Voice continues as we see a typing class working on all electric typewriters.

a) "That doesn't mean you're going to work as a typist. Hey, if you can't type, you can't talk to a computer . . ."

24. Visual montage of computer activity, with strong musical background. Start with students working on PCs and PC clones (Room 308).

25. Students at Wang word processors (Room 306).

26. See the Sperry mainframe system, with students (Room 307).

27. Computers with color monitors (Room 205). Student doing spreadsheets.

28. End computer sequence with System One Airline reservations computer. Voice of narrator explains:

    a) That this is the most modern airline reservation equipment. It's a real system, not a mock-up. Students are actually interacting with the professional reservations system. And when they've learned System One, they can use any system. Cannon's teaches the business systems of the future . . . now.

29. Now we see a futuristic background and graphics of the logos of major, interesting companies in "glamour" fields (which have hired Cannon's graduates) flash past: airlines, resort hotels, cruise lines, banks, advertising agencies, film/video production companies, music recording companies, etc. The music continues strong in the background, while the narrator tells us:

    a) That Cannon's prepares its graduates for careers in the most interesting and exciting fields in business, with an emphasis on the fastest growing fields where the jobs and good salaries will be from now to the year 2000. Twenty-five different programs in the fields of accounting and business administration, computer information systems, general office procedures and word processing, hotel and tourism (including airlines), and secretarial.

30. We see a group of students come into the library and begin to study, as the narrator continues.

    a) "You can start with your interests, and find their expression in the world of business. Earn an Associate in Science degree, and be started up the ladder to success, and earning money, in just 18 months."

31. Student:

    a) "What I like is, at Cannon's you don't have to take a lot of courses that are not directly related to your career goals."

32. Graduate:

    a) "A lot of people say don't make a career decision. Just go to college for four years and you'll get a good job when you graduate. But why waste all that time. Cannon's is the alternative for people who already know what they want."

33. Student:

    a) "You don't even have to have taken business classes in high school. Everything you need is right here."

34. Student:

    a) "I'm taking the secretarial course—and it's a lot more than typing and answering the phone. You learn the organizational skills that your boss may not have. A private secretary is well paid and today has a good chance to move into management."

35. Academic Dean:

    a) "Cannon's offers sound preparation. In addition to major courses, all students take accounting, college English, oral communication, typing, and success strategies."

36. Shelly:

    a) "Success Strategies is taken in the first semester. The students learn things like goal setting, some study skills—note taking, test taking—and the applied psychology of how to work for what you want."

37. At the Hotel Management check-in counter (mezzanine), students practicing. Nicely dressed. Music in.

38. Office procedures (Room 401) students on the phone. Nicely dressed. (Shelly's voice continues)

    a) "We have a dress code, because business has a dress code—whether it's written down or not."

39. School time clock. Nicely dressed students checking in or out.

    a) "We stress punctuality and courtesy, because business expects people to be on time, and to be courteous and considerate. We're teaching success habits. That's why Cannon people make it."

40. Class showing practice job placement interview techniques. Narrator's voice:

    a) "To get a job, you have to get past the job interview. Cannon's offers practice in job placement techniques—more habits of success."

41. We see a practice interview, with smiling students and a positive attitude, with theme music in full. Male student might arrive at the door. Girl meets him, checking her watch. Hands him a necktie. They

make it in time. Teacher counseling. Might pantomime a no-no.

42. Otto Lehrack:

    a) "How does the business world like our graduates? Last year we had three times as many jobs available to our graduates as we had people to fill them. Three times as many. That's why Cannon people make it."

43. Graduate in the downtown setting, from the opening scene.

    a) Says he had many job interviews/offers to pick from.

44. Another graduate in the downtown setting, from the opening scene.

    a) Says he/she felt really prepared in the job interview. "Used all the things I learned, and I got the job I wanted."

45. Exterior, graduate in a nice car.

    a) "I picked Cannon's because of the placement service. I got a good job in business. And I've already earned enough to buy my car."

46. Placement officer:

    a) "We offer lifetime placement service. If you want to make a career move, or if you should lose the job you have, we're always here to help."

47. Second floor student area. We see students at the snack bar and follow them into the lounge. Musical background. Students are smiling, well dressed, attractive. As we continue to watch student activities we begin to see people we've already seen on camera making a statement in friendly interaction. This is a montage of activities such as boy meets girl; a wave

across the room; someone comes up to a table and responds to a question about class work; a girl and boy walk arm in arm; etc. In between, at appropriate points in the music, we drop in statements:

a) "At Cannon's, you'll find a nice group of people to go to school with."

b) "A good student body allows a lot of teaching and learning to happen."

c) Older student: "Just because you've been out of high school for a while doesn't mean you won't fit in. All it takes is a sincere interest."

d) "I like the small classes. You can learn more."

e) "We have individual counseling on careers and courses. You stay on track."

f) "Cannon's has a lot of student groups, such as the Future Manager's Association, the Tropicannon Club, the Cannon Association of Legal Students . . . Just about every major has its own organization."

48. Beginning of "Battle of the Majors montage." Narrator says,

 a) "In the fall, we have the Battle of the Majors at Magic Island."

49. Montage of scenes from the Battle of the Majors, with musical background. Use some live sound as appropriate. A nice, one minute, kids-having-fun piece.

50. See students in a group at Battle of the Majors. Narrator says,

 a) "Forty-five to fifty percent of the students have some form of financial aid. Cannon's qualifies for all the student aid programs."

51. Placement officer:

    a) "We have a placement service for part-time jobs for students. Some go right from a part-time job to a full-time position with the same employer when they graduate."

52. Graduate:

    a) "I don't think I realized, until I graduated, just how good the faculty is."

53. Student:

    a) "It's not just book learning with our teachers. They have really strong professional experience in business."

54. Student:

    a) "They can tell you the things you really need to know."

55. Exterior, Admissions Office, student goes through the door and we follow him/her in. Narrator says,

    a) "You're interested in business. You want to make a good living, and you're willing to work hard to do it. You want to achieve, and you want to succeed. Come to Cannon's."

56. We see the student go into an admission officer's office. Narrator continues:

    a) "You'll find it easy to talk with the people in the admissions office. They can help you plan a program for success."

57. Student and admissions officer at the door, shaking hands. Narrator:

    a) "Remember, at Cannon's you can. For more information, call or write Cannon's International

Business College of Honolulu, 1500 Kapiolani Blvd., Honolulu, 96814. Telephone 955-1500."

58. Music up for a closing montage of fun shots from things we've already seen, while we hold the address and telephone number, accreditation information, etc., on the screen.

Appendix 5

Complete Treatment for *The Hawaiian Volcanoes: A Force for Creation*

A. DISCUSSION

1. What follows is a plan for a half-hour video centered on Hawaii's volcanoes. The video will weave together:

   a) Spectacular volcano footage of Kilauea and Mauna Loa.

   b) Native Hawaiian chants and hula dealing with creation and the stories of the volcanoes.

   c) Volcano science which has largely grown from the Hawaiian Volcano Observatory.

2. Theme: The video will show the awesome force of the volcano as creative rather than destructive. The volcano is the force which created the islands and adds to their size and number.

3. Chant: The chant is the history of Hawaii and its people. The background music will be the chant and the music of the hula. It will be established early in the

video in a natural way, so that it will be accepted by the viewer throughout the program.

4. Progression of volcano footage: Footage of volcanic activity will appear throughout the video. It will progress from slight activity, smoke, glow through skylights, etc., at the beginning to climax with large fountains and extensive rivers of fire at the end.

B. THE VIDEO

1. The opening of the video is a creation story:
2. Underwater footage. Fish swimming. Plant life. If possible the red glow of magma beneath the water. (Possibly available in footage from Mauna Ulu.)
3. A tremor. Fish scoot away.
   a) On the soundtrack: the beginning of a chant of creation. English subtitles translate the meaning.
4. Beneath the water, a seamount rises.
5. Steam. Smoke. Explosive tephra. An island breaks out of the sea.
   a) (The chant continues)
6. Against this we super the
   a) Opening titles
7. The chant ends. The fiery images dissolve to black lava desolation—aerial footage flying over Kilauea caldera. Wind sound. Emptiness.
   a) Narration: the worst is over. For now the volcano is calm. Dormant, but not dead.
8. Sulfur smoke. Steam.
   a) Narration: The awesome force of the volcano—which burns, crushes, or covers everything in its way—is the creative force of the islands.

9. Ocean at black sand beach or lava beach.

   a) Narration: the islands rose out of the ocean.

10. Images of a bird in flight, flotsam at the water's edge.

    a) Narration: the sea brings nutrients . . . Passing birds help fertilize the rock and may drop seeds.

11. Wave motion.

    a) Narration: Time is on the side of creation.

12. We see a tiny seed, borne on the wind, and follow it to find tiny bits of vegetation in the lava.

    a) A chant begins. It tells of the people living in harmony with the *aina*.

13. Montage of growth. Sparse bits of green in the lava field. Then more. Lush green foliage. Bright flowers. Then the green jungle cliffs of the Na Pali coast.

    a) The chant ends.

    b) Narration: Volcanoes created the chain of islands.

14. Dissolve to:
    Dubner graphics showing the Pacific Plate and the rim of fire around it. In the center is a lava hot spot in Hawaii's location. As we move closer, this becomes Kure Atoll, and as we watch, the chain of islands is slowly created and moves off to the northwest. We come even closer to see the inhabited islands and at the end pull out to see the entire archipelago.

    a) Narration: Explains how the oceans and continents sit on huge tectonic plates, which float on magma. Where the plates meet is the usual place for volcano and earthquake activity. Volcanoes along the edge of the plate create a "rim of fire" which circles the Pacific. In the center of the Pacific Plate is a "hot spot" so hot it can burn through the plate and release magma into the ocean. It grows into shield volcanoes, which become seamounts, and eventually islands. The plate moves at the rate of three to four inches a year. In 25 million years it would travel about 1,500 miles. And that's the distance from Kure Atoll to the rising seamount of Loihi, beyond Kilauea—which will be the next Hawaiian island. The story of Pele's search for a home is both good history and good science.

15. Hula of Pele, perhaps performed at the rim of the caldera, against the sky. This then becomes superimposed over pictures of volcanic activity.

    a) Chant: the story of Pele's flight down the chain of islands from Kauai to Kilauea, seeking a home.

16. Lava flow.

    a) Narration: Describes "Pele's hair"

17. Bubbling lava.

    a) Narration: Distinguishes types of lava

18. Lava flow

    a) Narration: lava tubes

19. Inside lava tube

20. Lava through the woods.

    a) Narration: tells about lava trees

21. Glowing volcano. Against it we see in silhouette or super the hula of Pele and Kamapuaa.

    a) Chant: The story of Pele and Kamapuaa—Pele burns, but Kamapuaa grows back

22. Dissolve to:
    Devastation Trail.

a) Narration: Says that this is a long-term study of the return of plant life from the devastation of a volcano.

23. See the regrowth along the trail.

24. Dissolve to:
Shoreline where vegetation grows to the water. Follow with plant life in the lava fields. Then thick growth.

 a) Narration: The ocean is a moat around the islands. Tells of the plant life on the islands before people came to Hawaii. Unique species—then, and even now. One in every 30,000 to 50,000 years was successfully established. Gentle plants. No predators. No need for thorns; didn't have to be poisonous.

25. Double-hulled canoe.

 a) Narration: Arrival of the Polynesians in 500 A.D. or before. Bringing with them imported plants and animals. 98% of the original flora is gone.

26. Volcano flow.

 a) Narration: Defines Kipuka, a small section of ground surrounded by recent lava flow. This is another kind of isolation. Left alone, some of the original flora asserts itself.

27. Botanists studying plant life on Devastation Trail.

 a) Narration: Some scientists study the behavior of plants in a volcanic area . . . while other scientists study the behavior of volcanoes.

28. Follow a wire to a seismograph.

 a) Narration: explain seismography

29. Reggie Okamura on camera.

 a) Says we are accurate in geologic terms.

30. Volcano begins an eruption
31. Inflation of the volcano
32. See tilt measurement with lasers.
    a) Narration: Explains tilt measurement and the use of lasers.
33. Volcano becoming active.
34. Gas measurement
    a) Narration: Explains careful monitoring of eruptive phase.
35. Observers—on foot and in helicopters
36. Gas venting.
37. Dissolve to:
    Hula halau at Halemaumau
    a) Narration: explains that *halaus* come annually, not out of fear but to honor Pele.
38. Volcano becomes more active.
39. Fountaining.
40. Hula silhouetted or supered in the fountain.
    a) Chant: with the hula
41. Fountain alone. We are watching active eruption. Long, slow looks at volcanic activity.
42. Lava flow. A scientist makes a temperature measurement.
    a) Narration: Taking Pele's temperature. How the instrument works. What the temperature is.
43. Flowing lava. Measuring the speed of the flow.
    a) Narration: How speed is measured. What the speed is.

44. Building in fury.
    a) Beneath the sound of the volcano, we hear a chant fading in and out.
45. Spectacular fountaining.
46. Rivers of fire at night.
47. Build to spectacular footage as climax.
48. Fade to black.
49. Fade in
50. Dead lava flow. Black.
    a) Chant, softly.
51. A bird flying.
52. A seed, blowing.
    a) Narration: The cycle of rebirth starts again.
53. In the black and burned out lava field, we find a glowing vent.
    a) Narration: And Pele waits . . .
    b) A chant begins
54. Fade out
55. Closing titles
    a) Chant continues
56. Fade out titles
    a) Fade out sound.
57. END

Appendix 6

Complete Script for *The Hawaiian Volcanoes: A Force for Creation* in Classic Screenplay Format

FADE IN

1 EXT. SKY—DAY

Blue Sky, Clouds, the Heavens, the start of any Hawaiian creation story.

SFX
(Wind sound)

NARRATOR
Long ago . . . Long before the
people came . . . there was
just the sky . . .
{S=0:10 || RT=00:10}

2 EXT. OCEAN—DAY

Empty Ocean, seen from above, through the clouds.

NARRATOR
and the sea.
{S=0:04 || RT=00:14}

3 EXT. OCEAN—DAY

Ocean in close-up, waves.

SFX
(Natural sound. Wind and waves.)
{S=0:03 || RT=00:17}

4 EXT. UNDERWATER—DAY

Underwater footage. Fish swimming. Plant life. If possible the red glow of magma beneath the water. (Possibly available in footage from Mauna Ulu.)

SFX
(Underwater sound)

NARRATOR
This is where Hawaii began . . .
{S=0:06 || RT=00:23}

5 EXT. UNDERWATER—DAY

A tremor. Image shakes. Fish scoot away.

SFX
(Volcanic rumble)

NARRATOR
Deep beneath the sea.
{S=0:04 || RT=00:27}

6 EXT. UNDERWATER—DAY

Beneath the water, the impression of a seamount rising.

SFX
(rumble continues)

NARRATOR
A volcano . . . creating a
seamount which slowly lifted
for centuries from the ocean
floor . . .
{S=0:06 || RT=00:33}

7 EXT. OCEAN—DAY

Images of steam. Smoke. Explosive tephra. An island breaking out of the sea.

SFX
(Loud volcanic noise)

NARRATOR
and became . . . Hawaii.

Images of heat, smoke, fire. Lava flow into the ocean. (These images are mostly smoke and blackness, and the meeting of volcano with sky and sea.)

SFX
(Volcano noise, wind, water)

SUPER:

THE HAWAIIAN VOLCANOES
A Force for Creation
A Presentation of

HARADA PRODUCTIONS
In Cooperation with The U.S. Geological Survey Hawaiian Volcano Observatory
Produced on location at Hawaii Volcanoes National Park and on the Islands of Hawaii, Maui, and Oahu

{S=0:22 || RT=0:55}
DISSOLVE TO:

8 EXT. KILAUEA—DAY

Black lava desolation—aerial footage flying over Kilauea Caldera. Emptiness.

SFX
(Wind sound)

NARRATOR
The volcano became calm.
Quiet . . . but not extinct . . .

{S=0:05 || RT=01:00}

9 EXT. LAVA FIELD—DAY

Close images of black pahoehoe lava. Smooth, flowing. Lava everywhere and nothing else.

NARRATOR
The power of the volcano was
a rich creative force in the
making of the islands, then
. . . as it is today.
{S=0:07 || RT=01:07}

10 EXT. BLACK SAND OR LAVA BEACH—DAY

Where the ocean meets the beach. Lava and water.

NARRATOR
From the sea these volcanic
islands rose to become a new
home for life on the earth. . . .
{S=0:05 || RT=01:12}

11 EXT. LAVA FIELD—DAY

Rain on a smoking, steaming lava field.

NARRATOR
Rich and fertile, which would
begin to support small forms
of life almost as soon as the
lava cooled.
{S=0:08 || RT=01:20}

12 EXT. BLACK SAND OR LAVA BEACH—DAY

At the edge of the beach, bits of flotsam carried in by the sea.

NARRATOR
And the sea brought things to
the new islands . . . bits of
plants . . . seeds . . .
{S=0:05 || RT=01:25}

13 EXT. BIRD IN FLIGHT—DAY

A sea bird over the island.

NARRATOR
birds came to the islands . . .
{S=0:05 || RT=01:30}

14 EXT. OCEAN SHORE—DAY

Wave motion.

NARRATOR
And time was on the side of
creation. Time . . . not in
hours or days . . .
{S=0:05 || RT=01:35}

15 EXT. VOLCANO—DAY

Pull down from mountains and greenery to lava bubbling from the ground, or a small flow of lava.

SFX
(natural sound)

NARRATOR
But geologic time, measured
in millions of years . . .

MUSIC
(Fade in theme)

NARRATOR
What causes a volcano?
For one thing, what we like to
call "solid earth" isn't quite
as solid as we might hope.
{S=0:15 || RT=01:50}
DISSOLVE TO:

16 INT. DUBNER GRAPHIC—DAY

World globe, slowly spinning, turns into a cross section of a globe. At the center is the inner core, in rocky blue-gray. Then the liquid outer core in glowing sun gold. Next is the mantle, perhaps white hot near the core, shading to yellow-orange near the surface, then the crust/plate in slate gray, with the surface of the earth outlined in blue, green and brown. As each section is talked about, it glows or pulses. (See Sketch #1R)

MUSIC
(Continues under)

NARRATOR
The center of the earth has an inner core and an outer core. Together, they are a little over 4,000 miles in diameter. The inner core seems to be solid. But the outer core acts like a very thick liquid.

Surrounding the outer core is the earth's mantle, about 1,800 miles thick. It's rock . . . but most of it is at an extremely high temperature. Finally there's a thin crust, ranging from three to 45 miles thick.

{S=0:50 || RT=02:40}
DISSOLVE TO:

17 EXT. VOLCANO—DAY

Some volcanic activity—smoke, steam, bubbling lava. Nothing big.

SFX
(Natural sound swells over the music)
{S=0:04 || RT=03:50}
DISSOLVE TO:

18 INT. DUBNER GRAPHIC—DAY

The outside of the globe, which then spreads out into a flat map showing the lithosphere plates of the earth. (Sketch #2)

MUSIC
(Continues under)

NARRATOR
The earth's surface is broken into a number of giant slabs or tectonic plates. These are made up of crust and mantle and are about fifty miles thick. And these plates are in motion. They don't move very fast—the rate varies with the different plates. The Pacific Plate, for instance, has been measured at a rate of about ten centimeters, or four inches, a year.

Highlight the plate boundaries.

{S=0:40 || RT=03:20}
DISSOLVE TO:

19 EXT. VOLCANO—DAY

Long shot of smoking volcano, or mild lava flow.

SFX
(Natural sound)

{S=0:03 || RT=03:23}
DISSOLVE TO:

20 INT. DUBNER GRAPHIC—DAY

Graphic showing the "Ring of Fire." This might start by rejoining the previous graphic into a cylindrical projection, rotating it until it shows the Pacific Plate in its entirety (Sketch #3), then flattening it and changing it to show the "Ring of Fire" (Sketch #4). Highlight volcano names such as Krakatau, Mt. Fuji, and Mount St. Helens.

MUSIC
(Continues under)

NARRATOR
Most of the world's active volcanoes are located along the boundaries of the plates. Several plates touch boundaries around the Pacific Basin . . . and so many volcanoes are located along these boundaries that this area has become known as the "Ring of Fire."

{S=0:14 || RT=03:37}
DISSOLVE TO:

21 EXT. VOLCANO—DAY

Along Kilauea Caldera. Smoke and heat, but no lava at first.

SFX
(natural sound in and under)

NARRATOR
At the edges, where one moving plate is pushed down beneath another, melting can occur. The hot, molten rock, called magma, may rise to the surface . . .

We see the flow of lava.

as part of a volcanic eruption. Magma that has reached the surface is called lava.

We see some interesting lava flow.

SFX
(natural sound)

{S=0:28 || RT=04:05}
DISSOLVE TO:

22 INT. DUBNER GRAPHICS—DAY

Zoom in from the Ring of Fire to see the Hawaiian Archipelago from Kure Atoll to the Big Island. (Sketch #5)

MUSIC
(Chant continues under)

NARRATOR
These islands sit in the center of the Ring of Fire . . . far from any plate boundary. And yet they were formed by volcanoes. How?

Zoom in to the Big Island, to the volcanoes.

{S=0:08 || RT=04:13}
DISSOLVE TO:

23 INT. DUBNER GRAPHICS—DAY

Graphic showing weak spot in the mantle, causing magma, which collects and rises (Sketch #6).

NARRATOR
The scientific explanation is that there is a weak spot in the mantle which lets through enough heat to melt the rock of the tectonic plate. The magma collects and finds its way to the surface, to erupt as a volcano. Over time, it builds up into an island.

{S=0:17 || RT=04:30}
DISSOLVE TO:

24 INT. DUBNER GRAPHICS—DAY

The Hawaiian Chain as in Sketch #5. Start with a CU of Kure Atoll and then pull back.

NARRATOR

The oldest island in the chain
is Kure Atoll, located the
farthest northwest of
Honolulu. It is at least
twenty-five million years old.

Show the Big Island and the location of Loihi.

The youngest is the Big
Island of Hawaii, whose
oldest areas are only about
half a million years old. And
to the southeast of the Big
Island, a new seamount,
Loihi, is rising about twenty
miles out to sea.

Animate to show plate movement over a hot spot from Kure to Kilauea.

Now, if the Pacific Plate
travels over a hot spot in the
mantle at a rate of about four
inches per year, then in
twenty-five million years it
would have moved close to
1,600 miles.

Show the measured distance from Kure to Kilauea.

And that is pretty close to the
distance from Kure Atoll to
the active Big Island
volcanoes of Kilauea and
Mauna Loa.

{S=0:50 || RT=05:20}

25 EXT. VOLCANO—NIGHT

An active eruption of the volcano. (Not yet the real "blockbusters," but good night scenes, small fountaining, and fireworks.)

SFX
(Natural sounds of the volcano)
{S = :40 || RT = 06:00}

26 EXT. VOLCANO—NIGHT

Fountaining.

SFX
(Natural sound)

NARRATOR
An exciting part of the eruption of a Hawaiian volcano is the spectacular fountaining which can force jets of lava a thousand feet or more into the air. Temperature of the lava is eleven hundred fifty degrees Centigrade. Fountaining is caused by the pressure of gas, seeking release, against fairly thick magma. Hawaii's volcanoes are considered relatively gentle because they fountain rather than have a violent explosion like that of Mount St. Helens.
{S = 0:20 || RT = 06:20}

27 EXT. VOLCANO—NIGHT

Mauna Loa fountaining.

SFX
(Natural sound)

NARRATOR
Mauna Loa's fountains of lava don't rise as high, because the magma is denser, and the gas pressure is lower.

{S=0:18 || RT=06:38}
DISSOLVE TO:

28 EXT. VOLCANO—DAY

Lava flow.

MUSIC
(Theme in)

{S=0:12 || RT=06:50}

29 EXT. VOLCANO—DAY

Pahoehoe lava. We see interesting forms and shapes of the lava.

MUSIC
(Continues under)

NARRATOR
Lava that cools in smooth, flowing shapes is called *pahoehoe.*

{S=0:20 || RT=07:10}

30 EXT. VOLCANO—DAY

We see *a'a* lava.

MUSIC
(Continues under)

NARRATOR
Rough jagged lava is called *a'a.*

{S=0:10 || RT=07:20}

31 EXT. VOLCANOES NATIONAL PARK—DAY

Scene deleted.

32 EXT. DEVASTATION TRAIL—DAY

The Cinder Cone.

NARRATOR
The fallout from one eruption
created a cinder cone that
rises over 840 feet high.
{S=0:06 || RT=07:26}

33 EXT. VOLCANO—DAY

Crab shot up Pu'u o'o.

SFX
(eruption noise)

NARRATOR
An eruption creates an area
of devastation. It can drop a
blanket of cinders and ash on
hundreds of acres of forest,
covering the floor of the
forest to a depth of anywhere
from eight inches to as much
as eight feet.
{S=0:17 || RT=07:43}

34 EXT. DEVASTATION TRAIL—DAY

An area of sparse plant life.

MUSIC
(Theme in)

NARRATOR
This will create a totally new
inorganic surface—
everything that had been
there before is covered up by
cinders and ash.
{S=0:09 || RT=07:52}

35 EXT. DEVASTATION TRAIL—DAY

Close-up of cinders and lava.

MUSIC
(Continues under)

NARRATOR
Lava actually makes a nutritious soil, except for a problem with nitrogen. For plants to grow, a nitrogen-fixing organism is needed. Fortunately, this is present in some algae.

{S=0:14 || RT=08:06}

36 EXT. DEVASTATION TRAIL—DAY

Close-up of a pool of water, or water on the lava and cinders.

MUSIC
(Continues under)

NARRATOR
And algae spores are everywhere. Growth began in the area as soon as the lava surface cooled. Algae are the first life forms found in this kind of rain-forest environment.

{S=0:12 || RT=08:18}

37 EXT. DEVASTATION TRAIL—DAY

Moss, ferns, lichens.

MUSIC
(Continues under)

NARRATOR
Then came mosses, ferns, and lichens.

{S=0:09 || RT=08:27}

38 EXT. DEVASTATION TRAIL—DAY

Isolated ohia plants, growing among the lava. Lehua flowers on the ohia.

MUSIC
(Continues under)

NARRATOR
After a number of years, the first seed producing plants appear. These will be ohia plants, the start of a new ohia-tree fern forest. The flower of the ohia is the beautiful lehua.

{S=0:16 || RT=08:43}

39 EXT. DEVASTATION TRAIL—DAY

Scene omitted

40 EXT. LAVA FIELD—DAY

We see a tiny feathered seed, borne on the wind. We follow it to see tiny bits of vegetation growing out of the lava.

SFX
(Wind noise)

NARRATOR
And this is how the islands have grown and become fertile.

Montage of growth. We see sparse bits of green in the lava field.

Then more.

Lush green foliage.

Bright flowers.

Rain forest.

Then the green jungle cliffs of the Na Pali coast.

{S=1:05 || RT=09:48}

DISSOLVE TO:

41 EXT. SHORELINE—DAY

A place along the shore where the vegetation grows right down to the water.

MUSIC
(Continues)

NARRATOR
Throughout most of the life of the islands, the ocean has protected them from the outside world.

{S=0:06 || RT=09:54}

42 EXT. VOLCANO—DAY

Plant life growing in a lava field.

MUSIC
(Continues under)

NARRATOR
The plant life that grew and evolved here was unique to these islands, not only then . . . but even today. Over the life of the islands, some 1,700 species and varieties of native plants have evolved.

{S=0:17 || RT=10:15}

43 EXT. THICK PLANT GROWTH—DAY

Lush vegetation.

MUSIC
(Continues under)

NARRATOR
These were gentle Hawaiian plants. They had no natural enemies . . . and they evolved few defenses.

{S=0:07 || RT=10:22}

44 EXT. STOCK FOOTAGE—DAY

Footage of Hokule'a or other Polynesian canoes at sea.

MUSIC
(Continues under)

NARRATOR
There were no thorn-bushes, no poisonous plants, here, when the first people came to Hawaii. That is estimated to have been about fifteen hundred years ago.
These Polynesians, who came to Hawaii from the south, brought with them plants and animals from their homeland.

{S=0:18 || RT=10:40}

45 EXT. BAMBOO GROVE—DAY

Thick stand of bamboo (it's an imported plant).

MUSIC
(Continues under)

NARRATOR
Eventually, some 4,000 new plants were brought to the islands by man over this period of fifteen hundred years. Bamboo was one, as well as many food plants and fruit trees . . . and a lot of weeds.

{S=0:12 || RT=10:52}

46A EXT. SHORE—DAY

Hokule'a or other canoe, different shot.

MUSIC
(Continues under)

NARRATOR
These were proto-Hawaiians, seeking new lands to conquer and settle, bringing with them their gods, traditions, and mana. The deity which stands foremost in the creation of new lands was Pelehonumea—which we know today as Pele—the goddess of the volcano. She came from the south, with members of her family in the canoe Honua-i-a-kea. This chant tells of Pele traveling to Hawaii. . . .

{S=0:23 || RT=11:15}

46B EXT. OCEAN SIDE—DAY

Pua's chant at the ocean.

{S=:30 | RT=11:45}

46C EXT. OCEAN SIDE—DAY

Transition shot, "ocean to land."

{S=:30 | RT=12:15}

46D EXT. VOLCANO—DAY

Chant at Volcano.

{S=:38 | RT=12:53}

47 EXT. AT SEA—DAY

An island, dimly seen from the water.

NARRATOR
The chant tells us that Pele and her party came first to little Nihoa Island, northwest of Kauai, and then worked their way down the chain of islands.

{S=0:08 || RT=13:01}

48 EXT. KAUAI—DAY

Kauai.

NARRATOR
They tested the islands of Niihau, Kauai, and Oahu with a divining rod to see if there was a suitable home for them there.

{S=0:08 || RT=13:09}

49 EXT. OAHU—DAY

Oahu, Diamond Head.

NARRATOR
They looked many places on Oahu. And Pele created the landmark craters at Diamond Head, Punchbowl, and Koko Head. But Oahu was not the home Pele was seeking.

{S=0:11 || RT=13:20}

50 EXT. MAUI—DAY

Haleakala.

NARRATOR
Pele moved on to explore Maui and its neighbor islands. Even Haleakala—the House of the Sun—was not acceptable to Pele. The legend says it is so large that Pele found herself unable to keep it warm.

{S=0:12 || RT=13:32}

51 EXT. BIG ISLAND—DAY

Kilauea.

NARRATOR
Pele found her home on the southern half of the island of Hawaii . . . claiming Mauna Loa, Hualalai, and Kilauea. Finding great comfort in the caldera of Kilauea, she created a home for herself there, in the crater of Halemaumau.

{S=0:16 || RT=13:48}

52 EXT. VOLCANO—DAY

Rim of the crater. Hula dancers. Pua chants about Pele. Dancers hula.

CHANTER
(Begins the chant)
(Narration to introduce the hula to come from Pua.)

{S=2:21 | RT=16:09}

53 EXT. VOLCANO—DAY

Scene merged into #52

54 EXT. VOLCANO—NIGHT

Scene omitted

55 EXT. VOLCANO—DAY

Scene omitted

DISSOLVE TO:

56 EXT. VOLCANO—DAY

Shots of "Pele's hair."

MUSIC
(Continues under)

NARRATOR
"Pele's hair" is finely extruded lava, often found after the volcano has been active.

{S=0:15 || RT=16:24}

57 EXT. VOLCANO—DAY

Pele's tears.

NARRATOR
Pele's tears . . . bits of liquid thrown up by a lava fountain that have solidified in teardrop shape.

{S=0:09 || RT=16:33}

58 EXT. VOLCANO—DAY

Lava flow.

SFX
(Natural sound)

NARRATOR
When the volcano erupts, sending out lava, the flow may follow a previous path . . .

{S=0:06 || RT=16:39}

59 EXT. VOLCANO—DAY

Lava traveling through trees, burning them.

SFX
(Natural sound)

NARRATOR
Or it may take a new route, burning and covering everything in its way.

{S=0:06 || RT=16:45}

60 EXT. HAWAII VOLCANOES PARK—DAY

Lava trees.

NARRATOR
Sometimes the flow of hot lava wraps around a tree, burning everything inside. As the lava flow recedes, the lava may cool in the shape of the tree it burned away. These formations are called "lava trees."

{S=0:15 || RT=17:00}

61 EXT. VOLCANO—NIGHT

Lava flow.

MUSIC
(Continues under)

NARRATOR
Sometimes the flow of lava during an eruptive episode will surround an area of vegetation without destroying it.

{S=0:07 || RT=17:07}

62 EXT. VOLCANO—DAY

A *kipuka* somewhere in the park. Shots of plant life.

MUSIC
(Continues under)

NARRATOR
Such an area is called a *kipuka.* It's like a little island in a sea of lava, cut off from the surrounding vegetation. In a kipuka the native plants often have a chance to reassert themselves, since they have evolved and adapted to survive best in the volcanic growing conditions of Hawaii.

{S=0:16 || RT=17:23}
DISSOLVE TO:

63 EXT. VOLCANO—DAY

A lava tube. Thurston or other, as long as the "tubeness" is clear in the picture.

MUSIC
(Continues under)

NARRATOR
This is called a lava tube. It's a cave, formed by the flow of lava. Lava tubes run underground, and sometimes out to sea.

{S=0:07 || RT=17:30}

64 EXT. SHORE—DAY

Blowhole or the equivalent.

MUSIC
(Continues under)

NARRATOR
The geyser effect of these "blowholes" along the shore is caused by waves rushing into an undersea lava tube and forcing water out the top.

{S=0:12 || RT=17:42}

65 EXT. HAWAIIAN VOLCANO OBSERVATORY—DAY

Exterior of the observatory, with a sign telling what it is.

MUSIC
(Theme in)

NARRATOR
The Hawaii volcanoes are the most watched in the world. The Hawaiian Volcano Observatory was established in 1912 . . .

{S=0:07 || RT=17:49}

66 INT. HAWAIIAN VOLCANO OBSERVATORY—DAY

Close-ups of seismograph recording instruments.

MUSIC
(Continues under)

NARRATOR
and has been operated by the
United States Geological
Survey since 1948. The
behavior of the volcanoes is
constantly monitored by
instruments located
throughout the volcanic area.
Seismographs measure and
record disturbances on the
surface, or below it.

{S=0:18 || RT=18:07}

67A INT. HAWAII VOLCANOES NATIONAL PARK—DAY

Develcorder film.

MUSIC
(Continues under)

NARRATOR
Most of the methods for
monitoring a volcano were
developed here. And some of
them are quite sophisticated.
Seismometers send their data
by telemetry to a
Develcorder, which records
the traces on film.
Measurements taken from
the film provide a
preliminary indication of the
location, depth, and
magnitude of the seismic
event.

{S=0:20 || RT=18:27}

67B INT. HAWAII VOLCANOES NATIONAL PARK—DAY

CUSP Display on Computer.

MUSIC
(Continues under)

NARRATOR
The data are also sent to a computer based system which processes the information quickly and displays it on the computer screen. The system, which supplements hand calculations from film, can plot the location of earthquakes very shortly after they occur. That's especially useful during earthquake swarms which often precede volcanic activity.

{S=0:22 || RT=18:49}

68 EXT. HAWAII VOLCANOES NATIONAL PARK—DAY

Scientist makes a laser measurement.

MUSIC
(Continues under)

NARRATOR
Laser instruments are used to measure the increase or decrease in the reservoir of magma beneath the volcano. As the reservoir inflates with magma, prior to an eruptive episode, the area around the volcano swells. . . . This can be detected by the tiltmeter, and by making an electronic distance measurement.

{S=0:22 || RT=19:11}

DISSOLVE TO:

69 EXT. VOLCANO—DAY

The beginning of an eruptive episode. Smoke, gas venting, etc.

SFX
(volcano noise)
{S=0:15 || RT=19:26}

70 INT. HAWAIIAN VOLCANO OBSERVATORY—DAY

Close-up of seismographic needles becoming very active.

SFX
(sounds of radio, intercom, etc., talking about the start of an eruptive episode.)
{S=0:10 || RT=19:36}

71 EXT. HAWAII VOLCANOES NATIONAL PARK—DAY

Montage of eruptive activities:

Helicopter flying into the caldera.

Men in hardhats with equipment packs going out to observe.

Etc.

SFX
(volcano noise)

NARRATOR
As the volcano becomes active, monitoring is stepped up. The observatory does not rely solely on instruments, but sends observers into the field to see what is actually happening.

SFX
(volcano noise)
{S=1:00 || RT=20:36}

72 EXT. VOLCANO—DAY

Scientist taking gas and temperature measurements.

SFX
(natural sound)

NARRATOR
From the temperature and composition of the gas emitted by the volcano, scientists can tell a great deal about the makeup of the magma building up below the surface.

{S=0:18 || RT=20:54}

73 (SCENE OMITTED)

74 EXT. VOLCANO—DAY

Volcano fountaining begins. Long shots. (From here, we build to the best and most spectacular footage.)

SFX
(volcano sounds)

NARRATOR
The Hawaiian Volcanoes offer a perfect laboratory for the study of volcanic behavior. In an ideal setting, filled with a rich tradition—and the mystic presence of Pele—the work goes on.

Hawaii Volcanoes National Park is one of the few places in the world where you can witness a volcanic eruption.

{S=0:40 || RT=21:34}

75 EXT. VOLCANO—DAY

Fountain alone. Long, slow looks at volcanic activity.

SFX
(volcano sounds)

{S=0:40 || RT=22:14}

LONG SLOW
DISSOLVE TO:

76 EXT. VOLCANO—DAY

Lava flow. Rivers of fire.

SFX
(volcano sounds)
{S=0:40 || RT=22:54}

77 EXT. VOLCANO—DAY

Scenes of human activity at the volcano:

Helicopter near the fountain.

Scientists taking measurements of temperature and speed of flow.

SFX
(volcano sounds)
{S=0:46 || RT=23:40}
LONG SLOW
DISSOLVE TO:

78 EXT. VOLCANO—NIGHT

Spectacular fountaining.

SFX
(volcano sounds)
{S=0:50 || RT=24:30}

79 EXT. VOLCANO—NIGHT

Lava flows—"rivers of fire."

SFX
(volcano sounds)
{S=0:50 || RT=25:20}

80 EXT. VOLCANO—NIGHT

Spectacular volcano footage at night.

SFX
(volcano sound builds)
{S=1:00 || RT=26:20}

81 EXT. VOLCANO—DAY

Best day footage of the volcano.

SFX
(natural sound)

{S=1:40 || RT=28:00}
FADE TO BLACK
FADE IN

82 EXT. VOLCANO—DAY

Dead lava flow. Black lava, cooling. Scenes of devastation and desolation.

NARRATOR
It's over . . . for now.

{S=0:10 || RT=28:10}

83 EXT. VOLCANO—DAY

A bird flying over the lava field.

A seed blowing in the wind.

NARRATOR
And the cycle of rebirth
begins again.

{S=0:20 || RT=28:30}

84 EXT. VOLCANO—DAY

We move across the lava field until we find a wisp of smoke, and then a glowing vent.

NARRATOR
The volcano continues . . .
and as long as smoke can
darken the sun, yes, so long
as there is a faint hint of
sulfur in the air, we will
continue to compose songs
and dances for the woman of
the pit . . . Pelehonumea will
live on.

{S=0:30 || RT=29:00}
FADE TO BLACK

85 INT. GRAPHICS—DAY

Closing titles:

HAWAII VOLCANOES
A Force for Creation

Producer-Director-Cameraman
JAY F. HARADA

Producer, Editor
CYRIL AKASHI

Written by
BARRY HAMPE

Volcano Technical Adviser
REGINALD OKAMURA

Chief of Operations
Hawaiian Volcano Observatory
U. S. Geological Survey
Hawaiiana Consultant and Chanter
KUMU HULA PUALANI KANAKA
'OLE KANAHELE

Hawaiian Botany Technical Adviser
DIETER MUELLER-DOMBOIS, PH.D.
Professor of Botany
University of Hawaii

Hula Dancers:

Narrator
GREGG MUELLER

Special Thanks to:
KGMB-TV Newsroom 9

HAWAII VOLCANOES NATIONAL
PARK

FADE OUT
END
{S=1:00 || RT=30:00}

Appendix 7

Resource Organizations

Here are several national organizations which you should know about, because your prospects may belong to one or more of them. You can contact the national offices, listed below, to find out about the local chapter nearest you.

American Advertising Federation (AAF)
1400 K Street, NW, #1000
Washington, DC 20005
Phone (202) 898-0089

American Association of Advertising Agencies (AAAA)
666 Third Avenue
New York, NY 10017
Phone (212) 682-2500
Fax: (212) 682-8136

American Society for Training and Development (ASTD)
Box 1443
1640 King Street
Alexandria, VA 22313
Phone (703) 683-8100
Fax: (703) 683-8103

International Association of Business Communicators (IABC)
1 Hallidie Plaza, #600
San Francisco, CA 94102
Phone (415) 433-3400
Fax: (415) 362-8762

International Television Association (ITVA)
International Office
6311 N. O'Connor Rd., LB-51
Irving, TX 75039
Phone (214) 869-1112
Fax: (214) 869-2980

Public Relations Society of America (PRSA)
33 Irving Place
New York, NY 10003-2376
Phone (212) 995-2230
Fax: (212) 995-0757

Women in Communications, Inc. (WICI)
2101 Wilson Blvd., Suite 417
Arlington, VA 22201
Phone (703) 528-4200
Fax: (703) 528-4205

Bibliography

Field, Syd. *Screenplay: The Foundations of Screenwriting*. New York: Dell Publishing Company. 1989.

———. *Selling a Screenplay: The Screenwriter's Guide to Hollywood*. New York: Dell Publishing Company. 1984.

Gillis, Joseph. *The Screenwriter's Guide: Second Edition*. New York: New York Zoetrope. 1987.

Haag, Judith H., and Hillis R. Cole. *The Complete Guide to Standard Script Formats, Part I: The Screenplay*. Los Angeles: CMC Publishing. 1980.

———, and ———. *The Complete Guide to Standard Script Formats, Part II: Taped Formats for TV*. Los Angeles: CMC Publishing. 1980.

Iuppa, Nicholas V. *Corporate Video Producer's Handbook*. White Plains, NY: Knowledge Industry Publications. 1991.

Nash, Constance, and Virginia Oakey. *The Screenwriter's Handbook: What to Write, How to Write It, Where to Sell It*. New York: Harper & Row, Publishers/Perennial Library. 1978.

Rawson, Hugh, and Margaret Miner. *The New International Dictionary of Quotations*. New York: New American Library. 1986.

Seger, Linda. *Making a Good Script Great*. New York: Dodd, Mead & Company. 1987.

Straczynski, J. Michael. *The Complete Book of Scriptwriting*. Cincinnati: Writer's Digest Books. 1982.

Van Nostran, William. *The Scriptwriter's Handbook.* White Plains, NY: Knowledge Industry Publications. 1989.

Walter, Richard. *Screenwriting: The Art, Craft and Business of Film and Television Writing.* New York: Plume/New American Library. 1988.

Writer's Market. Cincinnati: Writer's Digest Books. Published annually.

Sources of Excerpts and Interviews

For granting the interviews which served as the basis for Chapter 17, I am indebted to Jacqueline Albarella, president, Avid Productions, Buffalo; Tony Bond, president, Take One, Inc., Las Vegas; Tim Bradley, managing director, Quenzer Driscoll Dawson, Inc., and president, Tim Bradley Productions, Inc., Honolulu; Michael Davis, video production manager, City of Charlotte Public Service and Information Department, Charlotte; Jim Dotson, Take One Productions, New Orleans; Alan Foral, general manager, CMC Video, New Berlin, WI; Ron Kemp, director, Broadcast Services, North Carolina State University and owner of Southcoast Video, Raleigh; Bill McCarthy, video producer, White Bear Lake, MN; Chuck Neff, owner, Neff Productions, St. Louis; Verle Peterson, president, Envision Communications, Inc., Omaha; and Phil Schulman, owner, Phil Schulman Productions, Rosemont, PA.

The excerpts from the Associated Production Music catalogs (Figures 10-1, 10-2, 10-3, and 10-4) are reprinted with the permission of Associated Production Music, copyright 1990, Associated Production Music.

Excerpt from the Bank of Hawaii video (Figure 9-2), written in March 1989, reprinted with the permission of Bank of Hawaii.

The treatment for *At Cannon's You Can* appearing in Chapter 6 and Appendix 4, and excerpt from the script (Figure 7-1), all written in October 1987, reprinted with the permission of Cannon's International Business College of Honolulu.

Excerpt from the script *Safe and Healthful Working Conditions* (Figure 9-1), written in December 1990, reprinted with the permission of the State of Hawaii, Department of Labor and Industrial Relations.

Excerpts from the *First Night* footage log (Figure 4-1) and from the script, *First Night* (Figure 8-1), written in 1991, reprinted with the permission of First Night Honolulu.

Excerpt from the script *Hawaii Family Stress Center* (Figure 8-3) written in September 1989, reprinted with the permission of the Hawaii Family Stress Center.

Excerpt from the treatment for the script for a travel agent's video for Hilton Hawaiian Village (Figure 6-1), written in June 1988, reprinted with the permission of Hilton Hawaiian Village on Waikiki Beach.

Excerpt from the script *Operation Breakthrough* (Figure 11-1), written September 19, 1989, reprinted with the permission of Kentucky Fried Chicken.

Excerpts from the script *Light in Art* (Figure 7-2) and the narration script for *Light in Art* (Figure 11-2), written in August 1988, for the *Spectrum Hawaii* series, reprinted with the permission of KHET Hawaii Public Television.

Excerpt from the treatment *Kauai, Your Flight of Memories* (Figure 6-1), reprinted with the permission of Quenzer Driscoll Dawson.

Excerpts from the shooting script and the script *Sensational Sea Life Park* (Appendix 3), released as *Sea Life Park: Hawaii's Window into the Pacific*, copyright 1988, Bruce Benson Marketing, written in August 1987, reprinted with the permission of Bruce Benson Marketing.

Excerpts from the treatment and script *Ease the Squeeze* (Appendix 2), written in August 1990, reprinted with the permission of the State of Hawaii, Department of Transportation.

Excerpt from the proposal for the films *A Young Child Is . . .* and *Schools for Children* in Chapter 6 and the treatment for *A Young Child Is . . .* (Figure 6-3), copyright 1983, Educational Improvement Center—South Jersey Region, reprinted with the permission of the Educational Information and Resource Center, Sewell, NJ.

The complete treatment appearing in Appendix 5 and the complete script appearing in Appendix 6 for *The Hawaiian Volcanoes: A Force for Creation*, copyright 1989, Harada Productions, reprinted with permission of Harada Productions.

My thanks to the following computer software companies for providing samples of their word processing or scriptwriting software: Inherit the Earth Technologies for SuperScript; Lake Compuframes, Inc., for ShowScape; Reference Software International for Grammatik 5; Screenplay Systems for Scriptor; and WordPerfect Corporation for WordPerfect 5.1.

Glossary

2S, 3S Two-shot, two people in the frame, or three-shot with three people.

A and B rolls (1) Preprint materials used in printing film to provide clean splices and easy printing of fades, dissolves, and superimpositions. The first scene is printed from the A roll, the second from the B roll, continuing to alternate from one to the other until the end of the film. (2) Any system of switching from one roll to another in film or television.

above the line cost Pre-production costs such as script, supervision, cast salaries, music, royalties and commissions, and fixed costs.

animation Drawings or graphics that move. Once done with paintings on clear cells which were photographed one frame at a time. Now done in video with a computer.

answer print The first film print from preprint materials, it answers the question, Is the film properly timed and color-corrected? Also called a check print.

audio The sound recorded for a production.

audio engineer The technical person at an audio recording session.

audio recording (1) A sound recording on audiotape, record, or compact disc, as distinguished from sound recorded on film or videotape. (2) The process of recording sound on any medium.

audition A tryout for actors or other talent.

back story A brief biography of a character in a script which the writer creates to aid in characterization; what happened in the lives of the characters before the script begins.

below the line cost The expense of principal photography and post production: set construction, equipment, salaries of technical people, transportation, location costs, makeup, wardrobe, laboratory, special effects, editing.

BetaCam A videotape system which renders broadcast quality video on a half inch videocassette.

block (a scene) See **blocking.**

blocking The way the director places the actors, props, and camera for a scene.

boom A long pole, generally used to place a microphone into the set from outside and above, so it won't be seen by the camera.

camera operator The person who physically operates the camera; cameraman. May also be the cinematographer or director of photography, but need not be.

camera original (1) Film exposed in the camera. (2) Film or videotape shown exactly as it was exposed, without editing.

casting Selecting the actors and extras who will appear in the video or film.

casting director A professional who works with the director to select the talent for the production. A good casting director knows what actors are available at any given time, what their capabilities are, and roughly how much they will cost.

check print See **answer print.**

cinema vérité Literally "film truth." A style of making films and videos which tries to show everything and tell nothing.

cinematographer The person responsible for the look of the image on film or videotape. Controls the lighting and the camerawork. May or may not physically operate the camera.

clapper Originally the part of the slate shown at the beginning of a film scene which was slapped together to establish a synchronization point for sound and picture. Now any system that creates a sync point for sound and film.

client, the See **the client.**

client, your See **your client.**

close-up (CU) A shot showing just the face of an actor, or any close shot of something which fills the screen.

conflict Dramatically, any opposing forces which create tension and interest in a scene.

conforming editor In film, the editor who physically cuts the original and edits it into A and B rolls to match the work print.

cover shot See **master shot.**

CU Close-up.

cut The change from one shot to the next taking place within a single frame.

dailies See **rushes.**

decision list The computer memory of all videotape editing decisions, telling what roll of original each scene came from, where the scene starts, where it ends, and how it makes the transition to the next scene. The computerized editing system can recreate the editing process for a video from the decision list.

dialogue The words written for actors to say in a video or film.

director The person with overall creative control of a production from principal photography through to the end of editing.

director of photography (DP) The cinematographer or the person with overall responsibility for recording the image. May or may not operate the camera.

dissolve A transition in which the scene on the screen fades out as the next scene fades in. A dissolve can be slow, taking up to several seconds, or fast, ocurring in a few frames. A fast dissolve is sometimes called a soft cut.

dolly A wheeled camera support which can move the camera through the scene while shooting; the act of moving the camera on a dolly.

double-system sound In film production, sound which is recorded on an audio recorder rather than on the film itself.

dubbing Rerecording audio or video from one tape to another, or from a master tape to one or more copies.

dubs The copies made during dubbing.

ECU Extreme close-up. Any extremely tight shot of a person or object so that a very small part fills the screen.

edge numbers In film, reference numbers printed on the film original and all prints and sound tracks to facilitate synchronizing them.

edit bay The room in which videotape editing takes place. At a minimum it will contain several video recorders and monitors, the editing computer, and a console for selecting inputs and outputs.

editing The process of selecting and putting together the film or videotape scenes which make up the video or film.

editor The person in charge of editing.

establishing shot A long shot or wide shot which establishes the time of day and location of the scene. A shot of the Eiffel Tower immediately establishes the scene in Paris.

exteriors Scenes shot outdoors or meant to look and sound as if they were shot outdoors.

fade-in A transition in which the image gradually appears on the screen.

fade-out A transition in which the image gradually disappears from the screen.

filmstock The film used in motion picture photography and printing.

film-to-tape transfer The process of recording a film onto videotape.

fine cut The last stage in editing, in which the production is smoothed and tightened into its final form.

first draft (1) The first completed draft of a script or manuscript. (2) The first *official* draft of a script or manuscript, i.e., the one that is shown to the client.

footage Film or videotape on which images have been recorded.

frame In film, a single picture on the roll. Film runs normally at twenty-four frames per second. In video, one complete recording of all the lines on the video screen. Video runs normally at thirty frames per second.

freeze frame Stopping the action in a scene by repeating a single frame for as long as you want.

fx Any special effects in picture or sound.

gel A transparent colored material placed in front of a light to change its color or intensity.

graphics Drawings or text placed in the scene.

graphics camera A camera placed in an edit bay to record graphic elements such as photographs, drawings, art cards, and title boards.

grip A member of the crew responsible for moving and setting up props and lighting equipment.

grip equipment Lights, light stands, gels, and all the other artificial stuff the director of photography needs to make the scene look "natural."

interiors Scenes photographed indoors.

interlock (1) The process of playing back film and double-system sound synchronized together. (2) The point in film production at which the fine cut of the film and the mixed sound are shown for approval.

layback In video production, rerecording mixed or sweetened sound tracks onto the video master.

leader Blank film used for spacing in editing.

lip sync Film shot with picture and sound synchronized together; now often means the post-production technique of recording a voice synchronized to lip movements on film. This is also known as "post sync."

location Any physical site for principal photography outside a studio or sound stage.

log A record; specifically, a list of images or sounds recorded. A camera log is kept during principal photography. An editing log is created when the footage is reviewed in post production.

long shot (LS) A scene recorded with the camera at a distance or using a wide angle lens so that all or most of whatever is in the master scene is recorded. A long shot of a house would include the whole house and probably some of its surrounding environment. A long shot of a person shows the whole person.

LS Long shot.

magnetic film Motion picture film coated with a magnetic medium like that put on audiotape, for the purpose of recording audio. Magnetic film is used to synchronize double-system sound with picture during film editing.

master scene In a script, the description of what occurs during the scene without regard to blocking. In principal photography, a master shot or cover shot.

master shot (cover shot) Photographing or recording the scene, usually in a long shot, so that all the people and the action are shown. Following the master shot, individual close-ups, reaction shots, and other shots needed for editing are recorded.

master tape The first-generation audio tape or videotape made during editing.

medium shot (MS) It isn't an LS and it isn't a CU, it's in between. A medium shot of a person might be head and shoulders or from the waist up.

montage Literally, montage means editing. In present-day usage a montage is a series of shots, often edited to music, to create an artistic or emotional message. The "falling in love" sequence in a romantic film is often a montage set to a romantic song.

MOS Code for silent footage.

MS Medium shot.

narration The spoken words accompanying a video or film conveying the information the audience needs to know which cannot easily be inferred from the images.

negative Camera original from which a direct positive print can be made.

off-line editing Videotape editing in a simple edit bay, used for viewing, assembling, and making the rough cut. A relatively inexpensive way to do the long process of editing to rough cut. May lack the ability to do dissolves and supers or to add graphics or titles.

on-line editing The final stage of video post production, in which the program is assembled in its final form with all the bells and whistles. Most expensive form of video editing.

optical track A sound track printed on film which can be read by an optical audio system. The sound track on most 16mm prints, such as those shown in schools, is an optical track.

original The film originally recorded in the camera. It may be negative film or it may be reversal original which yields a positive image like a color slide.

pan Rotating the camera on a fixed axis from left to right or right to left.

paper edit An editing script detailing how to organize existing footage.

pickup shooting Additional shooting after principal photography to record a missed or needed scene.

post production Everything having to do with creating the final version of the program after the completion of principal photography. In addition to editing, post production includes recording narration and music, creating special effects, and all the mechanical and electronic processes involved in completing the video or film.

post sync See **lip sync.**

pre-production Everything prior to principal photography, including script development, location scouting, casting, and rehearsals.

preprint materials All the rolls of film and sound required to make a print of a motion picture.

principal photography The process of recording the live action of a video or film in front of the camera. Does not include pickup shooting or graphics and special effects which may be done at a different time.

producer The person with overall responsibility for the planning, execution, and completion of the video or film.

release print A finished print of a film for distribution.

reversal original Film which, when processed, yields a positive, rather than a negative image. Slide film is reversal original. The film which passes through the camera is the film which is mounted in the slide.

rough cut A first assembly edit of a video or film.

running time The actual time it takes for a scene or program to play, often expressed in minutes, seconds, and frames.

rushes (dailies) In film, the first print of the camera original, returned to the director for review.

scene (1) All the action taking place in a continuous span of time at a single location. (2) In film editing, the film from one splice to the next.

scouting Looking for locations.

segue In audio recording or editing, a transition fading from one audio source to another. The audio equivalent of a dissolve.

sequence Several shots (or scenes) which go together for a single purpose. An editing montage is a sequence.

setting The description in the script which tells where and under what conditions the scene takes place.

setup A camera and lighting position. Every time the camera moves to a different angle or the scene changes, a new setup is required.

shooting ratio The ratio of the footage shot during principal photography to the running length of the edited video or film.

shooting script A script which puts together all the scenes from the same location—or featuring the same players—so that they can be shot at the same time, regardless of where they appear in the original script.

shot The basic building block of video and film. In the camera, everything recorded from the time the camera is turned on until it is turned off again. In editing, everything from one splice to the next.

shot list A list of all the things that need to be recorded during principal photography. Many documentaries are shot from a shot list with the script written later from existing footage.

single-system sound Audio which is recorded directly onto the filmstock in the camera at the time the picture is recorded. Single-system sound may be recorded to an optical track or to a magnetic strip placed along the edge of the film.

slate The board with scene information held up at the start of each shot.

sound bite A short, pointed speech recorded on film or videotape; a piece of sound selected from a longer interview or speech for inclusion in the edited film or video.

sound mix In film, rerecording the sound from the edited sound tracks to a new composite sound track.

sound stage A studio in which a set can be constructed and scenes can be shot with minimum interference from outside sounds.

sound sweetening A process for video similar to the sound mix for film. All the audio is rerecorded to a multitrack audio recorder in sync with the videotape, so that each sound source is on a separate track. Narration, music, wild sound, and sound effects can be added, each on its own track. Then the tracks are blended to a single composite sound track for layback to the video master.

special effects Special photographic effects include explosions and camera magic. Special effects in post production range from superimpositions to removing people from one scene and adding them to another. Computer-generated effects can flip images, change them from positive to negative, and manipulate them in a variety of other ways.

stock shot Use of existing footage for a scene rather than recording a new shot. A stock shot of the Eiffel Tower may be all you need to convince the audience the action takes place in Paris. All the rest can be shot in the studio or at practical locations in your hometown. Stock shots are available from stock shot libraries.

storyboard An artist's rendering of the visual part of the script as a series of drawings.

superimposition (super) Recording one image on top of another.

swish pan A pan so fast that the image becomes blurred. Often used to create the impression that the camera has panned quickly from one location to a different location as a continuous action. For instance, the camera pans left from the scene at the first location until the image blurs. At the next location, the camera pans quickly in a blur to the left, then slows and stops at the incoming scene. In editing, you dissolve from one to the other during the blur. This has become a cliché.

sync The synchronization between picture and sound.

take One instance of recording a shot.

talent The actors and the people whose voices are used in the production.

talking heads Pejorative term for interview scenes in which there is no visual action, just people talking.

tape-to-film transfer The technical process of converting a video from videotape to film original.

TelePrompTer A piece of equipment which displays the words of the script to on-camera talent so they can read them while looking into the camera.

the client For the purpose of this book, the end user, the company or organization which commissioned the video or film. See also **your client.**

tight shot Another term for close-up.

time code A reference system recorded onto videotape which lets you locate any frame in any scene. Time code is expressed in hours, minutes, seconds, and frames, e.g., 01:23:44:12

treatment The description of the script that will be written. It states the purpose for making the video, lists important points to be included, describes the visual or cinematic style, and then outlines the content that will be included.

video master The first-generation videotape of the finished program made during editing.

voice-over A voice presented off-camera, or voice-over-picture. Narration is voice-over.

wide shot Similar to a long shot, a wide shot includes the whole scene or setting. Or it includes an object with lots of surrounding environment.

wild sound Audio recorded separately from picture.

window print A dub of videotape footage with the tape's time code displayed in an electronic "window" in the image.

wipe A transition in which one scene seems to slide off the screen as another slides on.

work print A low-cost film print made from the original for use in editing.

WS Wide shot.

your client For the purpose of this book, the company or organization which hired you to write the script. See **the client.** May be the same as **the client** or may be an advertising or P.R. agency or a production company working for **the client.**

zoom Rapidly changing focal length on a multiple focal length lens (originally called a Zoomar lens) so that the camera seems to be moving closer to or farther away from the scene.

Index